The Decolonial Abyss

John D. Caputo, *series editor*

PERSPECTIVES IN
CONTINENTAL
PHILOSOPHY

AN YOUNTAE

The Decolonial Abyss
Mysticism and Cosmopolitics from the Ruins

FORDHAM UNIVERSITY PRESS
New York ▪ *2017*

the
modern language
initiative

THIS BOOK IS MADE POSSIBLE BY A COLLABORATIVE GRANT
FROM THE ANDREW W. MELLON FOUNDATION.

Visit us online at www.fordhampress.com.

Library of Congress Cataloging-in-Publication Data

Names: An Yountae, author.
Title: The decolonial abyss : mysticism and cosmopolitics from the ruins / An
    Yountae.
Description: First edition. | New York, NY : Fordham University Press, 2016.
    | Series: Perspectives in Continental philosophy | Includes
    bibliographical references and index.
Identifiers: LCCN 2016014169 | ISBN 9780823273072 (cloth : alk. paper) | ISBN
    9780823273089 (pbk. : alk. paper)
Subjects: LCSH: Meaninglessness (Philosophy) | Postcolonialism. |
    Decolonization.
Classification: LCC B825.2 .A5 2016 | DDC 190—dc23
LC record available at https://lccn.loc.gov/2016014169

Printed in the United States of America

19 18 17   5 4 3 2 1

First edition

Contents

Introduction

Staring into the Abyss

> Afuera hay sol.
> No es más que un sol
> pero los hombres lo miran
> y después cantan.
> Yo no sé del sol
> Yo sé de la melodía del ángel
> y el sermón caliente
> del último viento.
> Sé gritar hasta el alba
> cuando la muerte se posa desnuda en mi sombra.
> Yo lloro debajo de mi nombre.
> Yo agito pañuelos en la noche y barcos sedientes de realidad
> bailan conmigo.
> Yo oculto clavos
> para escarnecer a mis sueños enfermos.
> Afuera hay sol.
> Yo me visto de cenizas.
>
> **—Alejandra Pizarnik, "La Jaula"**

With her gloomy poetic imagination, the twentieth-century Argentinian poet Alejandra Pizarnik delves into the depth of meaninglessness, the source of inspiration that marks her entire writing career through the 1950s and '60s. Her obsession with lack, also represented as the void, absence, and death, points to her existentialist poetic vision that privileges darkness and silence over the "sun" or "word."[1] However, the dark night of *nihil* does not seem capable of redeeming Pizarnik's despairing existential cry, for after her encounter with the void she confesses, "I cry beneath my

1

name" (Yo lloro debajo de mi nombre). Despite "the sun outside," her melancholic tone culminates in "I dress in ashes" (Afuera hay sol, yo me visto de cenizas). These ashes perhaps encode immense historical experience if we consider that she was born in 1936 to Russian-Jewish parents who had immigrated to Argentina in flight from the Nazi holocaust. Her desolation is further manifested by her tormenting life trajectory, one marked with severe borderline personality disorder that eventually led her to end her own life at the young age of thirty-six. In her abyssal poetic world, Pizarnik discloses the void as a site of revelation. However, it is not a revelation that leads to the reconstruction of ground and meaning. Rather, the poet's revelation gravitates around nothingness and emptiness, vacillating between silence and absence.[2]

The utterly negative character of the abyss depicted in Pizarnik's poems is indicative of the existential chasm encountered at the horizon of finite human existence. But such a view fails to capture another important aspect of the abyss: a space replete with potential. Facing the abyss, in this sense, is different from facing nothing or the void. Pizarnik's conflation of the abyss with a void covers over the abyss's complex polysemy and ambiguous nature. For the abyss does not signify a mere lack of meaning. It signifies something more material. In this regard, the abyss is not synonymous with finitude. It is rather a paradox. It puts you face to face with finitude, but this finitude at the same time signals possibility by revealing itself to be the passageway to infinitude, an absence (or lack) that can possibly lead to replenishment.

This might sound like a classic narrative of triumphalism, the story of the resilient self who (re)discovers and reconstructs itself after a series of failures. Such stories are usually accompanied by teleological accounts of theologies that regard evil and suffering as a necessity. It is from this perspective that the early church apologetic Irenaeus viewed suffering and evil as part of the process of growth to maturity in God, and the world as the "vale of soul-making."[3] These stories regard finitude as a necessary component of the progressive cycle of life. Experiences of finitude may shatter one's horizon of life, but there is a promise of reward, of growth and self-discovery: reconstruction of what has been dismantled and compensation for what was lost.

What this book is about to unfold is not stories of victorious reconciliation. Rather, I attempt to examine the shuttling movement of the self, the oscillation between the two opposites across the abyssal chasm, the possible and the impossible, finitude and infinitude. When we accept the shadow of the abyss not as a necessity but as a reality, a constitutive element of the self conditioning its existence, numerous questions and possibilities are opened up for a new understanding of the self—with implications for philosophy, theology, ethics, and possibly politics. Briefly speaking, that the self is the result of an incessant dialectical tension and movement raises important philosophical and ethical questions about the place of the "other" in the constitution of the self. To what extent is the self indebted to or implicated in the other(s)? Is it possible to build a coherent and cogent account of the self who is clearly demarcated from the other? If the answer is no, in what ways does this reshape the philosophical discourse of God and ethics in relation to the other?

Another important question that I encounter in the face of the abyss concerns the restlessness of the self who negates finitude, namely the self who (counter)negates negation. For the abyss often induces the self, who is confronted by negation (whether we call it finitude or loss) and is agonizing in despair, to gather herself resiliently. This is why the abyss designates passion rather than resignation. I am here by no means trying to contradict my own statement above by invoking a narrative of the self who successfully conquers the shadows of darkness and rises above her limits. Rather, my intention is to probe the work of negation that displaces the self and her old world and gives birth to a new self at the same time. The work of the negative or the way negation works is complex. For it is neither a mere antithesis conducive to resignation, nor a magical remedy that heals the irreparable breach. Negation does not guarantee a triumphant and predictable outcome. Yet the power of negation lies in its evocation of the self as a relentless and insistent movement, the restless movement of struggle, becoming, and dialectical mediation across the valley of the abyss. We no longer imagine the self as a determinate substance but as a force: a movement of incessant self-creation and unfolding.

If the double move implied in the abyss nurtures a sense of possibility for thinking newly about the self in her ethical and political relation to the other, my hope is to carefully explore such possibility by relocating theological and philosophical texts to the contextualized horizon of history. For as much as philosophy builds universalized theories of reality, these thoughts do not simply transcend the historical contexts out of which they are constructed. After all, the self in trial in the different philosophical inquiries I engage here is not a disembodied notion but a living body with a specific shape, flesh, and history.

The familiar tone of metaphysical narratives of the abyss reverberates in an intriguing way with stories of survival that are marked by historical loss and physical suffering. At the intersection of such similarity among dissimilarities, I wonder about the possible crossings between these two distinct kinds of stories of loss and finitude, one shaped by metaphysical contours, the other marked by sociopolitical conditions. These questions extend my inquiry further to the divide lying between the spiritual and the political. The spiritual, or, to be more specific, mystical spirituality, has long been misperceived as a privatizing affair, a self-absorbed form of religious experience unable to make an ethical/political offering to the community in despair. And to push the "political" even further, my query extends to the divide between the West and the global South, the subject of knowledge production and the colonial other. Indeed, as the Portuguese sociologist Bonaventura de Sousa Santos remarks, the gap between the West and the global South indicates an "abyssal" divide. The word *abyssal* here has pessimistic overtones suggesting an unbridgeable gap, for Santos is describing a separation of the social reality of the West from that the global South in which whatever lies on "the other side of the line" is deemed nonexistent and radically excluded.[4]

Globalization is a reality that shapes us all today. If continental philosophy of religion has opened the new millennium with its distinctive orientation toward ethics, it is imperative that it now respond to this new phenomenon, system, or configuration of the old world as we knew it. Globalization is perhaps not all that new when we remind ourselves of the legacy of the power network that has long exercised sovereign rule over those who live on the other side of the line: from the ancient Christian image of cosmopolitanism named the *Orbis Christianus* (the Christian cosmos) to the hegemonic installment of European modernity upon the back of its colonial other (the "New World"), and from imperialism, the expansion of the colonial order to the rest of the world through military force, to the planetary dominion of capitalist expansion, namely capitalist globalization. Pressing these questions in the philosophical discourse of religion is a daunting task. Yet leaving these questions unaddressed would perpetuate the abyssal divide between the Western philosophical discourse of religion and the political realities of the global South, and would fail to hold discourses about God, ethics, and political responsibilities accountable to the reality of global communities. How, then, can we bridge the mystical abyss of theology and the abyss of sociopolitical trauma engulfing the colonial subject?

The question that remains and haunts this book will largely rest on the unique perspective that the thematization of the abyss in each one of the different (con)texts opens. As my reading reconstructs the figure of the abyss, I will demonstrate how questions of theology, philosophy, ethics, and politics cut across these seemingly distant contexts. In other words, this book demonstrates that mystics' concern for union with the divine and decolonial thinkers' concern for the reconstruction of a collective identity share a common ground—or is it groundlessness?—in the abyss. The unquenchable passion (and the failure) to name the "unnameable" name of God need not be separated from the passion (and the failure) to name the unnameable historical trauma from which the fragile name of the community is born. In this strange crack, we witness the double work of the abyss that dissolves the self and opens up possibility. And precisely here the central question driving the narratives of this book intervenes. What kind of future does this crack open? Or does it open a future at all? For the universalizing accounts of dialectical becoming might certainly open a future, but a future perhaps all too familiar to us: one that does not break from the genealogy of the old Christian cosmopolitan world order that keeps reproducing itself each time with a different name: modernity, capitalism, liberal democracy, postmodernity, globalization, and so forth. Indeed, is this not the totalitarian future that (the misreading of) Hegel opens for us? Since my goal here is to write a different narrative of dispossession and reconstruction, accountable to the reality of the globalized world living under perpetual systems of violence and exploitation, it is crucial that my argument take on the structure of violence deeply embedded in the system. And this is why, in a way, this book suggests a form of political theology, or better, a cosmo-political theology, as it aims to displace the sovereignty of coloniality, which grounds the Eurocentric production of knowledge and West-led capitalist globalization.

The methods and disciplinary boundaries shaping the polyphonic voices of this book are often blurred as I navigate through philosophy, theology, postcolonial thought, and poetics. While largely philosophical, this book also invokes a theological discourse, a secular theology—if we may call it that—perhaps concerned less with making theological claims about dogmatic notions such as God or transcendence than with disclosing the overlooked political possibility lurking in mystical thought while probing the mystical depth implicated in political thought.

Chapter 1 of the book provides a general overview and definition of the key themes and questions of the book. It begins with the questions that Martinican thinkers Frantz Fanon and Édouard Glissant raise regarding the possibility of constructing being, self, and collective identity in the context of colonial oppression. A brief review of philosophical discourses and critical theories that address questions of race, (post)coloniality, and the global state of trans-spatiality such as theories of cosmopolitanism, postcolonial theory, and Latin American decolonial thought ("the decolonial turn") will provide the methodological framework for both theorizing some of the central terms of the book and reading the figure of the abyss from diverse perspectives.

Chapter 2 examines the notion of the abyss as it has been developed within the tradition of Western philosophy and theology. It traces the abyss back to its inception in Neoplatonic philosophy by Plato in his *Parmenides*, followed by Plotinus, who develops the traces of panentheist mysticism lurking in Plato's system into the seed of negative theology. In the Neoplatonic tradition and the medieval mysticism of Pseudo-Dionysius and Meister Eckhart, the abyss points to the theological crossroads where finitude and infinity, creaturely vulnerability and divine potency, intersect. The paradoxical path of the *via negativa* renders the abyss a site of uncertainty and unknowing in which both God and the self are uncreated (Eckhart). Subsequently, the ethical implication or potential of the abyss is probed via the works of contemporary philosophers (Jacques Derrida, Jean-Luc Marion, Slavoj Žižek) who engage negative theology from a postmodern perspective.

Chapter 3 examines explicitly the ethico-philosophical meaning of the abyss by locating its trace in German idealism and Hegel. Jakob Boehme's elaboration of the abyss as *Ungrund* (groundlessness) and Schelling's appropriation of it pave the way for the transition from mysticism to dialectic via Hegel. I then move to Hegel in order to examine the ethico-philosophical questions implicated in the abyss. My reading demonstrates that while the trace of the abyss is underdeveloped in Hegel, it nevertheless structures his dialectical system. The abyss signals the moment or movement of passage from the negative to the positive, through which the shattered self transforms its eroded ground into the condition of a new possibility. I interrogate the terms of such reconstruction or passage by engaging both Judith Butler's feminist and Slavoj Žižek's materialist readings of Hegel.

Chapter 4 extends the meaning of the abyss by giving it a specific contextual shape. By investigating the colonial impasse from which the Afro-Caribbean decolonial imagination of the (post)*Négritude* movement emerges, I probe the complex crossings that take place between the mystical and the political. In the writings of Caribbean thinkers one witnesses an understanding of identity based on relational ontology; the story of the shattered other shapes the very contours of the collective history from which the traumatized self emerges. In this middle, the groundless site lying between the devastating past and the equally impaired present, one begins to reflect upon the possibility of *passage*, of *beginning* after trauma. I explore the possibility of reconstructing the traumatized self in the extended notion of identity based on relational ontology found in Édouard Glissant's philosophy of creolization.

Finally, chapter 5 explores the possibility of using the reconceptualized notion of groundless ground as a new framework from which to envision a new form of self and of thinking and inhabiting the world. A comparative reading of Glissant's poetics, a poetic of resistance he calls a "forced poetic," and of continental philosophers' theopoetics (Jacques Derrida, John Caputo, Richard Kearney, Catherine Keller) suggests the poetic as an epistemological alternative and political instrument that makes possible an open future and a relational self born from the wombs of pain and trauma. Poetics in the colonial abyss is not a glamorous, apolitical escapism but a mode of being in the world, a mode of recreating the self amid unrealized possibilities, and hence is inescapably political. (Theo)poetics of creolization thus leads us ineluctably to cosmopolitics. If this cosmopolitics offers some kind of theological possibility, it indicates perhaps the possibility of conceiving the name of the divine right at the site where the cosmopolitical struggle of the creolized masses creates, uncreates, and recreates itself and its ground for a future of cosmopolitan justice and solidarity.

Situating the Self in the Abyss

Since its inception in the Neoplatonic tradition, the abyss points primarily to the gap between the world and the radically transcendent God. At the same time, the abyss also denotes the internal crack within the self, that is, the irrevocable inner gap splitting the self. As David Coe tells us, for Augustine, the abyss was "related to the inwardness of man's soul, to his freedom to choose his own concerns, and to his openness to the possibilities before him."[1] This gap is not pertinent only to the human soul or self. It also indicates the inner fissure within Godself, that is the hiddenness of God from Godself, as Luther would say, or the groundlessness (*Ungrund*) inscribed in God before God emerges as Godself (Boehme and Schelling).

The *Oxford English Dictionary* defines *abyss* as the bottomless chasm that bears a direct association with the primal formless chaos and the subterranean source of water in ancient Hebrew cosmology. Its archaic form, *abysm*, was borrowed from the Old French *abisme*, which means a very deep hole. While the Latin root of *abisme* is the vulgar term *abismus*, it was later replaced by the late Latin *abyssus*, which comes from the Greek word *abyssos*, signifying bottomlessness (*a* = without, *byssos* = bottom), the unfathomed, boundless, and great deep.[2] However, the abyss has often been conflated with the void or nothing, and these two concepts need to be distinguished from each other. The *OED* defines *void* as an adjective indicating vacancy, the state of being unoccupied (either by a person or by any other visible content), empty, lacking, destitute of, and deprived of. The notion of the void plays an important role in shaping ancient Greek cosmology through the debates among the atomists in pre-Socratic philosophy. Represented by Leucippus, Democritus, and Epicurus, the atomists viewed the universe as composed of being and nonbeing, that is, body and void.[3] For the atomists, the void can mean both the "space" of emptiness and emptiness itself. But *void* does not simply denote the "unoccupied space" separating bodies. Rather, for Epicurus, the term refers to "intangible substance" (ἀναφὴς φύσις, *anaphes phusis*) "surrounding the distinct, constantly moving atoms,"[4] without which "bodies would not have anywhere to be or to move through as they are observed to move."[5] The Latin etymological root of *void, vacuus,* also means the state of being empty, occupied, and nothingness. In this sense, *void* is close to *nothing,* the state of having no part, share, or quantity of a thing. If *nothing* points to the null state of existence, whether a person or a thing/matter, *void* presumes a previously occupied or filled state, if not an expectation of presence. While *nothing* can be free of value and affect, *void* may imply a sense of intense frustration caused by an unexpected or unforeseeable emptiness. Contrastingly, *abyss* indicates a sense of indeterminacy in which the rigid boundary between the finite and the infinite, presence and absence, no longer holds.

The often puzzling relation or overlap between *abyss* and *void* finds its theological ground in the very first chapter of Genesis. The long-standing tradition of *creatio ex nihilo* (creation out of nothing) has, for millennia, dominated the popular theological imagination with its interpretation of the *tohu-vabohu* (formless and void) state of precreation as "nothing." Denouncing Western theology's negligence of, or rather deep-seated aversion to, darkness/chaos, the interstitial *tehom* of Genesis 1:2, Catherine Keller helps us distinguish *tehom* as the abyss, the primal chaos of creation, from the notion of the void as mere nothing: "A churning, complicated darkness was wedged right between the two verses . . . 'in the beginning God created the heaven and the earth' and 'God said: let there be light . . .' This interstitial darkness refuses to disappear. It refuses to appear as nothing, as vacuum, as mere absence."[6] Despite the dominant theology's consistent attempts to nullify it, the abyss, Keller tells us, survives.[7]

The polysemic nature of the abyss figures prominently in the long history of mystical literature. If Pizarnik's abyss points unidirectionally at absence, or what Grace Jantzen calls the "nihilistic abyss," the long history of the Western mystical tradition testifies to the more complex meaning of the term, which often associates bottomlessness with an overwhelming ravishment .[8] The sixteenth-century French mystic Francois-Louis Blosius describes the abyss as a space of unfathomable potential in which the ecstatic experience of the union with the divine takes place:

For when, through love, the soul goes beyond all works of the intellect and all images in the mind . . . it flows into God. . . . The loving
soul, as I have said, flows out of itself, and completely swoons away;
and, as if brought to nothing, it sinks down into the abyss of the
divine love, where, dead to itself, it lives in God, knowing nothing,
feeling nothing, save only the love that it experiences. It loses itself
in the infinite solitude and darkness of the Godhead; but so to lose
itself is rather to find itself.[9]

Although this mystical union signals unfathomable abundance, it is first
characterized by infinite solitude and darkness. Plunging into the abyss
thus involves facing the negative experience of loss, which is followed by
the rewarding realization of the self's truth, that finding the self in God
(union with God) necessarily involves the loss of the self.[10] In this sense,
the abyss indicates double movement: loss and discovery; dissolution of
the self followed by replenishment of the self. It signifies both lack and
abundance.

The imagery of the abyss as overwhelming plentitude and bliss figures
perhaps most prominently in the writings of the thirteenth-century Bel-
gian mystic and poet Hadewijch. The main theme of Hadewijch's poetry is
love between the lover (herself) and her object (God); the poems are filled
with the joys and frustrations of longing for her object of love. Thus it is
not surprising that she associates the abyss with love: "O Beloved, why has
love not sufficiently overwhelmed you and engulfed you in her abyss? Alas!
when Love is so sweet, why do you not fall deep into her? And why do
you not touch God deeply enough in the abyss of his Nature, which is so
unfathomable?"[11] As the unfathomable depth of and within love, the abyss
is the indefinite possibility of renewal in love:

My soul melts away
In the Madness of Love
The abyss into which she hurls me
Is deeper than the sea
For Love's new deep abyss
Renews my wound.[12]

At times hinting at a positive meaning, at times signifying the negative, the
abyss implies both, and *neither*. It is the space or state of ultimate indeterminacy. But this is not a static space or state in which one is perpetually
trapped in-between. My reading suggests that the one who encounters the
abyss is the self in its movement or "passage." In other words, the abyss is
inseparably connected to what I call the movement of passage, that is, the
self's passage into and out of the abyss: from loss to possibility, from fini-

tude to infinity. Meanwhile, the trope of the abyss has long been popular in the philosophical and literary traditions. This is because the figure of the abyss creates mystical repercussions in a wide range of contexts in which the finitude of human existence is experienced. The trope of the abyss employed by novelists and philosophers, for instance, resonates with that employed by theologians.

The Philosophical investigation of the abyss shares a similar concern or ground with theology. In both cases, the abyss indicates the indeterminate—if not finite—structure of being, the precariousness of the human epistemological and ontological foundation. What sparks my interest, then, is the use of this trope to describe the concrete sociopolitical situation of human existence that is "the lived experience" of the body. The Brazilian ecofeminist theologian Ivone Gebara uses the trope of the abyss to describe the vulnerable matrix of our existence, where systematic, everyday evil and good are "inextricably present and commingled in our own bodies."[13] Holocaust survivor and Nobel laureate Elie Wiesel also uses the trope of the abyss when narrating the horrifying experience of deportation to the concentration camp: "We were still trembling, and with every screech of the wheels, we felt the abyss opening beneath us. Unable to still our anguish, we tried to reassure each other."[14] I wonder, here, about the intriguing connection between the mystical experience and the experience of suffering born at this juncture. The common ground that these two different experiences share in the space of groundlessness is perhaps the failure of language to name the overwhelming nature of this indeterminacy. But in another context the abyss also becomes the womb of creative potential, as it bears witness to the resilient spirit that strives to speak the unspeakable. What lies at the intersection between the desperate attempt to name the unnameable name of God and the desperate attempt to express the agony born in the context of traumatic suffering and violence? The existential chasm of the colonized subject, the "ontological quandary" of the colonized, has surprising resonances with the trope of the abyss in the long tradition of theological and philosophical inquiry into the finitude of the self and its relation to the divine. These resonances are the central theme of the current project.

The trope of the abyss has often expressed the historical pain of the colonial wound that many decolonial thinkers have struggled to articulate. Looking at the tradition of Afro-Caribbean decolonial thought in particular, we find in the writings of the French-Martinican philosopher Édouard Glissant the figure of the abyss merging with the historical reality of colonialism, particularly the historical memory of the traumatic middle passage. Capturing the experience and the meaning of the middle passage,

Glissant writes, "Experience of the abyss lies inside and outside the abyss. The torment of those who never escaped it; straight from the belly of the slave ship into the violent belly of the ocean depths they went. But their ordeal did not die; it quickened into this continuous/discontinuous thing; the panic of the new land, the haunting of the former land, finally the alliance with the imposed land, suffered and redeemed. The unconscious memory of the abyss served as the alluvium for these metamorphoses."[15] The abyss conveys the unspeakable: both the unspeakable pain of the colonial wound *and* the unspeakable state of the self who lives in the suspended present, awaiting for the unforeseeable future to unfold. Despite horror, the abyss of the middle passage beckons toward the future. Trauma opens possibility: "This experience of the abyss can now be said to be the best element of exchange."[16]

Another French Martinican thinker, the psychiatrist and revolutionary Frantz Fanon, also links the abyss to the reality of colonial violence and political devastation. Commenting on the violence of the French militia in Algeria, he writes: "But isn't the colonial status the organized enslavement of an entire people? The Algerian Revolution is precisely the living challenge to this enslavement and this abyss."[17] What does such a political rendition of the abyss say about the *apolitical* reading of the mystical abyss? Do these two radically different readings and uses not share a common ground at all? Why a separation between the mystical and the political in the first place? What happens when we reconcile the mystical depth of the abyss with the political potential lurking in it?

By examining the works of Latin American/Caribbean decolonial thinkers, this book reevaluates questions of selfhood from the standpoint of extreme violence and oppression. Specifically, I reflect upon the experience of subjects whose textures of being are imprinted with the indelible trauma of colonial history. Despite the bursting emergence of academic discourses addressing the worldwide phenomenon of globalization and transnationalism, these discussions present an ambiguous view of the political effects and consequences of the capitalist globalization, as their critique is often conflated with celebration of this universally sweeping force. But more importantly, these contemporary discussions of globalization miss, if not overlook, the crucial connection between modernity and the current regime of globalization, namely coloniality at large. I will in later discuss in more detail the importance of coloniality for the current project by engaging the ideas of the Latin American decolonial philosophers Enrique Dussel and Walter Mignolo, but suffice it for now to point out one of the many shortcomings that the failure to address coloniality creates: the (re) production of counterglobalization theories grounded in the experience of privileged transnational citizens. The critique of coloniality helps us open our theoretical horizon to the often overlooked reality of many people who live in the extended sociohistorical web of coloniality in the age of globalization. My own experience of being displaced at an early age and growing up in a foreign land (Argentina) not only as a racialized subject but also as an undocumented immigrant in a working-class family informs perhaps my personal perspective on the topic.[18]

Rethinking the place of the self in the matrix of coloniality allows me to explore the possibility of reconstructing the fragmented sense of the self after traumatic ruins. Over and against a metaphysics that views the self as internally undifferentiated and unchanging, I follow the tradition that views the self as internally incoherent, fractured, contradictory, and always in the process of becoming. By situating the self in the politicized space of neocolonial globalization, I seek to identify it as embodied, that is, as a racialized and gendered category constitutive of the global order of epistemological/ontological hierarchy. I examine the process through which the self emerges from the dialectical tension lurking in the abyss. The emergence of the self entails the movement of passage, from negative to positive, from finite to infinite, from death to life. By *passage* I do not mean a simple movement of either entering or exiting the abyss. Rather, I imply the whole process of plunging into and reemerging out of the abyss. This is by no means unidirectional and linear, nor does it take place as a one-time event. Passage does not conclude its wayward trajectory once the self emerges out of the depths. There will always be yet another face of the abyss to stare at, hence another movement back into the abyss.

To address questions of the self's passage through the complex matrix of coloniality, I relocate the movement of passage—as suggested by the metaphysical accounts of both the mystical tradition and the continental tradition of philosophy—in the spatiotemporality of the "middle passage," and I question the meaning of the abyss, political subjectivity, and spirituality in relation to collective historical trauma. In other words, I rethink the movement of passage from the standpoint of the middle passage. The central question guiding the book will be: How to gather the self after a history of suffering, transportation, discontinuity, slavery, and death? In other words, how is selfhood possible for a colonized subject whose very horizon of existence is breached by the ongoing effects of "coloniality"? What happens when the abyss is not merely a metaphysical figure but a social, historical, and political one that emerges from the terrain marked by coloniality? In what ways and in which directions do theological and political concerns evolve when we relocate the account of the self to the colonial abyss?

The notion of the abyss interweaves three different disciplinary threads constituting this book: *theologically*, it denotes the blurring boundary between human finitude and divine potency; *philosophically*, it points to the incompleteness of the self (before "the other"); *politically*, it bears a wider politico-historical meaning emerging from the history of suffering, the reality of coloniality, and a fragmented sense of collective identity. The many abysses that open up as the book unfolds might seem to point to different types of abysses each time, and indeed the abyss might offer different shapes and meanings in different contexts. However, there is an important continuity among these many abysses, a common element or effect on the self and her passage through it. In other words, the commonality of the diverse abysses in my reading concerns the movement of the self who, dispossessed by its encounter with the abyss, emerges eventually as a reconstructed self. What does this process of remaking the self consist of? How is the newly emerging self different from the preabyssal self? While my reading in the following chapters provide answers to these questions, let me clarify here a few key points that my reading brings up.

The self who is undone in the encounter with the abyss, that is, the preabyssal self, lives with a misguided consciousness. Without having faced or embraced the vertiginous depths beneath the precarious ground of its being, this self views itself as coherent and independent. I am here referring to the self who operates in clearly demarcated binaries and boundaries, the self who views God as distinct from the world, the other as separate from the "I," the spiritual as distant from the political. Conversely, the new self that emerges—if it does at all—from the abyss understands its nature not as an immutable substance but as multiple, fragmented, and always-in-becoming. In the abyss the old self is dissolved, emptied, abandoned, annihilated, lost, crushed, dismembered, shattered, and drowned. The newly emerging self is "reconstructed," but not because it is fully and completely repaired or reassembled. Rather, as the Saint Lucian poet Derek Walcott writes, the gathering of the broken pieces is a work of love that, at the same time, reveals the pain of its scars.[19] In this sense, reconstruction refers not to the state but to the process. Such a trajectory of becoming and passage that culminates in the reemergence or reconstruction of the self takes a different shape in each context—despite the significant similarities they share—that I examine in the following chapters. That is, we observe in the three different abysses the self's passage from the old self to a new consciousness: from the self trapped in a dualistic illusion that valorizes purity, completeness, and stasis over and against impurity, incompleteness, and change to a creolized self that finds its truth in the never-ending, plurisingular acts of becoming in relation to the other; and from the self living with a teleological cosmology to a self who understands the end as a new beginning. Nevertheless, the differences marking off these abysses complicate and interrogate the different readings of the abyss and their relation to theology, ethics, and politics.

If the subject of the Hegelian narrative is characterized by an indomitable spirit, persistence in resiliently gathering itself each time it is crushed, the self reemerging at the shorelines of the colonial abyss is the one who *survives* the passage, disclosing the scars that hold its disparate pieces together. The reconstructed self of the colonial abyss, in essence, interrogates both the sociopolitical conditions that enable the passage and the seamless reconstruction of the self—*and* the theologico-philosophical implications that such a passage and such a self carry for the countercolonial narrative of cosmopolitan theory that I develop here. Meanwhile, the passage of the self in the mystical abyss is distinct in being an unidirectional process—a way of negation, namely self-abandonment and self-emptying. It is perhaps debatable whether the self is actually "reconstructed" in the mystical abyss, as it finds its truth only in total loss, the complete effacement of the self. The self in the mystical abyss, unlike the self in the Hegelian or the colonial abyss, materializes itself in complete undoing and total dispossession. Despite these differences, however, the dialectical movement of passage in the mystic abyss and the passage we witness in the Hegelian or the colonial abyss show telling parallels. If these similarities unify and support my thematization of the abyss and its passage, the multiple differences inscribing the multiple abysses and passages provide critical perspectives to analyze the political and the theological significance of such differences in the matrix of global, capitalist, neocolonial power. At any rate, whether the mystic self eventually reassembles itself or not, we find in the mystics a sense of self-consciousness retained even after their full self-dispossession. But this is not merely the preservation of the old consciousness. Rather, the postabyssal consciousness of the mystic is a new consciousness that allows one to realize the coincidence of opposites (Nicholas of Cusa), the ontological inseparability of God from the human (Eckhart), and the incompleteness of reason and knowledge (Pseudo-Dionysius).

Exploring all of the above questions will eventually let me move beyond the narrowly defined trope of the abyss, often restricted to metaphysical and existential meanings in its popular usage. In conversation with Enrique Dussel, Aimé Césaire, Franz Fanon, and Édouard Glissant, the authors of the (post)*Négritude* movement and Latin American liberation philosophy, I argue that the notion of the abyss warrants a wider ethico-political application in the global context of (post/neo)coloniality. I read the abyss as an all-pervading ontological groundlessness of being that involves an insurmountable material and political devastation, thereby inventing a new idiom for articulating in the same term both the spiritual/existential quandary and a political reality marked with violence and suffering.

Theorizing Coloniality: Cosmopolitanism, Postcolonial Theory, and Latin American Decolonial Thought

The crucial significance for the present project of tracing the trajectory of passage through the abyss lies in examining the passage's possibilities—and its possible resignification. While both the medieval and the continental thinkers agree on its possibilities, their response to the question of *how* such passage happens differ dramatically. These differences condition the responses that emerge from the particular context or community of interpretation. This is, perhaps, why Hegel's highly speculative account of the abyss presupposes a magically resilient subject who is able to gather itself despite uncountable failures. For the Hegelian-Marxist philosopher Slavoj Žižek, the passage through the abyss is the crucial event that gives birth to the political subject; for the American philosopher Judith Butler, the abyss is indicative of the loss constituting the self, which in turn reveals one's ties to unknown others to be the condition of her survivability.[20] The answer to these questions—that is, *how* the movement of passage takes place—shows greater differences and deeper complications when we extend this ethical/philosophical question to a different geopolitical location, specifically those sites marked by colonial difference. While I turn to Latin American decolonial theorists' elaboration of colonial difference and their discussion of coloniality/modernity later, it is important to note here the link between the theological construction of the abyss and the geopolitical difference that shapes the political contours of such theological thought.

The key argument of this book is that the trope of the abyss warrants a wider political and theological application in the global context of (post/neo)colonialism. One might perhaps question the significance of emphasizing colonial difference to contextualize or read the abyss in the politicized space of globalization. Why should this Western theological and philosophical notion be reread and rethought through the lens of colonialism and globalization in the first place? What is the possible link between the history and legacy of colonialism and the current world order framed by capitalist globalization? What is the relation between the sociopolitical articulation of this universalizing phenomenon (globalization) and the philosophical-theological construction of God, self, and other?

The clear link between European modernity/coloniality and the unstoppable expansion of globalization suggests the need to examine the history of imperialism and colonial violence when European/Western ideas are articulated in the global context. The restructuring of the world order in the past three decades under the name of globalization has given rise to numerous theories and discourses that attempt to address the abrupt shift this phenomenon has created in our conceptions of national boundaries, sovereignty, identity, culture, labor, and capital. Among many others who interrogate the terms of cultural difference, global justice, and cultural identity in the age of globalization, theorists of cosmopolitanism have advanced important theoretical foundations for a critical reading of globalization.

Rooted in the Greek term *kosmopolites* (citizens of the world), cosmopolitanism is the idea that all human beings, regardless of their political and geographical associations, are citizens of a single world community —with equal rights and status. While discussions of the major ideas of cosmopolitanism have always been central to Western social/political philosophy, the first full-fledged form of cosmopolitanism is attributed to the Stoics, who believed that one could achieve goodness by serving other human beings through political engagement. What provided the basis for this human community, for the Stoics, was "reason" in every human being.[21] This service, according to the Stoics, could not be limited to one's own state, for being human had a universal significance that transcended the geopolitical affiliation of the individual being. In Marcus Aurelius's words, "It makes no difference whether a person lives here or there, provided that, wherever he lives, he lives as a citizen of the world."[22]

Kant laid the foundation of the cosmopolitan ideas that have shaped the modern and contemporary discussions of cosmopolitanism. In *Toward Perpetual Peace*, Kant lays out the ground principles for a moral cosmopolitanism based on the notion of "hospitality." He writes, "Hospitality means the right of a stranger not to be treated in a hostile manner by another upon his arrival on the other's territory."[23] Kant's claim is based in the somewhat urgent geopolitical and judicial concern of his time that traditional understandings of sovereign states and citizenship are being challenged: "The people of the earth have entered in varying degrees into a universal community, and it is developed to the point where a violation of laws in one part of the world is felt everywhere."[24] But while the Kantian model of cosmopolitanism has been the backbone of the predominant discourses of moral and political cosmopolitanism, it goes often unnoticed, as David Harvey points out, that Kant's cosmopolitan vision is paralleled by his self-contradicting understanding of geography and anthropology, which is informed by prejudicial knowledge about race, class, gender, and nation.[25] In "The Difference between the Races," Kant writes, "The Indians have a dominating taste of the grotesque. . . . Even their paintings are grotesque and portray strange and unnatural figures such as are encountered nowhere in the world. . . . The negroes of Africa have by nature no feeling that rises above the trifling. . . . Although many of them have been set free, still not a single one has ever been found who presented anything great in art or science or any other praiseworthy quality."[26] Harvey expresses his suspicion of Kantian cosmopolitanism given that Kant's universal ethic presents a direct conflict with his anthropology and geography: "How do we apply a universal ethic to a world in which some people are considered immature or inferior and others are thought indolent, smelly, or just plain untrustworthy?"[27] Thus it is not surprising, Harvey comments, that we see in contemporary international politics a certain political power (The United States, for example) presenting "itself as the bearer of universal principles of justice, democracy, liberty, freedom, and goodness while in practice operating in an intensely discriminatory way against others" who are perceived as morally inferior and as lacking the same qualifications.[28] The problem that Harvey finds in cosmopolitanism is that it is sometimes not clear whether cosmopolitanism is a critical engagement with the current global order or a mere reflection of it. Without critically engaging the current order, Harvey contends, "seemingly radical critiques (as in the field of human rights) covertly support further neoliberalization and enhanced class domination."[29] Here Harvey targets Ulrich Beck and David Held, whose works on cosmopolitanism have had a major impact on the shaping of the contemporary discussions of judicial and political cosmopolitanism that focus especially on international human rights. The problem with their version of cosmopolitanism, for Harvey, is that their definition of human rights is too individualistic while at the same time their theories lack a critical engagement with the ways neoliberal capitalism and imperialism shape supposedly cosmopolitan practices.[30]

Walter Mignolo also raises some critical questions regarding the mainstream discourse of cosmopolitanism based in Kantian vision. His critical stance parallels Harvey's in that he too reads Kant's cosmopolitan vision against his racist anthropology and Eurocentric geography. What is innovative about Mignolo's historico-literary approach is that he sees the connection between contemporary forms of the cosmopolitan ideal and the ancient imperialistic vision of the *Orbis Christianus* (the Christian cosmos). If the historical origin of the *Orbis Christianus* dates back to the ancient Roman Empire, its cosmopolitan vision was revivified in the sixteenth century as Europe encountered its "truly" cosmopolitan horizon: the New World. Thus began the debate at the University of Salamanca in which legal theologians tried to determine "to what extent Indians in the

New World were Human, and to what extent, as a consequence, they had property rights."[31] Mignolo turns to Francisco de Vitoria, the Spanish legal theologian who was influential in shaping international law in sixteenth-century Europe. De Vitoria's humanist stance on *ius gentium* (rights of peoples or nations) held that "nations, that is, communities of people, were bound by natural law and therefore had the rights of the people" and consequently concluded there was no difference "between the Spaniards and the Indians in regard to *ium gentium*."[32] However, the problem arose when de Vitoria had to provide a logical justification for the Spaniards' appropriation of the Indian lands. His solution was to acknowledge the humanness of the Indians but to suggest that "they 'lacked' something."[33] In this way, Mignolo observes, de Vitoria inscribed colonial difference in the cosmopolitanism of sixteenth-century Europe.

Thus the Kantian cosmopolitan ideal has a trajectory of continuity that stretches from the *Orbis Romanus Christianus* via the Spanish cosmopolitan debate all the way to the contemporary cosmopolitan account called globalization. Mignolo's view resonates with Harvey's in that their uneasiness with certain contemporary versions of cosmopolitanism lies in their apprehension that globalism and cosmopolitanism may be two faces of the same coin. However, Mignolo does not reject cosmopolitan ideas altogether. The critical approach to cosmopolitanism does not indicate its ineffectuality. Rather, I argue with Harvey and Mignolo, cosmopolitanism needs to be grounded in a critique of the fundamental structure of modernity/coloniality and the destructive forces of the capitalist globalization.

Postcolonial theory has played a critical role in interrogating and reconsidering the colonial legacy and the sociocultural impact of the Western, capitalism-driven phenomenon of globalization after the "decolonial wave" that took place across the globe following the world wars. Postcolonial criticism questions the Eurocentric regime of knowledge built upon the social, historical, and ontological texture of coloniality from which the subject of knowledge is constructed. In line with poststructuralist thought, postcolonial criticism harnessed critical theoretical tools for unveiling the dark side of the phenomenon of West-led globalism that has framed the sociocultural order of signification of the postmodern age. At a theoretical level, the significance of postcolonial theory lies in its extension of the philosophical criticism of totalitarian metaphysics to the realm of historical and sociocultural discourse. On a more political level, its contribution lies in its effort to reconfigure the asymmetrical power dynamics between what has been so far perceived as the subject of power/knowledge and its others.

For the purpose of the critical analysis that this book pursues, reading the self's place (along with the place of the other) in the colonial abyss is, therefore, an endeavor that takes the character of a critical cosmopolitan project, conceived upon the horizon of postcolonial vision. Critical cosmopolitanism in the age of capitalist globalization cannot be articulated apart from the critique of coloniality undergirding and conditioning the very phenomenon of globalization, which creates an irremediable structure of inequality that precludes the cosmopolitan platform for the reinvention of citizens of the world with equal rights. Despite the significant impact and crucial contribution of postcolonial theory to the global project of counterhegemonic/modernity criticism, its political angle has been a matter of scholarly debate. Among many of its critical readers, a cluster of Latin American/Caribbean thinkers—who insist on the term *decolonial thinking* or *decolonial turn* over *postcolonialism*—have been developing a coherent body of literature that offers another constructive version of countercolonial/modern discourse.

I offer here a summary of some key points of their critique. First, Latin American/Caribbean decolonial thinkers point out the Eurocentric nature of postcolonial theory by arguing that postcolonial criticism has been theorized mainly by Third World intellectuals writing from First World metropolises that how these theorists were indifferent to the critiques emerging from the so-called peripheries.[34] While postcolonial theory, predominantly led by Asian theorists, relies heavily on French poststructuralism, Latin American and Caribbean decolonial thought grounds itself in the long tradition of countercolonial thought that began with the first colonial encounter.[35] Second, postcolonial criticism's perception of colonialism is limited to nineteenth-century European imperialism. Consequently, it tends to restrict the resource of anticolonial thinking to early twentieth-century postcolonial literature. Contrastingly, Latin American/Caribbean decolonial thinkers extend the history of colonialism to the so-called discovery of the America, which goes back to the fifteenth and sixteenth centuries. By this, they not only link the expansion of modern capitalism with the history of colonialism but also show how Europe's invention and the domination of its "other" made the universalization of Eurocentric logic, that is, European modernity, possible. In other words, colonialism is not the result of modernity, as postcolonial critics have argued. Rather, modernity is the starting point of coloniality, and coloniality is such a constitutive element of modernity so that one cannot be articulated without the other.[36]

The third and last point targets postcolonial theory's inability to address, if not its lack of interest toward, the issue of neocolonialism. Because of its literary-theoretical bent, it tends to focus on the issues of the production (or the representation) of otherness and the psychoanalytic dynamics of racial and gender identity formation, so it has not always been very successful in detecting the effects of the new historical phase of neocolonialism that has succeeded colonialism. Challenging neocolonialism, which has continued to rely on the paradigm of Eurocentric logic and which features an even more intensified system of capitalist expansion, requires perhaps more than the deconstruction of colonial binaries that many postcolonial critics have been preoccupied with. In contrast, Latin American/Caribbean decolonial thinkers place the connection between race and economy/labor at the heart of their critical analysis. As the works of founding figures such as Enrique Dussel and Anibal Quijano have demonstrated, Latin American decolonial thought attempts to link the cultural/philosophical analysis of race relations and coloniality with the historical/economic analysis of capitalist expansion accompanied by the exploitation of labor.

The differentiation of Latin American theory's particularity, according to Mabel Moraña, Enrique Dussel, and Carlos Jauregui's introduction to *Coloniality at Large*, lies not in a claim of exceptionalism but in "an attempt to elaborate on colonial difference."[37] Here *colonial difference* is a key term in Latin American decolonial thinking that points to the irreducible difference of the colonial configuration marked by the spatial articulation of power. In other words, as defined by Walter Mignolo, it is the consequence of the "coloniality of power" (Anibal Quijano) born out of the collusive tie between modernity and coloniality (Enrique Dussel).[38] It follows that the primary focus of colonial difference as outlined by Latin American philosophers has been power asymmetry between Europe and its other as it affects epistemological, geopolitical, and economic differences between the two locations. Both Quijano's and Mignolo's works have played a key role in shaping the geopolitical and sociohistorical design of colonial difference. Particularly important is Quijano's contribution showing how race was invented as a tool of domination by colonial ideology. Quijano's main contention is that race was used as a category of social classification in order to justify the colonial relationship in which the system of forced labor was legitimized.[39] On the basis of this colonial difference, the racist distribution of social identities—with its main axes being, first, the racial difference between the conqueror and the conquered, and second, the control of labor on the basis of both capital and racial difference—labor distribution provided the basis for the consolidation of a structure of exploitation that became the key generating power of colonial capitalism.[40]

Another facet of colonial difference can be articulated in ontological and existential terms. Enrique Dussel views America as the other of Europe, whose exploited labor and resources provided the material ground for the cultural hegemony or universalization of European modernity. Dussel adopts the notion of the other from Emmanuel Levinas and connects it with the concrete sociopolitical context of Latin America. In his influential critique of metaphysics, Levinas points out the totalitarian tendency of metaphysics, which appropriates and reduces the other into the same. For Levinas, "The other is neither initially nor ultimately what we grasp or what we thematize."[41] Rather, it signifies exteriority, an "alterity" and a "radical heterogeneity," an "absolutely other [that] is the Other."[42] Dussel then interprets the Levinasian other as the poor, the "wretched one who suffers traumatically in her corporeality the oppression and exclusion from the benefits of the totality."[43] Therefore, Dussel clarifies, Latin America does not fit into the frame of modernity, whether pre-, anti, or postmodern. Latin America *is* the exteriority of European modernity. Following Levinas's critique of totalitarian metaphysics, Dussel asserts the critique of the totalitarian regime of European modernity as the central project of Liberation philosophy. The affirmation of the other, the exteriority of the totalitarian system, is the basis and the ground from which Liberation philosophy begins.[44]

Dussel claims that exteriority originates from a place "other" than European and American modernity. Cultures that were excluded and negated by European modernity but that developed and survived are "transmodern," as they are beyond European modernity. The Caribbean existential thinkers further complexify and probe the notion of colonial difference with an added layer of ontological coloniality. They articulate a decolonial vision out of the traces of trauma imprinted on the deepest existential texture of (colonized) being, whose ontological horizon is conditioned by the threat of what Frantz Fanon calls "omnipresent death."[45] It is not my intention, however, to suggest the superiority of Latin American decolonial thought over the more Asian postcolonial theory. Rather, I see these methods as complementing each other. In other words, the multidisciplinary journey of this book is born out of my interest in probing the philosophical, theological, ethical, and political significance of the abyss from the standpoint of coloniality. Cosmopolitanism, postcolonial criticism, and Latin American decolonial thought serve as the guiding theoretical tools that facilitate this journey.

In effect, this book attempts to achieve a multidisciplinary dialogue that is largely missing in the crucial junctures where different theological and philosophical threads emerge and intersect. Indeed, despite its strong impact in the overall field of the humanities, postcolonial/decolonial theory has seldom been taken as a serious conversation partner by the philosophical discourse of religion. In theology, on the other hand, postcolonial theory started to have relatively significant repercussions from the end of the last century. However, the Latin American (Pan-American) brand of decolonial thinking remains a discourse foreign to contemporary theology and philosophy of religion.[46] In the current debates of continental philosophy of religion and political theology particularly, an in-depth analysis of the conditions and political effects of ongoing "coloniality" at a global level is, to a large degree, missing.[47] By exploring the diverse forms of political theologies arising from the colonial context, I aim to bring the experience of the ongoing reality of colonialism to the forefront of theological and philosophical reasoning.

Taking on Theology from the Ruins

If political theology articulates a form of thought geared toward addressing cultural and political questions in their relation to religion, its scope has been mostly limited to discourses emerging from the continental philosophy of religion. Despite the growing interest in the phenomena of globalization and cosmopolitanism within the ongoing debates of political theology, a substantive analysis of the relation between politics and the all-pervading conditions of (neo)colonialism is largely absent. This book therefore proposes a form of political—or better, cosmopolitical— theology that thinks through the ideas of religion, ethics, and politics from the contextualized standpoint of sociohistorical trauma and structural violence affecting disenfranchised communities around the globe. To do this, I ground my critical analysis of coloniality in the writings of the post-*Négritude* movement, particularly in Glissant's work. If the Hegelian journey of dialectical becoming is characterized by the enigmatic resilience of the subject who reconstructs itself despite constant failures, Glissant presents an account of becoming that opens a significant line of contrast. The question that Glissant presents is, What happens when the self (or self-consciousness for Hegel) is born in and conditioned by coloniality? In what ways might the trajectory of becoming differ when the abyss from which the self emerges is not just a theological and mystical indeterminacy but a colonial groundlessness?

For Glissant, the reconstruction of the self in the colonial context seems to be an impossible project. Glissant's writings are characterized by the notion of the abyss and a language akin to that of mysticism; in its excessiveness the colonial abyss resembles the theological abyss of mysticism. Marked by the horrifying memory of death and the shock of transportation, slavery, and dehumanization, the history of Martinique and the Afro-Caribbean diaspora still fails to find expression in language. At the deadlock between the memory of the unspeakable trauma and the still-impaired present, between "a past order that is rejected" and an "absurd present," Glissant turns to the power of poetics.[48] His notion of "counter-poetics" or "forced poetics" conceives poetics as a strategy of survival and resistance, a way of naming and remembering the unbearable memory of historical trauma that constitutes the abyss of the present Afro-Caribbean reality. By welcoming the haunting memory of terror and affirming the impaired present, Glissant ventures to construct a collective sense of identity out of the abyssal trauma of fragmentation.

At the juncture where ontology and politics fail, (theo)poetics offers a fresh perspective as I strive to negotiate the delicate boundary between the spiritual and the political with the end of articulating the unnameable name of the divine and the unbearable memory of pain and suffering in the same term. Glissant's secular poetics of creolization becomes a more relevant reference for the reconciliation of the spiritual and the political after its dialogue with contemporary theopoetics, as my comparative reading uncovers the theological implication implicit in Glissant's poetics while equally uncovering the political implication lying beneath theopoetics. Of particular importance will be the comparative reading of Glissant and the feminist theologian Catherine Keller, since Glissant's view on the past and future of Caribbean identity finds deep resonance with Catherine Keller's constructive theological vision. Common to both authors is the metaphor of the depth of the ocean as it denotes the abyss, which, for both authors, signifies a middle space of becoming. More importantly, Keller's endeavor to politicize apophaticism and her theopoetics of *tehom*—and more recently her "cloudy" theology—provides important insights for unveiling the theological potential of Glissant's secular mysticism and thus for rethinking the very notion of theology and the divine in postsecular terms. For both Keller and Glissant, the abyssal depth of the middle is the matrix, the "groundless ground" for the self's relational becoming that inescapably leads to cosmopolitics: the creolized world in Relation (Glissant), ceaselessly struggling to found a "planetary convivencia" (Keller).[49]

This loop of relational becoming is neither merely a result of a constructive interpretation nor a cross-disciplinary invention foreign to the old theological and philosophical tradition. Rather, as I have briefly summarized above, there is a long tradition of intellectual history that testifies to such a rich polysemy of the abyss. By tracing its trajectory of development within the tradition, we might, perhaps, see a new politico-theological horizon emerge: an oceanic depth of possibility in which the experience of loss and trauma opens the door to the cosmopolitical future.

The Mystical Abyss

Via Negativa

The trope of the abyss evokes both the images and the sentiments of mysticism. The mystical underpinning of the abyss does not, however, exclusively derive from philosophical and religious writings. Rather, the figure of the abyss has mystical repercussions in a wide variety of literatures that scrutinize the human experience of finitude. The mystical language of the abyss is appropriated by many writers who seek a way of translating the sense of finitude caused by the material and political conditions of human existence. But the gap between the philosophical or religious question and the ethical question emerging from the political context might seem to be irremediable, particularly when the tie binding these two distant contexts is woven out of mystical language. What is the point of intersection between the mystical experience conditioning the theological pursuit of God (or the metaphysical inquiry into the One) and the experience of agony born in the contexts of suffering and violence? In what ways does the abyss accommodate the failure of language, thought, or categories of being to articulate the untranslatable nature of the "all-transcending absolute" experienced in the two seemingly distant contexts of the mystical and the historical/political?

Theorizing trauma is a project that has not been paid the attention it deserves in contemporary political theology. In many cases, liberationist or radical forms of thinking have failed to consider the wounds of trauma and suffering as a resource for a radical political imagination. Theorizing trauma tends to be disregarded as a project restricted to psychoanalysis and as nonpolitical, privatizing, and even reactionary. Exploring the abyssal gap between the mystical and the historical/political from the site of colonial violence demands theorization of the history and reality of suffering, a sobering reflection on wounds and remains—that is, the very site where the history of a collective consciousness has been traumatically ruptured by colonial violence.

Further, there seems to be a conspicuous dichotomy between the mystical and the political. According to this division, the mystical rarely intersects with the political, as it usually amounts to an apolitical and privatized obsession with the self and God. Taking the writings of the Neoplatonic mystics in particular, one might indeed find many of them, to a certain degree, to be self-absorbed and apolitical. The mystics' theologies are apolitical to the extent that they are not deliberately politicized. Nevertheless, their theologies, more often than not, *are* political—even when articulated apolitically—in that they inevitably give birth to particular forms of politics. That is, it is unlikely that a theology based in a hierarchal cosmology is not somehow connected to a political ideal grounded in hierarchal values. My use of the term *apolitical*, therefore, designates the fact that the mystical writings are not molded by explicit political languages. However, I insist that a significant range of mystical texts bear traces of radical forms of thought for rethinking the political. In particular, Neoplatonic mysticism develops in the form of its negative theology the seeds of an innovative frame of a cosmology that in surprising ways opposes the dominant, Platonic form of metaphysics that has shaped the main tradition of Western philosophy and theology. Specifically, I submit that negative theology's understanding of the self, that is the insistence on the dispossession of the self, the negation of speech and representation, and the openness to uncertainty or exteriority, bears important implications for the project of (cosmo)political theology that I seek to develop. Therefore, by engaging the writings of the mystical thinkers, this chapter draws a parallel and creates resonance with chapter 4, in which I read the abyss as an experience of finitude conditioned by the political and historical predicament. While the connection between these two different contexts will become more explicit in chapter 4, the apophatic way articulated by mystical thinkers lays the groundwork for the further exploration of this surprising connection. For now, suffice it to name a few points that mystical thought suggests for the general direction of this book. First, by looking at the implications of "finitude" in mysticism, I intend to examine the fine line that divides finitude and plenitude, or vulnerability and potency, against the one-sided understanding of finitude as a negative characteristic destitute of any positive significance. My reading of the mystics will lift up human finitude as the gateway into the "beyond" of finitude itself. Consequently, this point will set the stage for my project of looking into wounds and theorizing trauma in order to turn them into the very site or womb that gives birth to new political possibility. Second, the apophatic move that mystics take when confronted with the impasse of the unspeakable experience signals the overthrowing of all given names and representations, including one's own sense of self and, by implication, sociopolitical reality. This might further point to the potential embedded in the unexplored connection between apophatic theology and political theology, while the work of naming the unnameable would amount to what Derrida calls the "impossible." Impossibility, however, does not indicate the renunciation of hope. Rather, it points to the tireless work of striving for the *possibility* of the impossible. This last point will be a recurring theme in the following chapters as I read the abyss articulated in the ethico-philosophical context (post-Kantian continental philosophy) and in the political context (Latin American/Caribbean tradition). That is, one of my central agendas here is to demonstrate, through my constructive reading of the three different contexts (mystical, philosophical, and political) of the abyss, the complex tension between the possible and impossible, naming and the unnameable, hope and despair, or future (beginning) and trauma. Third and last, the dispossession of the self in mystical thought entails the self's submission to her limits, to the realm of the unknown and uncertainty. It implies openness to exteriority, to the other, that is, *relation*.

In effect, reading the mystical and the political together helps us rediscover not only the political potential of the mystical and the mystical dimension of the political but the need to further politicize the mystical and to further mystify (spiritualize) the political. The abyss, in this sense, is the gap between these two poles (the mystical and the political) that reveals both the limits of each when they are articulated separately and, conversely, the potential that opens up when the boundary between the two is collapsed.

Stepping into the Abyss

The most remarkable development of the conception of the abyss took place within the long unfolding of medieval mysticism. The abyss becomes an important metaphor in the works of the mystics whose main preoccupation lies in finding an analogy, a way of articulating the ineffable character of the divine mystery. One of the main procedures that marks the trajectory of theological and philosophical development in Neoplatonism is negative theology. The tradition of negative or apophatic theology parallels the course of the conceptualization of the abyss since its inception in Neoplatonism. First developed by the early church fathers and the Neoplatonists in late antiquity, negative theology becomes a full-fledged theological methodology in the writings of Pseudo-Dionysius and medieval mystics such as Meister Eckhart, Hadewijch, Margarite Porete, Nicholas of Cusa, and John of the Cross. If the major contribution in the conceptualization of the abyss comes from the tradition of negative theology, it is in the work of the Neoplatonic thinkers that we find the traces of the inception of negative theology. It would be indispensable to discuss Plato before examining the writings of Neoplatonic thinkers. This is not simply because Neoplatonism is philosophically rooted in Plato but also because Plato's writings already bear some traces of negative theology. Plato's notion of the all-transcendent God provides the ground for Plotinus's further radicalization of the transcendence of the One, which is the womb of negative theology.

The irony of Plato's philosophy is that his works lay out the foundation of two competing philosophical traditions. Plato is commonly charged with grounding the foundational structure of the major trajectory of Western metaphysics. His theory of forms assumes the main responsibility for the dominance of idealism based on metaphysical dualism. Yet at the same time the nonsystematic—if not inconsistent—nature of Plato's thought reflected in works such as *Parmenides* and the *Republic* reveals the genesis of important philosophical ideas that contradict his own theory of forms—or at least the dominant interpretations of it. His construction of the One in *Parmenides*, for instance, presents a clear opposite of ontotheology as he negates all attributes that might subject the Good to being. The Good, Plato writes in the *Republic*, is beyond being (*epekeina tes ousias*): "Goodness isn't actually the state of being, but surpasses being in majesty and might" (*Republic* 509b). According to *Parmenides* the One is not compatible with the categories of being. In a way, the seed of negative theology is planted by the architect of the very form of thought against which negative theology emerged as a reaction.

The basic framework of Plato's philosophy lies in his dyadic analysis. He presents the world as composed of the material world of temporality and the ideal world of order and rationality. Whereas the former is contingent, visible, changeable, and mortal, the latter is divine, constant, intelligible, and changeless (*Phaedo* 78c–80b). The latter is also called the world of Forms or Ideal Forms by Plato in his Socratic dialogues, and it refers to the highest reality, which exists beyond any defective reality lying in the realm of the temporal, material order. Meanwhile, the sensible world of becoming has been fashioned on an eternal Idea and "formed to be like that reality" but is only a likeness (*Republic* 29 c). Lacking fundamental reality, the material world is the reflection or shadow emulating these forms (ideas). As the famous allegory of the cave he presents in the *Republic* tells us, people see only the shadows of reality without even realizing it. The Good, as the most fundamental and highest of all forms, represents perfection and immutability. Truth, for Plato, is eternal, and what is eternal never changes. Therefore, goodness, as the ultimate and unchanging reality, should not be equated with the knowledge of it (*Republic* 508c), since the visible, sensible realm is inherently defective. In the cosmological account he provides in *Timaeus*, Plato draws the distinction between being and becoming, between that which never changes and that which comes to be. He reinforces the dualistic hierarchy more concretely by associating being (the unchanging reality) with understanding and reason while linking becoming with unreasoned sense perception: "It comes to be and passes away but never really is" (*Timaeus* 28a).

We know perhaps all too clearly how such a dualistic view of the world has served as the foundation for the dominant dualistic epistemology of the Western philosophical tradition, which has operated upon the irreconcilable split between the spheres of mind and body, reason and sense, idea and matter. The trouble with this dualism is not only the false ontological hierarchy and separation it creates but also the epistemological—and the further ethico-political—implication that its idea of immutability and transcendence alludes to. The logic of colonial domination and its constant attempts to annihilate alterity/difference has been exercised under the principle of such totalitarian thought; it is characterized by a hierarchy that grants the "transcendent" qualities of unalterable being and reason to the colonizer while associating the colonial other with sense, body, and change. The colonial agenda was then about incorporating these deficiencies, differences, and deviations into the eternal perfection of sameness, that is, the unchanging One.

But the stern dualism characterizing the essence of the One and its relation to the universe is complicated by the modality of sheer transcendence framing Plato's cosmology. The logical consequence that Plato derives from the notion of sheer transcendence is the contradiction caused by the (in)compatibility of the One with the categories of being. In the *Republic* (509b), for instance, Plato famously claims that the Good is not being but transcends the category of being. As William Franke rightly points out, the notion of "a Good beyond being, and therefore equally beyond speech and reason (Logos)," undergirds the apophatic tradition.[1] Plato attempts to articulate this dilemma in detail in one of his late dialogues, *Parmenides*, and we find there the most explicit and systematic hints of negative theology. Perhaps the most remarkable aspect of *Parmenides* is Plato's use of negative language to describe ultimate reality. Except in the *Symposium*, where he employs negative terms to describe the mystery of inconceivable beauty, *Parmenides* is the only text where Plato uses the negative method to articulate the One. In what seems to be a challenge to his own theory of forms, Plato demonstrates, by the method of negation, how different attributes of being are not compatible with the One because the One is *One*. Having neither beginning nor end, Plato writes, "it would have no shape" (*Parmenides* 137d). The series of conversations involving logical exercise or inquiry and the method of negation develops further as the main interlocutor, Parmenides of Elea, claims that such a One would be nowhere, as "it would be neither in another nor in itself" (*Parmenides* 138a–b). The dialogue culminates with the strongest apopohatic statement, which comes toward the end, after Plato deprives the One of all its main attributes: "And so, the one in no way is. It appears not. So it is not even such as to be one; for otherwise it would at once be and participate in being; but the one, as it seems, is not one and is not" (*Parmenides* 141e). Plato concludes the first section of the dialogue by pointing to the ultimate mystery of the One who lies in the realm of the unknowable and unspeakable: "And that which is not . . . it is not named or spoken of, nor is it an object of opinion, nor is it known, nor does any of the things that are perceive it" (*Parmenides* 142a).

The relation between negative theology and the abyss is important not only because apophaticism is responsible for the dynamic ramification of the notion of the abyss within religious and philosophical discourses. The marriage of apophaticism and the abyss in mystical thought finds its irreplaceable significance in its (anti)metaphysical implication. The abyss, as reflected in the Neoplatonic mystics' writings, creates the possibility of deconstructing the very idea of substance, self, and even God. Just as the radical transcendence of the One results in its paradoxical immanence in all, the impossibility of articulating the transcendent Godhead turns in a radical reconfiguration of all previously established knowledge, including the conception of being and God. This is why Jacques Derrida affirms that his famous project of deconstruction resembles negative theology,[2] and further remarks that the essential traits of negative theology are "passing to the limit, then crossing a frontier, including that of a community, thus of a sociopolitical, institutional, ecclesial reason or *raison d'etre*."[3]

The radically transcendent God of negative theology finds its linguistic home in the language of "bottomlessness," as both notions point to the multifaceted paradox and the overwhelming mystery of divinity. The abyss denotes the converging point or the blurred demarcation between finitude and infinity, between the negative and the positive. Similarly, the path of the *via negativa* is also paved with seemingly contradictory qualities in such a way that *unknowing* is the only way leading one to true knowledge, and all creation is contained in the transcendent One who lies *beyond* all. The method of negation testifies to the fact that truth can be glimpsed only through a humble epistemological surrender to one's limits. No sense of a solid foundation and self-certainty survives the *via negativa*. All forms of knowledge, including the very assured sense of the self, are radically displaced in the journey of negation. The knowledge of both God and the self can be reached only beyond oppositions and boundaries as the uncontainable nature of the divine mystery cuts across the apparent sets of contradictions. For mystical thinkers, what lies at the heart of the journey on the *via negativa*, which is filled with denials and abandonment of all established categories of knowledge, is the abyss—the unfathomable depth of the Godhead.

However, throughout the history of the Western religious tradition the abyss refers to the depth(lessness) not only of God but also of the human soul. According to Grace Jantzen, Augustine formulates, on the ground of Psalm 42:7, the idea of "reciprocity of the unfathomable abyss of the divine nature and the abyss of the human heart."[4] Thus, for Augustine, the abyss also refers to the heart of human beings. As David Coe comments, it is related to the inward dimension of the soul, that is, the soul's unsearchable depths, where innumerable thresholds point to both limits (finitude) and new possibilities. Interesting here is Augustine's association of the abyss with freedom, for the conventional perception of freedom in contemporary usages draws, almost exclusively, on a boundless sense of liberty, without any restriction or any sense of negativity in it.[5] For the medieval mystic Meister Eckhart too, the abyss relates to both God and the human soul. Eckhart calls the abyss the ground that God and human soul share and writes that in their mystical union God and the soul are both uncreated.[6] In this sense, the abyss as gap, boundary, split, and indeterminacy manifests everywhere: both inside and outside God, between God and the world, and inside the human soul.

A close examination of negative theology, then, reveals the key traits of the abyss. These traits become more apparent as my reading of the abyss evolves and branches in multiple directions, particularly by examining the abyss's relation to God, the Other, and the context of oppression (suffering). One distinctive characteristic of the abyss is the unspeakable dimension of the experience (the encounter with the divine), its failure to find mediation in common language. At the impasse of unspeakability, mystics turn not to mere silence but to apophasis. Apophasis opened up at the limit of metaphysics offers a new way of knowing and thinking about being. Apophatic theology signals not only an alternative to ontotheology, as many of its postmodern readers suggest, but also the inadequacy of language to describe the unfathomable depths of both the self and God. Before the failure of predication, apophasis offers a twofold movement: it signals the resignation of the categories of being (including the self), while at the same time it indicates the self's indomitable desire to name the un-nameable, to speak the unspeakable. Hope arises somewhere in between these two movements, and they offer transition to a second trait of the abyss: the paradoxical relation between finitude and mystery, or wonder. The abyss, rather than pointing to *either* finitude *or* infinity, points to both of them at once. The key texts of negative theology illuminate the process in which the self's submission to her limit is followed by the opening of wonder. In other words, I want to highlight the fact that for the medieval mystics, divine mystery, or what Eckhart calls the "mystic union," cannot be glimpsed without the self's surrender to finitude.

Third and last, submission to finitude results in the dispossession of the self. And it is not only the self who is dissolved in the abyss but God. The absence of the ground (groundlessness) for the assertion of the self evokes another mode of knowing and being that is based in *relation*. The self who dissolves in the abyss and reemerges realizes that she is inseparably tied to the other(s). Relation testifies to the interdependence and the incompleteness of the self. The notion of the self as a totalitarian whole, purity, and essence is undone in the abyss. The abyss undoes the notion of being as an unchangeable essence. As Catherine Malabou tells us in her reading of Heidegger, before being there is change: "a change that finally changes essence into what it is—a place of exchange."[7] Thus embracing finitude in the abyss leads not only to the opening of wonder but also to relation. I hope to demonstrate how these characteristics of the abyss are articulated in the writings of apophatic theologians, particularly Plotinus, Pseudo-Dionysius, and Meister Eckhart.

Radical Transcendence of the One: The Neoplatonic Inception

Negative theology begins with Plotinus, who develops the underdeveloped trace of negativity lurking in Plato into a full-fledged philosophical system known as Neoplatonism. Plotinus develops a unified cosmology in which everything hierarchically emanates from the One. The basic structure of Plotinus's philosophy is indubitably Platonic. He inherits the major common themes of Platonic tradition, such as beauty, the good, the immortality of the soul, and the immateriality of reality, and affirms them in his major philosophical work, the *Enneads*.[8] Following Plato, Plotinus emphasizes the role of the One, which he also refers to as the "Good" or the "Ideal Form." Plotinus advances the notion of the all-transcending One, which remains underdeveloped and somewhat nebulous in Plato. The radical and unique aspect of the Plotinian view lies in the fact that the One, because of its absolutely transcendent nature, no longer contains a distinction within itself. Rather, as the prototype of all Forms, the One is "differing from all its sequel, self-gathered not interblended with the forms that rise from it."[9] At the same time, as the transcendent One it is also the cause of everything. It (the One) is "base to all, cause of universal existence and of ordered station."[10] The strict binary of transcendence and immanence is blurred, since Plotinus, as Baine Harris remarks, "does not set the knower off from his objects. Rather, he makes the intelligible universe within the subject the object of knowledge."[11] More specifically, the inexpressible transcendence of the One blurs the boundary between transcendence and immanence, subject and object, inside and outside, as the One is both "beyond" and the "ground" of everything.

In Plotinus's cosmology, the One, as the source of all the universe, emanates into another, less perfect level of being without necessarily affecting its perfect and unchanging nature. More interestingly, everything that derives from the One, in Plotinian cosmology, seeks to return to it. Plotinus therefore adds a relational attribute to the God of Greek metaphysics, "in which divine perfection meant indifference to the world."[12] The three cosmological principles inherited from Plato that Plotinus further develops are categorized as the One (Good), the Intellect, and the Soul. First is the One, which transcends all and exists outside all things. The One is by no means definable or namable. The crucial moment in the history of apophatic theology begins here, where "Plotinus actually bequeaths this term [apophaticism] to the tradition."[13] In the *Enneads*, he asserts that "generative of all, The Unity is none of all; neither thing nor quantity nor quality nor intellect nor soul; not in motion, not at rest, not in place, not in time: it is the self-defined, unique in form or, better, formless, existing before Form was, or Movement or Rest, all of which are attachments of Being and make Being the manifold it is."[14] Eloquently defined by Plotinus, apophatic theology presupposes an epistemological humbleness in which the solipsistic sense of a knower and a solid sense of meaning give way to uncertainty.

Second, the Intellect is derived from the One. Through the Intellect we know the One, for it represents, as with Plato's Ideal world, the image of the One.[15] The Intellectual Principle is the all-embracing archetype, the ideal archetype. In Philippus Pistorius's words, the Intellectual Principle is the "teleological goal of the universe," the universe as it should be, or "the plan according to which the development of the universe takes place."[16] The final component that enables the realization of the Divine Idea in the material realm is the Soul. The Soul expresses all the Forms by incarnating itself in the cosmos. It materializes particular entities in their pluralities, yet it grounds them in unity. Just as the Intellect seeks to approximate the One, the Soul strives back toward the One. Thus Plotinus rewrites Plato's blurry cosmology in a much clearer and more hierarchical form. This complex cosmology, which straddles multiple contradictory terms, along with the attempt to mediate the Platonic notion of the immutable One with the becoming world of matter, leads Plotinus to the abyss of apophasis. In *Enneads* 5.3, Plotinus articulates the apophatic nature of the One. The all-transcending One has no name and is unsayable. It "is not a thing among things; we can give it no name because that would imply predication."[17] The unsayability of the One indicates the failure of language, but it does not signify the impossibility of our experience of the One altogether. At the juncture where knowledge and language fail, Plotinus resorts to apophasis, to the poetic language that signals the mystical space of negation and silence: "We do not, it is true, grasp it by knowledge, but that does not mean that we are utterly void of it; we hold it not so as to state it, but so as to be able to speak about it. And we can and do state what it is not, while we are silent as to what it is."[18]

Seen this way, apophasis entails the embrace of human finitude in which the self surrenders to the limits of her knowing and being. Nonetheless, the One is not completely inaccessible to the world. The strict dualism distinguishing between finitude and infinitude and between transcendence and immanence loses its meaning in the abyssal space of negation as submission to finitude gives birth to wonder, the opening of the divine mystery or what Plotinian scholars call the "mystical union."[19] This is the second trait of the abyss; Plotinus insists that finitude does not indicate the ultimate limit of being. Against the temptation of denial or resignation before finitude, apophaticism invites us to embrace our limits by way of self-dispossession.

Analogically, the One articulated by negative theology, in its all-transcending nature and ungraspable mystery, bears a remarkable similarity with trauma. Just as the Neoplatonic One is characterized by ineffability and unknowability, trauma, in contemporary clinical and psychoanalytic understanding, is characterized by indescribability and unrepresentability. As I already stated earlier, the connection between God and trauma become clearer in the following chapters as it enables me to extend the theological-philosophical question of the abyss into the political questions of finitude experienced in situations of violence and suffering. Despite the absence of language to describe it, the crucial step involved in overcoming trauma entails *naming* the traumatic event—that is, acknowledging one's engulfment in the overwhelming force of trauma. In other words, the beginning point for addressing trauma is perhaps the act of embracing one's finitude experienced in one's encounter with the unspeakable event.

Embracing finitude also implies acknowledging the impossibility of being a complete self. As will become more explicit in Meister Eckhart's writings, the abyss exposed at the heart of Neoplatonic apophaticism points to the absence of the ground for a solid and coherent sense of the self. For Plotinus, therefore, the ecstatic encounter with the divine, or the "mystic union," implies acknowledgment of one's limit, for something greater than oneself takes control over the self: "Those who are divinely possessed and inspired have at least knowledge that they hold some greater thing within them though they cannot tell what it is; from the movements that stir them and the utterances that come from them they perceive the power, not themselves, that moves them."[20] Plotinus thus turns the limits of human existence into the threshold of transcendence. But the dispossession of the self or the collapse of the boundary between self and other also indicates the beginning of relation, the third characteristic of the abyss. Plotinus does not thematize relation or employ the language of relation. Nevertheless, one of his important contributions to the trajectory of Western intellectual history is the creation of a space for relation in the Platonic system. His effort to mediate the relation between the immutable One and the living universe resulted in the innovation of a pan*en*theist cosmology, which views God and the world as mutually enfolding each other. However, the potential for the advancement of a relational angle is already embedded in Plotinus's notion of the One. As Baine Harris remarks in discussing the nature of the One in relation to unity, the Plotinian One is itself the unity (rather than *having* unity), and it bequeaths being to its "participants."[21] The philosophical significance of Plotinus's notion of participation lies in the distinctive implication that "participation in the divine" bears, since it sets a clear difference from the Platonic term of merely "reflecting the divine."[22] Because the One is the source from which everything is generated and the goal toward which everything moves, the only way of being real is by sharing in the One, by participating in the "mystical union."[23]

Nevertheless, Plotinian cosmology remains largely undivorced from the Platonic system. Even after bequeathing form to other beings, the Plotinian One remains intact, unaffected by the emanation. Such principle puts a fundamental curb on identifying the relational side of Plotinus's cosmology. His cosmology is certainly more relational when compared to Plato's cosmology. But we are somehow left unconvinced about the ethics that this kind of relation evokes. For a relation centered on the sameness of the pivotal One and ontological hierarchy seems far from capable of undoing the ontotheological foundations of Platonic metaphysics. Whatever form of relation we see taking shape, it seems that the kind of relation we can envision from a cosmology in which everything issues from the immutable, pivotal One shows significant difference from the relation characterizing the self in the abyss. Despite this disparity, Plotinus's Neoplatonism is significant for the current conversation in that it opens the possibility for rethinking the robust dualism structuring the Platonic metaphysics.

Speaking of the One in Neoplatonic apophaticism carries a much wider meaning than just talking about the divine. With apophatic theology, we learn that (un)speaking of God involves acknowledging our creaturely finitude and the vulnerability of incompleteness ingrained in the edifice of our being. Speaking of the One implies speaking of our human limits of lack and contingency before the One: "Note, similarly, that, when we speak of this First as Cause, we are affirming something happening *not to it but to us*, the fact that we take from this Self-Enclosed: strictly we should put neither a This nor a That to it; we hover, as it were, about it, seeking the statement of an experience of our own, sometimes nearing this Reality, sometimes baffled by the enigma in which it dwells."[24] The dual failure of language and selfhood in the face of the overwhelming presence/absence of the One reflects the fundamental quandary that cuts through the writings of negative theologians. Ontotheology fails at this juncture because the very notion of being—including the Supreme Being, namely the One (God)—cannot be accommodated in ontological/theological terms. Instead, being finds expression within a fuzzy cosmological picture under a participatory and somewhat relational frame where the distinction between knower and known, subject and object, becomes elusive.[25] More importantly, the absolutely transcendent and radically immanent nature of the One makes all languages and images about God futile. In this sense, Plotinus can be seen as the progenitor of negative theology. However, Plotinus's successors will be the ones to establish the foundational ground of negative theology. Particularly Pseudo-Dionysius is an indispensable resource in negative theology, as he is considered to have made the first systematic attempt to build an intentional account of negative theology. Dionysius, whose real identity is appropriately unknown, was a Neoplatonist from the late fifth or early sixth century who transposed Neoplatonism, particularly that of Plotinus and Proclus, into the Christian tradition.

Darkness So Far above Light

In his attempt to develop a philosophical explanation of the One in its relation to the world, Dionysius sets the model for "apophatic rhetoric," as Franke suggests, characterized as "extremely provocative in its oxymorons, paradoxes, and neologisms."[26] He inherits the major themes of Neoplatonic philosophy from his predecessors and affirms the idea of an "utterly transcendent One" who nevertheless encompasses and grounds the creation. Consequently, the One contains contradictory qualities, grounding all things while transcending them all; it remains within itself even when it processes outward to create the universe; it is the boundary of all things while being itself the unbounded infinity.[27]

The theme of participation also occupies an important place in the Dionysian thought. Participation is the key principle that mediates transcendence and immanence or God and the world. God is both transcendent and immanent in all, and a unity and participation in the One becomes the absolute condition of the emanation of multiple forms in the universe. Dionysius further radicalizes the Neoplatonic dialectic of transcendence and immanence, which claims God to be the source of everything to the extent that the One is "virtually everything." The Dionysian One is more than an all-encompassing ground. The One materializes the "all" in itself: "So everything, and every part of everything, participates in the One. By being the One, it is all things."[28]

Following Plotinus, Dionysius takes on the *via negativa* in his attempt to articulate the all-transcendent One. No reason or language can ever find an appropriate articulation of the One: "The inscrutable one is out of the reach of every rational process. Nor can any words come up to the inexpressible Good." The absolute transcendence of the One lies beyond all human categories: "Mind beyond mind, word beyond speech, it is gathered up by no discourse, by no intuition, by no name. It is and it is as no other being is."[29] After acknowledging the limits of reason and language, which fail to contain the presence of God, Dionysius confesses the dilemma of the theologian who nevertheless strives to talk about God without knowing how to: "How can we do this if the Transcendent surpasses discourse and all knowledge, if it abides beyond the reach of mind and of being . . . how can we enter upon this undertaking if the Godhead is superior to being and is unspeakable and unnameable?"[30] Following Plotinus's mystic union, Dionysius also suggests the possibility of encountering the divine wisdom, what he calls the "Light beyond all deity."[31] Such union, Dionysius tells us, is possible only through the halt of reason, "through the denial of all beings."[32] The finitude of *being*, Dionysius shows us, is ineluctably connected to the finitude of *knowing*.

Plotinus's apophatic take on the finitude of being/knowing and his acknowledgment of the power of "something greater than oneself" are advanced by Dionysius into a full-blown system of apophatic epistemology. Negation takes a more active and concrete expression in Dionysian theology to the extent that the highest knowledge of God "comes through unknowing."[33] Self-dispossession or cessation of the act of knowing and speaking becomes a deliberate gesture in Dionysius as he suggests that before the mystery of the One we remove from ourselves all the previously established knowledge and understanding of the divine. Consequently, the self is also deconstructed at its encounter with its limits. Dionysius suggests that one can be uplifted to the ray of the divine shadow by an "absolute abandonment" of not only oneself but everything.[34] Truth is unreachable unless one throws oneself into the abyss and travels to the limits of reason and speech.

Dionysius's apophatic gesture culminates in his celebration of the complete surrender of the self before the mystery of the hidden One. The central focus of his apophaticism is not the dialectical mediation of Truth. Rather, his interest seems to lie in the sheer transcendence of the absolute Other and the concurrent failure of reason to grasp its mystery. If Plotinus's philosophical agenda lies in mediating the One with the human experience, Dionysius's negative theology hints at the complete surrender of reason and the humble praise of the ineffability of the One: "With our minds made prudent and holy, we offer worship to that which lies hidden beyond thought and beyond being. With a wise silence we do honor to the inexpressible."[35] A decentering epistemological gesture grounds Dionysius's theological vision as he alludes to the fact that the main purpose of his negative method is not to understand, name, or grasp that which lies beyond, not to reveal the reality of the ungraspable truth or to describe the indescribable. Rather, his intention is "to sing a hymn of praise" to the wholly other.[36]

Even though Dionysius pushes the apophatic method further than any of his other predecessors, his theological perspective is not necessarily any more pessimistic than that of his Neoplatonic ancestors. Rather, one finds in Dionysius the evocation of a beautiful poetic language that exalts the irremediable ontological gap between God and the world. Dionysius welcomes and even celebrates the failure of human language and reason before the fleeting traces of the transcendent One. The abyssal impossibility of knowing and naming God is largely covered by or inverted into a sense of excess caused by the overwhelming presence of the divine. As in the writings of Plotinus, the limits of being and knowing signal, in Dionysius, an unmediated potential for infinitude. Darkness and shadow are privileged over light and clarity so that the ecstatic moment of transcendence, followed by an absolute abandonment of both the self and the world, is characterized as being "uplifted to the ray of the divine *shadow*."[37] In the same vein, Dionysius claims that Moses, in encountering the divine revelation, "plunge[d] into the truly mysterious darkness of unknowing."[38]

The striking aspect of the Dionysian darkness is that it is not posited as a passageway to light. Darkness is not conceived as a stepping-stone or a process or through which one finally comes to the firm ground of certainty. Rather, Dionysius places darkness above everything: "I pray we could come to this darkness so far above light."[39] The act of knowing coincides with the place of being in that Dionysius subscribes unknowing or "inactivity of all knowledge" to an ecstatic dissolution of the self, a state of "being neither oneself nor someone else."[40]

The ontological finitude of both knowing and being is consistently upheld in Dionysius's writings. He turns the dark abyss of the unknown into the horizon of the encounter with the divine without inscribing a sense of teleology or reinscribing an all-transcendent essence beyond being. According to Jean-Luc Marion's reading, Dionysius's apophatic theology signals a nonpredicative discourse against the long tradition of ontotheology, which articulates God as a supreme being who provides the ground of all other beings.[41] Marion grounds his point in his reading of Dionysius's praise and prayer in *Divine Names*, where he finds an articulation of a "God without Being," beyond speech and thought.[42] On the other hand, Jacques Derrida presents his disagreement with Marion's reading of Dionysius by pointing out the danger of "hyperessentialism" lurking in negative theology. Contrary to Marion, who finds in negative theology a "break" from ontotheology, Derrida argues that the "hyper-" terms in Dionysius's writings might, as Thomas Carlson comments, "aim at speaking of the divine 'properly,' instead of avoiding to speak of it."[43] In other words, Derrida sees in negative theology the danger of reinscribing the hyper-, all-transcendent essence beyond name, speech, and Being, instead of freeing God from the thinking of Being. Derrida further insists that the negation of negative theology does not signal an absence but an overabundance.[44]

Derrida's reading of negative theology and Dionysius provides a new lens for reading the relation or (dis)continuity between the postmodern critique of ontotheology and negative theology. His analysis warns against any hasty attempt to reinstate the premodern (mono)theistic pursuit of the transcendent essence as an alternative to the dead end of Western metaphysics. However, while I do not disagree with Derrida's analysis of Dionysius's praise and prayer in its basic ideas, I hold some reservations on his warning that praise is prone to harbor a hyperessentialism. Derrida may be right when he points out the predicative nature of praise and the fact that praise may signal "determination" as "it says something about someone."[45] Nevertheless, it is worth considering Thomas Carlson's insightful suggestion that there is a deep continuity or correlation between negative theology and negative anthropology to the extent that the line between the two is indistinguishable.[46] With Carlson's suggestion in mind, Dionysius's praise needs to be read from the standpoint of the self—that is, keeping in mind the performative effects that apophatic praise produces in the self. From the self's standpoint, praising the other in place of attempting to grasp it signifies resignation of the self. By shifting focus from "naming the wholly other" to resigning the self, praise can be understood in the same line as prayer. Both praise and prayer indicate the negative move of self-effacement or self-abandonment while keeping the wholly other as an indestructible open-endedness, an endless deconstruction of all established images. This is because for Dionysius the very moment one encounters the divine light one does not come to the grips with an "essence" or a true image of it. Instead, one is immediately thrown into a darkness that eventually leads one to a further denial of all things and a self-emptying before the radical alterity of the Other. Consequently, we could read Dionysian prayer as pointing to the "beyond" of essence instead of to hyperessence. In the same way, Derrida's observation that the "negative" in negative theology is closer to overabundance than to absence must be reevaluated under Carlson's assertion that through the lens of desire the dividing line between overabundance and lack/absence is indistinguishable. As Carlson puts it, when "I" desire, "the intensity of excessive desire devastates me to the point of unknowing—beyond the simple alternative of presence and absence."[47]

The possible ethical consequence that we can derive from Dionysius's negative theology is an "ethical turn" to the other, followed by a radical self-denial. In this turn, the self gives up its agenda to grasp or to identify the other and passes to apophatic praise: "unseeing and unknowing, that which lies beyond all vision and knowledge. For this would be really to see and know: praise the One through denying all things."[48] The three elemental traits or movements of the abyss discussed earlier are all implicated in this picture, where the absolute transcendence of the other sweeps over the self, plunging it into the limits of knowing and being. Before the abyss, the self takes refuge in apophasis, the silence of unsaying and unknowing, the radical negation and denial of the self that results in the dispossession of the self. Dionysius's writings epitomize the fundamental character of the abyss—that is, the abyss as the passage from finitude to infinity and from infinity back to finitude yet again. My aim throughout the rest of this chapter and this book is to examine the above-mentioned movements of passage in different thinkers, their texts and contexts, borrowing insights from the ethical, political, and theological implications that these different accounts of passage present.

The Ground of the Soul and Self-Abandonment

The notion of the abyss comes to the surface of the Western theological tradition with Meister Eckhart. His frequent reference to the abyss makes the connection between apophatic theology and the abyss more explicit. A peculiar characteristic of Meister Eckhart's mystical theology is his distinction between Godhead and the revealed God. Godhead points to the deeper or wholly transcendent reality of God that lies beyond the revealed triune God. It is then the unknown, all-transcending nature of God that paves the way for the employment of the trope of the abyss in Eckhart's theology. He follows Augustine in linking the abyss not only with God but also with the human heart, thus making the abyss the shared space of the unsearchable depths of both God and the human soul. As Franke comments, for Eckhart "the ground of the soul" is at the same time "the abyss of deity."[49] The abyss refers to this depthless ground in which both God and the human soul are inscrutably lost, dissolved, and finally found in each other, undone, entwined, and ultimately in union.

Eckhart's understanding of the abyss is also undergirded by his idea of birth and breakthrough. His view on the relationship between God and creation is structured by a model similar to that of the Neoplatonic emanation, as he asserts that God flows into the whole creation. God's outflow coincides with God's inflow, in effect blurring the boundary between God and creation, between God and the self. This flow of the soul into the depths of God, in which the soul's inflow and God's outflow are indistinguishable, is named by Eckhart "breakthrough" (*Durchbruch*): "But in the breaking-through, when I come to be free of will of myself and of God's will and of all his works and of God himself, then I am above all created things, and I am neither God, nor creature."[50] Eckhart's breakthrough is possible, as Sigridur Gundmarsdottir comments, only through the groundlessness that is also the ground of God/soul in which both God and the soul are ceased or uncreated.[51] The ground of God/soul, therefore, uncovers the absolute groundlessness of God/soul. Negation in Eckhart's thoughts also leads to the dispossession of the self—as I have already observed in the writings of other Neoplatonic thinkers—so that the ground as an abyss represents the site of rupture and dispossession in which previously known identities and realities are dissipated.

A crucial element in the soul's journey into the unsearchable depth of the ground(lessness) is what Eckhart calls "detachment" (*Abgeschieden-*

heit). Eckhart's understanding of detachment is remarkably innovative and radical as he breaks down the distinction between God and creation. *Detachment* refers to the abandonment of the self: that is, the self as an autonomous subject of knowing and being. It is impossible to understand God or even to grasp one's self without abandoning oneself to the extent of becoming nothing, since God's nature is untranslatable to human beings. As Eckhart remarks, "Since it is God's nature that he is like no one, we must of necessity come to the point that we are nothing in order to be placed into the same being that he is himself. Therefore, when I come to the point that I form myself into nothing and form nothing into myself, and if I remove and throw out whatever is in me, then I can be placed into the bare being of God, and this is the bare being of the spirit."[52] The encounter with the unmediated presence of God takes place, in Bernard McGinn's parlance, "silently in the ground of the soul." By a total abandonment of the self, McGinn adds, one "create[s] the inner void that draws God into one."[53] Strikingly, Eckhart associates the void or nothingness not only with the human self but also with God. That there is no distinction between God and the human soul in the ground implies opening to each other on both sides. One of perhaps the most radical ideas in Western theology is conceived at this juncture where Eckhart gets rid of the distinction between God, human beings, and nothingness—and this move opens a loop of paradox, since the abandonment of finite being leads to the collapse of finite being altogether. As Charlotte Radler comments on this revolutionary conception of the divine, in the "ground of the soul" that is also the abyss of God where God and the human soul converge, God is "realized as an absolute transcendent nothingness through detachment; the soul flows into this nothingness and becomes a perfect nothing just as God is nothing."[54] Nothingness is posited not only as a part of the divine quality but as the goal toward which God moves. Subsequently, absolute self-negation leads to the abandonment of all images and words, which takes one to the creative space of plentitude, namely *nothing*: "You are seeking nothing, and so you also find nothing."[55]

The Hegelian-Marxist philosopher Slavoj Žižek associates Eckhart's "nothing" with the abyss and explains that it is not a mere meaningless void. Intriguingly, Žižek, instead of viewing the Godhead as being "beyond" God, follows Schelling in speaking of "the abyss of godhead *prior to* God."[56] Žižek agrees with other Eckhartian scholars that the abyss is the site where "the very difference between God and man is annihilated-obliterated."[57] He draws upon Reiner Schurmann, who comments that for Eckhart "God is opposed to non-God" instead of to the "world" or to "man."[58] The breakdown of the opposition that takes place in the abyss

is, then, for Žižek, the collapse of a boundary not between two different kinds "but between God as some(thing) and God as nothing."[59] Since
the abyss is characterized by the mutual dynamic of self-dispossession and
conversion between God and the human soul, it follows that God's act of
self-creation, God's becoming-something, happens only through human
beings' act of self-detachment. Žižek, however, presses this point perhaps
too hard by claiming that "God is nothing outside man."[60] In Žižek's radical materialist vision, the importance of Eckhart's mystical thought lies in
the fact that human beings are the medium through which God actualizes
Godself and that God lacks its ontological ground outside human beings.
Žižek further claims that "it is man who gives birth to God" and therefore
that "I am the only site of God."[61]

Žižek's reading of Eckhart has a certain validity inasmuch as Eckhart's
account of the ground and breakthrough could justify such an inference
as Žižek is drawing. His perspective also provides a refreshed mystico-
theological link to the revolutionary theo-political argument that he is
drawing out of the Hegelian dialectic. He reads God's abyss as the otherness of God lying prior to God, the nothingness inherent in God that
God needs to negate in order to become Godself. This dia-logic is mate-
rialized more explicitly in Jakob Boehme and Schelling, to whom Žižek
turns in order to build his materialist dialectic. However, despite the innovative breakdown of the human-divine dichotomy in his mystical thought,
Eckhart's writings show that he retains the essential theistic frame of the
Neoplatonic worldview. Eckhart maintains that the One remains the same
even after it flows into creatures and that the Godhead's substance does not
contain relation or an exteriority. This goes against Žižek's statement that
God has "a dark side," which is "an unfathomable otherness to himself."[62]
Eckhart adds that even in its most relational moment of flowing into the
creation God remains static in its substance "because God's substance does
not imply the idea of a relation."[63] The Neoplatonic model of emanation
upon which Eckhart grounds his theology maintains a panentheistic cosmology in which God contains the whole world within Godself, rather
than having an "unfathomable otherness" to itself, as Žižek argues.

In conclusion, Eckhart's mystical theology develops the trope of the
abyss into the primary material and resource for theology. For Eckhart, the
abyss is the ambiguous space of paradox in which the ontological finitude
of the human soul reflects the unsearchable depth of divinity. The ground
as the abyss denotes the end of the distinction between the divine and
creation. Self and God, creator and creation, subject and object no longer
exist in strict binary terms within the abyss. The threshold of the abyss is
marked by absolute negation and abandonment: the death of the self. Yet

what Eckhart shows is that reality no longer ends with death; rather, it begins there. The moment of the self's annihilation, the moment the self reaches nothingness, coincides with God's self-detachment and God's act of becoming nothing. In the unfathomable ground, God and the self are lost in each other and find themselves in each other, undone and uncreated, yet *incarnated* in each other. The once uncreated soul is now given a new birth, as Franke formulates, "in and as God," which renders God "nothing but generated Logos and living Spirit in us."[64] The traditional tension regarding God as the impossible object of knowing takes a new shape with Eckhart, whose theological query shifts the question from *knowing* God to *being* God.[65]

The abyss symbolizes the seemingly irremediable gap between finitude and infinity, creation and God, as well as the internal split within the self, human and divine. At the same time, the abyss indicates the passage or the crossing of this gap, the boundary between the two poles. As my reading demonstrates, the distinctive aspects of the abyss highlighted above characterize the mystical writings of the three Neoplatonic thinkers. Apophasis, first of all, beckons to us at the gap between self and language, speakable and unspeakable, or possible and impossible. Aside from overthrowing ontotheology and revealing the failure of ontology, apophasis opens space for reconsideration of the relation between reality and poetic imagination. If the unspeakable (either trauma or the divine) disrupts the boundary between imagination and reality, apophasis opens a porous passageway within the crack between these two. In a way, apophaticism serves as the historical root of theopoetics, the poetics of/about God, the poetic reconstruction of the self and the world—which I will examine closely in chapter 5.

Second and most importantly, the creative tension between the unspeakable and apophatic speech is succeeded by the self's surrender to darkness, to its finitude and the embrace of its groundlessness. I insist that submitting to finitude, the act of self-loss or self-emptying, is not escapism or an evasion of one's ethical responsibility. Rather, it is an ethical response, a bold act of diving into the vortical abyss in which one discovers oneself to be the very site where the crossing of the irremediable gap or the ecstatic movement of becoming-divine takes place. This leads to the third and last movement, which involves the dispossession of the self on both human and divine sides. It gives birth to a new subject who is conditioned by alterity. The passage from the impossible to the possible, from finitude (stasis) to infinitude (*ek*-stasis), reveals the self's contingency; it alludes to the fact that the self's becoming in groundlessness is conditioned by the other. Might this hint at the possibility of locating relation in Neoplatonic mysticism? If it does, it would arguably not be a relationality gesturing toward equality, multiplicity, and becoming over against the hierarchy, oneness/ sameness, and being of Platonic cosmology. Similarly, the Neoplatonic cosmology structuring Eckhart's understanding of God limits our reading of the relational aspect ingrained in his conception of the human-divine relation. He defends the immutability of the Neoplatonic One by keeping the notion of relation away from the divine substance. If we take Eckhart's claim seriously, then the divine/human event of becoming-nothing-in-groundlessness needs to be read as a convergence of one dissolved entity with another: difference is absorbed into the unifying totality of the One disguised as nothing; multiplicity is subsumed by the sameness of the (Neo)Platonic One. However, Eckhart's radical conception of the divine-human dynamic and the process of *Durchburch* troubles his own defiant claim. Can we call a God who effaces itself completely in the other absolutely self-sufficient and nonrelational? Might we not argue that at least the collaborative dynamic between the self and God creates the possibility of some sort of relationality in Eckhartian mysticism?

The relation we detect in the mystical tradition falls arguably short of "relationality" and openness. But one should not underestimate its significance within the history of Western philosophy, as it marks the beginning of an important break from the all-transcending and self-sufficient One. Despite its strong Platonic foundation, Neoplatonic cosmology and the apophatic tradition it fosters carve out the possibility of relation within the texture of both the self and God. This relation—which is underdeveloped yet harbored in mystical thought—will be recalibrated by the model of relation—as the modus operandi of the self—that I develop in this book. The models of relation that we draw from the Hegelian abyss and the colonial abyss offer, in my reading, ways of understanding the self that bear on the cosmopolitical project this book proposes: reconstructing the self in the colonial abyss.

In a way, the radical materialist reading that Žižek practices might seem to gesture toward a relational angle, as he builds the link between the human and the divine in a dialectical fashion so that God's self-actualization takes place only through the human person. For Žižek, this human person, like its divine counterpart, becomes "something," or, as he consistently evokes, "the subject," by negating its a priori otherness, namely nothingness. The problem lies not only in Žižek's misreading of Eckhart's Neoplatonic view of God, as I showed earlier, but also in the unambiguous difference between the relational ontology implicated in Eckhart's panentheistic cosmology and the atheist theology implicit in Žižek's materialist reading. As he consistently argues elsewhere, for Žižek the void, nothing, or the death of God *is* the starting point of the genesis of the subject. God, or the

Real, in Žižek's Lacanian term, is "nothing but an embodiment of a certain void, lack, radical negativity."[66] That the subject unmasks the illusion of the transcendent God and realizes that there lies nothing behind the Real is, however, a positive condition, since this indicates that what is missing in the place of the illusionary Real *is* the subject herself. In other words, what really matters for Žižek is that the subject *becomes* herself as she encounters the void and negates this nothingness. As he writes, "Behind the subject, there is nothing."[67]

It is, therefore, not the case that God's negation of nothingness and the human negation of nothingness share their trajectory of dialectical becoming. What Žižek fails to catch is the reciprocal nature of the divine-human relation in Eckhartian theology. In Žižek's reading, the negation of otherness (nothing) and the subsequent becoming of the subject (something) do not involve a co-participatory process. Rather, the almost heroic account of the political subject takes over the empty place of the (illusion of the) Other. Contrary to Žižek, I argue that there is a grain or trace of relationality in Eckhartian and Neoplatonic mysticism as it refers to the process in which the self strives to become nothing (Eckhart) or to come to the darkness above light (Dionysius), where the self disappears and only an apophasis of praise and prayer to the other remains. Thus the dialectical dynamic of the threefold movement through the abyss is brought full circle. This dialectical movement will be developed more fully in the next two chapters with a clearer focus on ethico-political questions.

The Dialectical Abyss

The Restless Negative of Hegel

> But the life of spirit is not the life that shrinks from death and keeps itself untouched by devastation, but rather the life that endures it and maintains itself in it. It wins its truth only when, in utter dismemberment, it finds itself.
>
> **—Hegel,** *Phenomenology of Spirit*

> Dialectics is the self-consciousness of the objective context of delusion; it does not mean to have escaped from that context. Its objective goal is to break out of the context from within. The strength required from the break grows in dialectics from the context of immanence.
>
> **—Theodor Adorno,** *Negative Dialectics*

Through the works of G. W. F. Hegel the trope of the abyss acquires a new or rather a wider meaning within the tradition of philosophical thinking. Most importantly, Hegel frees the trope of the abyss from the theological constraints reflected in the works of the Neoplatonic mystics. Hegel places the abyss or groundlessness (*Ungrund*) at the center of his dialectical worldview. As Jon Mills observes, the abyss is the central principle of *Phenomenology of Spirit*, remaining always in the shadow of the dialectical progress without ever being abandoned.[1] Within Neoplatonic mysticism—and all the way through Schelling and Hegel—the trope of the abyss straddles theology and philosophy, without drawing a clear distinction between the two. After all, the abyss has always remained a theological trope, an inquiry into questions of the self and its finitude but most importantly of *God*. Only following Hegel is the abyss divorced, at least in a particular sense, from the notion of God to drive the question of the self, particularly the irremediable incompleteness inherent within the structure of the self.

However, questions of the self and subjectivity in Hegel do not derive from a philosophical obsession with the solipsistic self. Rather, they are inseparable from the questions of "the other." As Hegel himself emphasizes in *Phenomenology*, and as numerous commentators have attested, the structure of the Hegelian dialectic rests on the foundational notion of "mutual recognition." As Jean Hyppolite, one of the major French commentators of Hegel, puts it, "the simple meaning of [Hegel's] entire dialectic" is that "human desire occurs only when it bears on another desire and becomes the desire to be recognized and hence itself to recognize."[2] In this dialectical structure of recognition I read the abyss as that which signals both the gap between self and other and the gap creating the internal split within the self, that is between the self and its consciousness.

To be clear, Hegel rarely uses the term *abyss* (*Ungrund*) in his works. Nevertheless, I follow Jon Mills, who identifies the abyss as the central principle of Hegel's system of dialectics. However, while Mills reads *Schaft* (shaft, pit, mine)—the often recurring term in Hegel's later works, particularly, the *Science of Logic*—as the abyss, I read the traces of the abyss mainly in *Phenomenology*.[3] Despite its limited number of appearances, the abyss —that is, the dispossession of the self in its encounter with the shattering power of the negative—is key to the Hegelian dialectic. The few times it makes its appearance in *Phenomenology*, it refer to the boundless depth and shadow haunting the journey of the Hegelian subject, whose path is marked by constant encounters with the unknown other. As the unknown makes its appearance on the horizon of being, and as this other immediately reveals itself to be the site of the subject's truth, the subject loses itself, becoming inscrutable to its own self, as its personality is now "dependent on the contingent personality of another."[4] Therefore, the abyss signals this state where self-identity, "having become divided against itself, all identity, all existence, is disrupted."[5] Such a moment of utter despair and loss of the self is translated in the same passage by Hegel as the *abyss*. Self-consciousness (the subject), Hegel writes, "stands on the very edge of this innermost abyss, of this bottomless depth, in which all stability and Substance have vanished."[6] The abyss, in this sense, is the site of negativity in Hegel, which signals, at the same time, the possibility of a new beginning. But the vital role that negativity plays in Hegel's thought is often misinterpreted, if not downplayed: over the past two centuries he has featured largely as a thinker of totalitarian progress and as a proponent of a closed absolute. Over against this underestimation of negativity in Hegel, I argue that in Hegel's system the negative is neither a mere temporary rupture on the way to a completed synthesis nor an expansionist negation of the other. With the so-called leftist readers of Hegel, I identify the negative as the structure of the constant dialectical tension between desire and satisfaction, absence and presence, or finitude and infinitude. My reading therefore is mainly informed by the Marxism-inflected, existentialist reading of Hegel of early twentieth-century France, a tradition that played a paramount role in shaping the leftist interpretation of Hegel within contemporary continental philosophy. Accordingly, the Hegelian negative represents the ineluctable and constant failure of subjectivity that is the subject's confrontation with the limits of its own knowing and being; it renders finitude a constitutive structure of being.[7] But paradoxically the work of the negative is what drives the subject toward the reconstruction of itself despite innumerable failures.[8]

The aim of this chapter is twofold. First, through my reading of Hegel, I show how the theological notion of the abyss plays out in the becoming of (self)consciousness (the Hegelian term for *subject*). The role of the abyss in the Hegelian system is very similar to its role in Neoplatonic mysticism: it points to the ambiguous boundary between subject and object, inside and outside, finitude and infinitude. The Hegelian subject constantly oscillates between these two poles, the opposites. The crux of the Hegelian dialectic is to hint at this movement of crossing or passage as the site and temporality in which the truth of the subject is *revealed*. Second, the abyss as the site of the negative signals the inversion of the negative into a new possibility, not only as a one-time event but as a continuous and open-ended movement. I pay particular attention to this resilience or persistence, which carries important implications for the further politicization of the abyss. In the first part of the chapter I examine the significance of Hegel's philosophy (dialectic) in both its ethico-philosophical and theo-political senses. If the ethico-philosophical element rests on the fact that the Hegelian dialectic incorporates exteriority/otherness into the structure of being (and knowing), the theo-political significance lies in the fact that Hegel's system renders God inconceivable outside the political.

The second and third parts of this chapter engage two contemporary readers of Hegel. Slavoj Žižek and Judith Butler provide guidance for reading the Hegelian dialectic in relation to the self, the abyss, and ethics/politics. Žižek's materialist reading uncovers the notion of the abyss implicit in Hegel's thought by identifying the abyss as the nucleus of negativity. Thus Hegel's dialectic acquires a refreshing perspective and a strong political edge. Žižek's Marxist/materialist reading translates the dialectic into the arduous struggle, or what he calls the "critical engagement," of the restless spirit/subject who seeks to negate the disrupting power of negation.[9] Quite differently, Butler engages Hegel from a feminist and deconstructionist perspective and inscribes the notion of loss in the place of the abyss. With loss as the constitutive element of its being, Butler's subject makes a gesture of ethical/political resistance guided by the alterity of the other, thus setting both vulnerability and the relational ties of our human existence as the parameters for the construction of a "political community of complex order."[10]

From Mysticism to Dialectic

While both the dialectic and historical materialism are often attributed to Hegel, the basic framework of these ideas is rooted in the tradition of German idealism in which Hegel himself is grounded. In particular, the mystical theosophy of Jakob Boehme provides the backbone of the Hegelian dialectic. Boehme's thought is significant in that it connects medieval mysticism and German idealism/continental philosophy. One finds in Boehme's mystical vision, described in image-saturated language, the convergence of mysticism and the dialectic, or better, the passage from the gradual dissipation of mystical thought to the birth of the dialectic.[11] Similarly, the missing link between the abyss's prevalence in Neoplatonic mysticism and its relative absence in Hegel may be found in Boehme, who develops the structure of a protodialectic upon the soil of mystical theosophy.[12] To be clear, in discussions of the direct influences on Hegel's thought, the most commonly invoked thinker is Schelling. However, Schelling's thought is anchored in Boehme, since the primal form of dialectic that Boehme develops plays a central role in Schelling's system too.

The starting point of Boehme is the supposition that nothing can emerge from nothing. What lies at the heart of God for Boehme is the desire to reveal itself. The desire for self-manifestation or self-actualization is not one among many attributes of God. Rather, self-revelation is God's essence. The key notion that frames Boehme's thought is *Ungrund*, the a priori space, the eternal nothingness within God, which, as Eric Trozzo defines it, "may be God or might be a non-divine darkness within the divine."[13] The *Ungrund* therefore signals an absolute indeterminacy, a "ground without a ground," as Alexandre Koyré has brilliantly called it.[14] This indeterminacy, however, derives from the polarities that constitute the essence of the divine. The divine contains opposition, the polarity of Byss (ground) and Abyss (groundlessness), as Boehme terms them. In other words, the emergence of the self-actualization of God, God's coming-to-be-itself, happens only through a confrontation with opposition. The seeds of the radical theological idea in both Augustine and Eckhart that the abyss signals the groundlessness not only of the human mind but also of God is reconceived and further radicalized by Boehme, who grounds the divine in the groundlessness of indeterminacy, the nonbeing, the nothing and everything before being. To clarify, the negative attributes with which Boehme characterizes the divine significantly differ from those of Neoplatonic apophaticism. If the negative in Neoplatonism indicates the insurmountable distance/gap between the divine and the human soul, the negative in Boehme amounts to the internal gap within the divine being itself or the within subject itself.

With the abyss, Boehme renders God the result of a dynamic movement. Thus *who* God is cannot be separated from God's own act of self-positing through which the divine achieves itself by overcoming the opposition inherent to its internal structure. Even though the evolutionary process of God's becoming is central to Boehme, he pays equal attention to the epigenetic womb of this becoming, namely the *Ungrund*. Perhaps Boehme's formulation of the protodialectic signals a teleological orientation geared toward the unfolding or becoming of God. But he does not move with haste across the depth of the mystical negative. Rather, he theorizes the negative, the abyss, in such a way that the haunting shadow of the *Ungrund* becomes the constitutive component of God's self-revelation.[15] But despite its intricate connection to God's self-actualization, the *Ungrund* is, paradoxically, unsearchable, since it represents the uncertainty preceding "the divine will's arousing itself to self-awareness."[16] In this unfathomable *Ungrund*, says Boehme, "even God would therefore not be manifest to Himself."[17]

The most daring conception of Boehme's theosophy is born here as he claims, "In his depth, God himself does not know what he is. For he knows not beginning, and also nothing like himself, and also no end."[18] God suffers God's own indeterminacy in the abyss, for God does not know what God is: God remains hidden or other to Godself. Just as the medieval mystics strove to name the unnameable essence of God, Boehme proceeds to give a form to the inconceivable *Ungrund* and the subsequent emergence of God out of it. However, unlike the mystics who take the way of negation (*via negativa*) into both the self and the other, Boehme's negation takes a constructive form in that negation is posited toward negation, to its otherness, as a form of "negation of negation." In other words, negativity in Boehme leads to positivity, since the act of negation enables self-positing or self-actualization.

In the eternal nothingness of the *Ungrund*, therefore, the desire for self-actualization is born. The undifferentiated nonbeingness of God now sets out to differentiate itself through its unquenchable desire or hunger to know itself,[19] and this is why, as Robert Brown remarks, "The *Ungrund* also contains within its undifferentiated wholeness the possibilities of all things that are to be."[20] Boehme's *Ungrund* is itself the desire, the desiring subject who seeks its full self-manifestation. The unfathomable negativity contained in the *Ungrund* is at the same time the infinite potential and drive to unfold, actualize, and manifest itself.

Schelling develops the basic contours of Boehme's theosophy into a more systematic form of dialectical and transcendental idealism through which he mediates the distance between human beings and nature and between God and the world by conceiving the relation between them as the self-manifestation of the absolute. The primary backdrop of Schelling's philosophy is Spinozism. Schelling places everything in God and claims that there is nothing outside God. But Schelling goes beyond Spinoza by turning the almost deterministic or mechanistic view of the Spinozan God into a more dynamic and personal subject. If, for Spinoza, God loses its subjectivity at the expense of a pantheistic naturalism, hence almost becoming the object of articulation by reason, Schelling restores the agency of the absolute by combining Spinozism with Neoplatonism, and particularly with Boehme's theosophy. The main attribute of God that Schelling inherits from Spinoza is that of infinity. God, for Schelling, is the ultimate ground of all being and reality. Since the infinite is constitutive of the finite, it follows that the finite cannot be separate from the infinite and instead must be contained within it. The same structure of opposition in the primal abyss of God found in Boehme structures Schelling's philosophy: God is the agent of its self-unfolding in nature. Because of its essence as freedom, God must be a dynamic essence of infinite becoming. Schelling blends the strong mystical element of Boehme's theosophy with idealist rationalism. Not only is his discussion of Byss and Abyss slightly different from Boehme's, but also he gives a more rational philosophical explanation by claiming that God cannot be static; God needs to unfold itself in history because, "if the full existence of God were already actual and perfectly fulfilled, then everything related to God would also already be completely determined."[21]

In this regard, the main attribute of God for Schelling is *freedom*, and God's ultimate purpose is its self-actualization in and through the world. However, this freedom also signifies groundlessness, since for Schelling, like Boehme, "Ground fails to ground."[22] In other words, God's infinite nature is grounded, paradoxically, in its own groundlessness. As Boehme writes, "This unsearchable, inconceivable Will without Nature which is only one, having nothing before it, nor after it, which in itself is but one, which is as nothing, and yet all Things; this is, and is called the one only

God."[23] In this sense, groundlessness becomes for Schelling the very source of infinity.

The dual nature of God persisting in Schelling's thought entails that God is, on the one hand, the abyss, darkness, the nonground, nonbeing. On the other hand, God's essence is the principle of being, reason, and positivity. While the *Ungrund* is the primordial aspect of the deity for Schelling, God is the unity of the two polarities, as Robert Brown affirms.[24] The actuality of God, then, is this synthesis of polarities.[25] The significance of Schelling's idea of God is that it provides the basis for Hegel's dialectic by redefining essence or God's being as God's act of self-unfolding/becoming. Nonbeing or otherness becomes the constitutive element of essence without which God cannot become Godself. As Žižek comments, Schelling shows us that the beginning of any movement is predicated on a negation, a decision and confrontation with the opposite.[26] God, as the synthesis of the opposites, the mediation between nonground and ground, irrational and rational, unfolds Godself in and through nature and history. Nevertheless, while the influence of Boehme's idea of absolute as *Ungrund* prior to all duality and existence leads Schelling to affirm the ineluctable presence of otherness or nonbeing in the dialectical (or dipolar) unfolding of God, the pole of being and reason is still the guiding force and principle of this movement. Reason does not give way to the abyss, and the dialectic becomes the movement of this reason, which is God.[27]

Into the Passage of the Negative

> Spirit is this power only by looking the negative in the face, and tarrying with it. This tarrying with the negative is the magical power that converts it into being.
>
> —Hegel, *Phenomenology of Spirit*

Jean Hyppolite emphasizes the central place of the negative in Hegel when he claims that "Hegel's philosophy is a philosophy of negation and of negativity."[28] Hyppolite's recurring emphasis on Hegel's negativity is reflected in the fact that the very first chapter of his commentary on Hegel, where he discusses the "meaning and the methods of the *Phenomenology*," is primarily dedicated to the analysis of the negative in Hegel's dialectic. Similarly, Alexandre Kojeve, whose lecture exercised an unparalleled influence on the subsequent generation of continental philosophers including Hyppolite, states that for Hegel the "I," the essence of being human, is born in the negating action, "which transforms given Being and, by transforming it, transforms itself."[29]

If Kojeve understands the axiom of the Hegelian dialectic in anthro-pocentric terms by translating the negative as "man's action for transfor-mation," Hyppolite "extends the domain of negation" by relocating the negative in the longer trajectory of human history and experience.[30] In Hyppolite's reading, the negative is the motor that generates the move-ment of dialectic, since the genesis of a new truth, the birth of new knowl-edge or/and being, is inconceivable without the negation of the immediate truth, the negation of the error, so that "the death of what [consciousness] held as its truth is the appearance of a new truth."[31] Meanwhile, the abyss is inseparable from the central axiom of Hegel's dialectic.

There is no simple definition of the abyss. The abyss eludes all names. Within the long tradition of Neoplatonism, it symbolizes the unsearchable unknowability and indeterminacy at the heart of being. At the same time, it is inseparably characterized by the movement of crossing, or "passage," from determinacy to indeterminacy and then to a renewed form of deter-minacy again: a dialectical journey that entails both *de*-construction and *re*-construction. Similarly, negation or the work of the negative in Hegel cannot be articulated apart from the abyss. To be clear, the negative should not be equated with the abyss. Whereas the abyss, in my reading, refers to the space, site, or state (temporality) of indeterminacy, the negative is the subject of its own movement, since it indicates the *act* of negation.

If the abyss is underdeveloped by Hegel himself, the central role of negativity in Hegel's system is further downplayed by his commentators. One reason why the place of the negative in Hegel is overlooked could be that Hegel has been often read as a thinker of totalitarian reconciliation, a proponent of the teleological movement toward the incorporation of difference into unity. Such readings can be attributed to the long-standing tradition of "right-wing Hegelians" who, against Marx's interpretation, were reading Hegel as the thinker of dialectical "unity" rather than dialec-tical "antagonism." As Jean Wahl's influential reading demonstrates, such a view erases, if it does not neutralize, the place of the negative in Hegel; for Wahl "what is negative in him [Hegel] is something absolutely positive . . . We can say that the unhappy consciousness is but the darkened image of the happy consciousness."[32] This tendency has prevailed in Hegelian schol-arship over its long development in philosophical and religious studies. Its predominance is best reflected in Karl Popper's famous denunciation of Hegel as the advocate of a straightforward totalitarianism.[33] However, not only the opponents of Hegel or the right-wing Hegelians read Hegel through a teleological lens. Faithful adherents of the existentialist reading of Hegel also often read Hegel as a thinker who espouses the movement of progression toward an absolute goal, from darkness to light, as is the case with Robert Solomon, who points to "growth" and "education" as the central metaphor of Hegel.[34]

Second, when the negative is taken seriously its significance is largely reduced to its deconstructive side only. But for Hegel the disruptive power of the negative is what gives birth to desire and drives it forward: the desire for recognition; the desire to overcome (negate) the negative and come to self-definition as a subject. Loss caused by the devastating effects of negation gives birth, in return, to the restless spirit, who despite its innumerable failures rises up and gathers its shattered self in order to proceed again. Therefore, we may here identify negation as the central principle of the Hegelian dialectic as described in *Phenomenology*. The negative, or the entire structure and scope of Hegel's dialectic in *Phenomenology*, concerns the problem regarding the gap and the unity between Truth and the subject or between epistemology (knowing) and ontology (being) in their relation to Truth. From this, I concur with Kojeve's compelling statement that negativity is "a constant deferral of the phenomenological truth, the given."[35] This is not, however, a mere phenomenological distance between the subject and the object but an active "event" or "encounter" with negation in which consciousness loses its truth by abandoning its first, illusory belief in the given, immediate truth.[36] Consciousness's initial encounter with exteriority, its limits, is not merely a cognitive issue involving questions of "knowing" but an existential anguish entailing the whole of one's being and existence.[37] It is not surprising, then, that the loss of truth, for Hegel, does not refer merely to the loss of the object of knowledge. Rather, loss of one's truth equals loss of the self, whose path is consequently attended by doubt or regarded famously as "the way of despair."[38] Loss, therefore, is one of the primary and essential characteristics of negativity. In Hegel it becomes the key, constitutive element of the subject, which subsequently carves the abyss at the heart of being.

The Abyss of the Other: Finitude, Loss, and Recognition

The moment of the fall is also the moment of salvation.
—Jean Hyppolite, *Genesis and Structure of Hegel's "Phenomenology of Spirit"*

The subject's immersion in groundlessness caused by the loss of self takes place in consciousness's encounter with the other. This means that the other for Hegel is directly indicative of *loss*. The unavoidable encounter with the other reveals the failure of the illusion of Cartesian subjectivity. This is because the dialectic points to the fact that consciousness can relate to truth or meaning only through the mediation of the other. However, the abyssal gap of negation refers not only to the disparity in the subject-object relationship but to the internal gap, the split within the self. This is why consciousness realizes, as Robert Williams writes, that even "the self's relation to itself is mediated by its relation to the other."[39] The given, immediate truth present in the knowing subject dissipates as the subject loses him- or herself in the object or as "the man who contemplates is absorbed by what he contemplates."[40] The contingent possibility of the emergence of the subject now depends on the outside, the other, who "must approach and call for it to turn in upon itself."[41] Meanwhile, what this implies for the (re)construction of subject is that the affirmation of the subject can take place only through the negation of the given.

The Hegelian subject's encounter with the other invokes a dynamic riddled with ambiguities and ambivalences; it hints at numerous bifurcating points regarding the place of the other within the structure of the self and vice versa. The dialectical journey is guided by the principle of reversal or paradox in such a way that the opposite, the exterior, and the nonreal are indispensable for comprehending and grasping the real. Thus it is not odd that loss, dispossession, finitude, and contradiction are essential for the affirmation or emergence of the subject: the "I" finds itself in the other, and the other finds itself in the "I." From this, the other in Hegel can be understood as the threshold of the abyss, the gateway to the abyss, serving both as the limit of being in which all stability and sense of substance dissipate *and* the soil for a new beginning from which a new subject and reality emerge.

This is perhaps why numerous commentators of Hegel contend that one of the central meanings of the dialectic comes into play as *recognition*. We observe in *Phenomenology* the development of a dialectical movement "from the abstract to the concrete" in which, at the same time, the prior movement of the principle of recognition from the "I" to "the other" and from "the other" back to the "I" is reproduced.[42] Therefore, Hegel writes, "What the object immediately was in itself . . . proves to be in truth, not this at all; instead, this *in-itself* turns out to be a mode in which the object is only *for an other*."[43] This highly original trope of recognition and intersubjectivity is further radicalized as he claims, more emphatically, "It is clear that being-*in-itself* and being-*for-an-other* are one and the same."[44]

Nevertheless, it is important to note the danger couched in the idea of mutual recognition and intersubjectivity that might lead to the temptation of simplifying recognition into a finalizing synthesis or a teleological achievement. Williams's remark regarding this point is illuminating: "Hegel denies immediate access to other. There is immediate confrontation with the other, but not an immediate knowledge of the other."[45] To this, I would add, following Williams, that Hegel denies not only immediate knowledge of the other but also an immediate reconciliation with or discovery of one's own self. The Hegelian subject is, therefore, bound to double contradiction and failure: its initial encounter with the other signifies loss and dispossession of the self.

The dynamic drama of self-consciousness's journey characterized by its self-positing, its encounter with the other, the dissolution of the self, and the recognition of itself in the other is best illustrated in the famous section of "Lordship and Bondage" that is also known as the "master-slave dialectic." The master-slave dialectic illustrates the tension structuring the subject and the object (or the two subjects), created by the mutual desire to affirm one's self via negation of the other. The primary dynamic framing the dialectical methodology is well reflected in the master-slave dialectic characterized by self-consciousness's encounter with another self-consciousness. As Hegel writes, "The 'other' is also self-consciousness; one individual is confronted by another individual."[46] The initial encounter with the other results in the loss of the self, the loss of self-certainty: "The knowing subject loses himself in the object that is known."[47] In his or her encounter with the outside world (the other), the subject is dispossessed, and Otherness reveals the inscrutable externality inherent in the structure of its being. As Judith Butler remarks, instead of consuming the other, self-consciousness "is instead consumed by the other."[48]

Butler's reading of Hegel, in particular her analysis of "Lordship and Bondage," provides an insightful perspective for reading Hegel in line with the notions of loss, self-dispossession, and desire. Since I will engage Butler's work in more detail later, suffice it to say for now that her reading underscores the centrality of loss, dissolution, and undoing of the self in Hegel. Indeed, Hegel himself privileges the importance of dissolution (*Auflösung*) by calling it "the most astonishing and mightiest of powers, or rather the absolute power," of *Understanding*.[49] The boundless power of the negative is inscribed in its work of the dissolution of substance and any reference of the world and being. This means, in reverse, that any act of positivity, namely positing of the self and creating of the world, entails, or rather must first go through, the passage of radical negation, including the dissolution of the self.

On this note, Jean-Luc Nancy writes how the Hegelian subject is "essentially, what (or the one who) dissolves all substance."[50] What Nancy sees in Hegel is a movement that breaks from Cartesian subjectivity and opens to an ontology of relation, a new subject whose essence consists of the movement of relation and becoming. This is, however, not a becoming that leads from one point to another. Rather, it refers to the *passage* itself, which in itself is the principle or condition of being while at the same time it demarcates the disavowal of the ontology founded upon substance metaphysics. Nancy's reading of *Phenomenology* sheds light on the trope of the abyss in the Hegelian dialectic. In describing the function and the effects of passage, Nancy writes that within this passage "One finds its truth in the other" and at the same time one "touches upon and unsettles its ground."[51] It is interesting to note that Nancy refers to "finding its truth in the other" and "unsettling its ground" in one and the same line without distinguishing between the two. Recognition and unsettling of the ground are articulated as parts of one and the same process. Furthermore, the absence of the separating line between the two is indicative not only of semantic homogeneity but also of temporal indiscretion. This means that—against the common expectation that "unsettling of the ground" is followed by "finding of the truth"—the temporal arrangement of the two processes is not laid out in a linear way. By removing the temporal distinction between deconstruction and reconstruction or between alienation and reconciliation, Nancy alludes to the fact that the Hegelian passage into the journey of its becoming is itself the depth, the unfathomable groundlessness. In other words, it is not the case that the abyss leads one to recognition and self-definition. Rather, perhaps recognition and becoming are the unsettling and destabilizing work of the abyss. Therefore, Nancy writes, "This ground founds only to the extent that it sinks in itself."[52] Ground destabilizes the ground, while, paradoxically, groundlessness founds the ground.

It is not my intention to argue that the abyss or otherness (nonbeing) occupies the primary place in Hegel's system. Hegel clearly seems to grant ontological priority to being and reason over irrationality and nonbeing. Reason, for Hegel, is the name for synthesis, that is, Absolute Knowing. As Robert Solomon indicates, reason is the "demand for unity," which is "the aim of the universe to unify itself."[53] Morris Cohen and Hyppolite too affirm this view, held by the majority of Hegelian scholars. One cannot deny, contends Cohen, that "reconciliation terminates in a reality which is completely rational."[54] Likewise, Hyppolite points out that reason is the name for the dialectical synthesis: "Reason is the supreme unification of consciousness and self-consciousness, of knowledge of an object and knowledge of self."[55] Consequently, despite the shadowing presence of the abyss and the crucial role it plays in Hegel's system, the abyss or nonbeing does not assume the primary place in his dialectic. My intention, then, is not to propose a shift of perspective but to assert, despite the priority Hegel grants to being and reason, a need to recognize the overlooked traces of the abyss imprinted in the progressively unfolding development of the dialectic. Hegel's reason does not designate a mere static signification of substance metaphysics. As Christopher Lauer notes, for Hegel reason is "not the unity of the concept that has brought all its otherness into itself. Rather, it is a relation to its other."[56] This implies that reason cannot come to know itself without otherness: "Reason can comprehend its necessity only through an encounter with its contingency."[57]

The Hegelian passage does not indicate a mere temporal process leading to a magical uplifting, suture, and reconciliation. Instead of reading the dialectic as a narrative of teleological progression, I concur with Hyppolite, who understands synthesis or the end as a momentary achievement.[58] Kojeve provides perhaps the most illuminating insight on this point by regarding the dialectical synthesis as "just one opinion among many others," instead of viewing it as a finalizing, once-and-for-all event of closure. In other words, synthesis does not lead to a final closure. Rather, "it arouses new antithesis,"[59] and "The final synthesis is also the initial thesis."[60] To this Hegel adds that the movement of becoming from substance to subject, the self-positing of substance as subject, has "its end also as its beginning."[61]

Such an idea of a constant struggle, alienation, and momentary reconciliation without closure might initially cause perplexity and raise questions regarding the ethical, political, and theological implications of the dialectic. If, as Hyppolite argues, Hegel's system indeed points to a cycle or circularity of "a conflict perpetually overcome and perpetually renewed," where can we locate the moments, in particular, of theological signification in such a system?[62] What are the registers of ethico-political possibility in a philosophical system that seems to perpetuate the negative as the structure of being and to foreclose all possibilities of positivity?

Infinite Restlessness

It is not surprising that the reciprocal and open-ended nature of Hegel's philosophy opens up questions of ethics regarding the other, or, more concretely, the place of the other in its relation to the self. If the Neoplatonic abyss refers to the ineffable distance between the self and divinity, in Hegel it is the evanescent presence of the other that points to the groundlessness of being. The other presents itself in an oppositional conflict with consciousness as consciousness realizes that it cannot gain the certainty of itself (that is, become a self-consciousness) without mediation by the other. Mediation, however, involves a painful renunciation of the subject's old world. In Williams's words, mediation is a tragic self-recognition that "comes with the demise of the self."[63] The presence of the other uncovers the epistemological and ontological finitude of the self who needs to confront the death of its world and the death of its own self in the face of the unassimilable other: "The simple meaning of dialectic: mutual recognition. . . . The other is a self and I see myself in the other. Two things: that I have gotten lost. I am for-an-other, and an other is for-me. And that I have lost the other, for I do not see the other as essence but see myself in the other."[64] As Hyppolite summarizes brilliantly, the irreversible distance between the self and the other reveals, paradoxically, the ineluctable structure of intersubjectivity connecting the self and the other, the subject and the other. Hegel's dialectic indicates the irruption of indestructible alterity, the unassimilable exteriority structuring the subject from *within*. But recognition of the self in the other cannot take place without the subsequent act of negation. To find itself and its self-certainty, the subject needs to *negate* negation. This means that renunciation or dissipation of the self is neither a perpetual dislocation nor a passive resignation of the self as a subject. Rather, the shattered subject realizes that his finitude, "his insufficiency[,] is at the same time his strength."[65] He proceeds toward "the negation of negation" by "enduring," "lingering over," and "tarrying with" the negative.[66] This process is often misunderstood as the negation of the other, a negation of the singularity of the other with the end of incorporating its difference into the totality of sameness. This reading is rooted in the master-slave dialectic, a narrative of antagonistic relation and constant struggle for recognition, which, however central to Hegel's entire system, is only the beginning of dialectic. Hegel's discussion, Williams clarifies, "proceeds from mutual exclusion and refusal, to mutual reciprocal recognition."[67]

I contend that the negation of negation is not negating the other, for this negation entails the dissolution of the self, the acceptance of its total loss, the death of the self, and the emergence of a new subject whose reality includes the nonreal, the opposite, the other. Rather, negation entails rejecting the perpetuation of the reality of loss and death, rejecting defeat as the permanent state of being by transforming it into a new possibility. I argue that it is this "disquiet" of the self, the "restlessness" of the negative, that the long and circulatory line of the Hegelian dialectic is signaling at its heart. It suggests that the subject no longer designates a fixed notion, an immutable substance. Rather, the subject points to the infinite spirit of restlessness that transforms its limits into the condition of a new meaning and a new reality. And this is precisely the passage that the Hegelian subject takes before the abyss. The dualistic separation between the finite and the infinite no longer holds its meaning, since finitude is the very condition of infinity: "The true nature of the finite is to be infinite. . . . The determinate has *no other essence than this absolute disquiet* not to be what it is."[68] The crucial significance of the negative in Hegel is that it evokes the power of transformation not by resorting to a transcendent synthesis but by presenting the structure of an immanent alterity/exteriority that deconstructs and transforms the structure from *within*. The subject's encounter with or exposure to its finitude opens the door to the discovery of its infinite self. The Hegelian passage parallels the work of the negative, which refers to the spirit of persistence, a tireless resilience "without renunciation or evasion, its praxis, and the conatus of its being."[69] Hegel thus provides the transition from the static notion of "substance" to the notion of "spirit" (subject) as a "whole" of the process of the dialectical movement.

Hegel regards the moment of dialectical synthesis as divine. The appearance of Spirit as subject is treated in the form of the historical manifestation of Spirit in art, religion, and philosophy. This process, in which Spirit discovers itself by way of externalization or self-manifestation, produces the "singular subject" whose life and existence embody and reveal the universal, namely "Absolute Being." It is important to observe here that the political struggle to *become* the subject hints at the theological moment of God's self-revelation/manifestation. Its divine quality rests on the fact that the Hegelian subject "neither seeks itself nor finds itself." Rather, as Nancy puts it, "*It effectuates itself*."[70] The world *is* what it creates, while "the subject is what it does."[71] Similarly, Žižek resonates with Nancy when he writes, "The only thing infinite about this subject is an interminable pursuit of the infinite."[72] The universal is manifested and actualized only in the concrete enactment of singular existence. One of the paramount philosophical contributions of Hegel, I would add, is that his system attempts to bring unity between knowing and being, being and becoming, and becoming and ethics/politics.

The Subject as Failure

The theo-political significance of Hegelian philosophy is further clarified by the Slovenian philosopher Slavoj Žižek. A proponent of radical-revolutionary philosophy, Žižek constructs his unique version of a materialist dialectic upon the edifice of the Hegelian system. By reading Hegel in tune with thinkers such as Kant, Schelling, Marx, and Lacan, Žižek refines the underdeveloped radical edges of the Hegelian dialectic. One focus of Žižek's thought is the notion of the subject. Following Hegel's account of the failed subject illustrated in *Phenomenology*, Žižek defines the subject as failure and self-contradiction. The rationale behind this is anchored in the Kantian antinomy; that is, the dilemma of the subject as an experience of finitude can be attributed to the questions of (the limits of) epistemology postulated by Kant. Kant's famous division of noumena and phenomena highlights the inaccessibility of "the Thing itself" (noumena) by phenom-enological reason, thus opening the gap between noumena, the "real," and its phenomena, that is, the form in which it is presented to our experience.

More importantly, the impasse of the subject rests on the fact that epis-temological finitude amounts to ontological finitude, that "the limitation of our knowledge is simultaneously the limitation of the very objects of our knowledge."[73] The fact that there exists an irremediable gap between noumena and phenomena indicates the incompleteness conditioning be-ing: the gap within the ontological structure means that there is an inher-ent gap within the ontological edifice. With this move, Žižek transitions from Kant to Hegel by conceiving Hegel as someone who transferred the epistemological project to ontology.[74] In this regard, Žižek resonates with the "nonmetaphysical/traditional reading" of Hegel and claims that He-gel's project is not to overcome the Kantian division but to expand Kant's project, or, better, to radicalize the Kantian division by "dropping the need for its overcoming."[75] The critical insight that Žižek provides for us in the transition from Kant to Hegel is that there is nothing beyond phe-nomenality. Although Žižek derives this insight primarily from Hegel, he deduces the idea from Kant as well. For Žižek, Kant can be also viewed as the one who, precisely because of his abyssal divide between noumena and phenomena, "re-conceives the noumenal as nonetheless a phenome-non *for-us*."[76] Žižek thus radicalizes Kant as someone who views the lim-its of knowing and being as the constitutive structure of being. In other words, the limit of human existence is the positive condition of reality.[77] But embracing finitude or accepting the material appearance as "real" and abandoning the illusion of the noumenal realm beyond appearance is con-stantly obstructed by the "transcendental illusion," the fantasy of the "big Other," to use Lacan's language, inscribed in the texture of the symbolic order. It is Lacan's thesis that participation in the symbolic order that is submission to the system of language and speech is derivative of "lack" and a subsequent "desire" to fill the emptiness. In other words, participation in the symbolic order reveals the desire for recognition. According to Žižek, what both Kant's transcendental illusion and Lacan's fantasy point to is the fundamental illusion of true signification, what Lacan also calls the "Real." Regarding this point, Lacan's argument is that no participant, no element of the symbolic order refers to the "Real." Rather, the linguistic signifier is a substitutive desire that always refers to another signifier and never to the signified. Nevertheless, Žižek points out, fantasy is an unavoidable el-ement that sustains and gives consistency to reality. In his words, "As soon as we renounce fiction and illusion, we lose reality itself."[78] On the other hand, another deceitful effect that fantasy produces is to conceal the absence of the subject by replacing this void with the transcendental illusion of the big Other.

What interests Žižek the most in this picture painted by Lacan is the fact that "the Real is therefore simultaneously both the hard, impenetrable kernel resisting symbolization and a pure chimerical entity which has in itself no ontological consistency."[79] Lacan's poststructuralist insight resonates with Žižek's radical materialist reading of Kant and Hegel in that Lacan embraces the impossibility of noumena (Real), which means that he embraces finitude as the horizon of human experience. Žižek radicalizes this point further and claims that the Real, in this sense, "is nothing but this impossibility of its inscription"; it is in itself a nothing, the embodiment of void, negativity, or emptiness.[80] In this vein Žižek finds ontological finitude a positive condition of being, for it is at the exposure to its limit that the self finally turns away from fantasy and takes the step toward the genesis of the subject. The Lacanian account of the subject Žižek draws upon finds its parallel in the Hegelian dialectic in which the birth of the subject is the result of the self's break from the void of the death of God.

The Void: Groundlessness and the Death of God

As I discussed earlier, Schelling provides Žižek with an important tool for developing the theo-political significance of the dialectic—a crucial conduit that facilitates the transition to Hegel. The theosophical depth of Schelling's thought serves for Žižek as vitally important material for weaving the theological and the political, as Schelling presents a cosmology framed by dialectical opposition and the becoming of God in nature/history. Schelling does not presuppose the subject as an a priori, a given. Rather, Žižek reads in Schelling a long and painful process of struggle for subjecthood, a tenacious account of self-actualization. To borrow Adrian Johnston's words, Schelling "attempts to sketch the (transcendental) subject's (ontogenetic) pre/proto history."[81]

To situate Schelling in the bigger picture of German idealism, while for Kant reason is the ultimate ground of reality itself, for Schelling reason "never begins in itself; its activity is never founded in itself."[82] There is an "archaic *Grund* beneath reason, giving rise to it and yet excluded from it," a groundless preontological drive in constant whirling motion or conflict within itself.[83] Žižek claims that Schelling's *Grund* does not presume a solid, consistent ontological foundation. Rather, it "corrodes the consistence of the ontological edifice of existence from within."[84] This means that *Grund* is preontological: it is hampered, fragmented, and inherently self-contradicted. Ground, in Schelling's thought, fails to ground, which indicates "that *Grund* is *Ungrund*, an abyssal groundlessness."[85] Beneath the seemingly calm and smooth surface of reality lies a perturbing vortex of drives (*Trieb*), a mass of conflicting darkness and chaos that Žižek, following Schelling, calls "horrible."[86] All of this suggests the existence of a temporality preceding beginning, a "true beginning" lying anterior to beginning. What does this true beginning look like? According to Schelling, this movement is an act of negation prompted by the perturbing, contradicting vortex of the (*Un*)*grund*. It is a movement of negation that turns toward the exit from the inconsistent mass of the ground(lessness). The importance of this movement for Žižek's theory of revolutionary materialism is specified as he explains that the Schellingian negation is brought about by what Schelling calls the "cision," *die Scheidung* (parting, divorce, separation).[87] Schelling's negation grabs Žižek's attention because it is born out of "decision," the elementary political gesture that enables the self to mark an authentic beginning toward becoming a political *subject* by way of breaking out of the vicious cycle of the rotary motion. Žižek writes, "In short, *at the beginning proper stands a resolution, an act of decision which, by differentiating between past and present, resolves the preceding unbearable tension of the rotary motion of drives*: the true Beginning is the passage from the 'closed' rotary motion to 'open' progress, from drive to desire—or, in Lacanian terms, from the Real to the Symbolic."[88] As Adrian Johnston puts it, this beginning alludes to a decision that *creates* the universe, rather than being *in* the universe.[89] Consequently, Johnston clarifies that "true beginning" is not the vortex itself but the "cancellation/negation" of it "through the gesture of the *Ent-Scheidung*."[90] But the reason why making the resolute step of *decision* is a task inscribed with difficulty is that a face-to-face encounter with the material substratum beneath reality is abyssal, hence traumatic. This is why, Žižek explains, Schelling calls freedom "abyssal": it is traumatic to accept that there lies nothing beneath matter (or beyond phenomena) but our *free will*. Encountering this ultimate freedom beneath the horizon of reality is abyssal and horrifying, since one realizes that one's ontological finitude is not the threshold for the passage to the Real, to the ultimate "Thing" lying beyond phenomena. Rather, one realizes that what awaits one is one's ultimate freedom to create the universe.

Žižek expands Schelling's vortex further by bringing in Lacan's insight and argues that the vortex is a fantasy, "a lure destined to distract us from the true traumatic cut, that of the abyssal act of *Ent-Scheidung*."[91] In other words, and to reiterate, what is terrifying for Žižek is not that there is a perturbing materiality beneath the symbolic reality. Rather, this palpitating mass of roiling matter is "a misleading, defensive distraction, in relation to the truly terrifying 'abyss of freedom,' the faceless void of (in)human autonomy."[92] Žižek defines Fantasy as the defense mechanism, the screen that conceals the abyss of the desire for the impossible Other, which is the Real that cannot be symbolized, the Real that is not a transcendental entity beyond the phenomena but a *nothing*, a *void*.[93] What is missing in this void is not the Thing or an ultimate Substance but the *subject*. On the other hand, Žižek opens up space for the advancement of theo-political thinking by highlighting (the death of) God in his radical materialist reading of Hegel. He transfers Lacan's notion of "the big Other as Fantasy" into a theological language and uses it to read Hegel's notion of the "death of God" that is, of God revealing itself to be a Fantasy. Here again, the same rationale that I discussed above applies: Fantasy allows the self to avoid the abyss of the traumatic encounter with the death/absence of God. The genesis of the subject is triggered by the self's encounter or realization of the void, namely the *death of God*. The Hegelian transition from *in-itself* to *for-itself* is born at this juncture as the self breaks from the vicious cycle of Fantasy by traversing the abyss of the vortex, thus becoming a self-conscious subject. Žižek emphasizes the terror that Hegel's abyss arouses by explaining that the political move of decision (scission) or the act of actualization entails "a jump into the unknown," a passage that "assume[s] the risk that what I am about to do will be inscribed into a framework whose contours eludes my grasp."[94] Žižek locates in Hegel the painful and almost violent rupture that accompanies the genesis of the subject. The birth of the subject is conceivable only upon the traumatic, bone-shattering pain of death: death of both God and of the self. This is why he writes that Hegel's abyss (night) is, "unlike the mystic void, a violent tearing apart, dismemberment."[95] Here Žižek's Kierkegaardian distinction between "Socratic reminiscence" and "Christian repetition" is insightful. According to Žižek, Socratic reminiscence subscribes to the idea of Truth as something that inherently dwells in oneself. On the other hand, Christian repetition understands Truth as an event, as something violently rupturing from the Outside "through a traumatic encounter that shatters the very foundations" of being.[96]

To recapitulate, the subject's journey of self-discovery begins with the void of the death of God, and *subject* is another name for the process and the struggle to fill the void, to "negate negation." This process ruptures the division between the theological and the political, since the subject realizes that what was missing in the void is not God but the subject him- or herself. In a theological language, we could argue that Žižek's thesis implies that the process of the subject's self-discovery carries a divine quality, just as God who died on the cross is incarnated in Spirit only in the community of believers (subjects) who "act."[97] The dialectical synthesis is, therefore, not a formula that can be fixed in a finalized form. Žižek thus maintains his faithful allegiance to the fundamental Hegelian thesis that the Universal becomes Universal only in the particular. However, the particular as subject is nothing but empty content, what Žižek calls (after Frederic Jameson) the "vanishing mediator." What is then left after the subject's act of traversal is not a static substance as/or subject, but "his own act of passage,"[98] while inscribed in substance is "an irreducible lack which forever prevents it from achieving full self-identity."[99]

Little Time for Grief: Žižek's Abyss and Trauma

It is important to remark that the abyss, along with the void, nothing, and trauma is one of the central metaphors in Žižek's Hegelian account. The abyss connotes the traumatic effect implicated in the subject's encounter with the void. For Žižek, the abyss is the violent rupture signifying both the dissolution of the subject and the birth of a new subject. But the Žižekian abyss fails to catch the rich complexity of the term in its original, mystical sense as it has been elaborated within the tradition of Neoplatonism. Despite his heavy emphasis on the singularity and the power of the negative, the subtle, yet persisting optimism couched in the Žižekian dialectic fails to provide us with a glimpse of the unfathomable depth produced by the pain and the shattering effects of the "traumatic abyss." How does the crushed subject manage to gather its fragmented self and rise up again amid endless series of traumatic encounters with the void? Can we simply and uncritically celebrate the shattering power of trauma and the void when considering the ongoing events of mass murder, violence, and sociohistorical trauma in the global world today? Along these lines I find Dominick LaCapra's critique of Žižek relevant as he problematizes Žižek's juxtaposition of historical loss/trauma (the concentration camp) and structural trauma or metaphysical absence (the Lacanian Real). LaCapra insists that loss needs to be distinguished from absence, since conflating these two could result in a misleading ethico-political attitude to context-specific historical loss. Likewise, historical trauma deserves a different reading practice than structural trauma, since the physico-material effects of these traumatic events are of a magnitude beyond devastation.[100]

Theologically, Žižek's account does not adequately explore the gap between the death of God and the resurrection or incarnation of the divine in history. God is murdered too prematurely, almost too easily, and what takes the place of God is the disguised optimism of a revolutionary political subjectivity. As a consequence, the vertiginous, ambiguous, and overwhelming depth of the abyss—lying between finitude and infinity, between immanence and transcendence—is largely absent from Žižek's account of the materialist dialectic. I would argue that one of the many things that contribute to the problem of Žižek's lack of a serious engagement with the abyss is that he often uses *void* and *abyss* interchangeably, thereby conflating the meanings of these two terms. In some instances he uses *abyss* in place of *void* when referring to the void as the site previously covered by Fantasy that now reveals itself to be nothing more than the "subject" itself.[101] In another instance, when discussing Butler's reading of "stubborn attachment"—a process of excessive attachment to a particular object that, according to Freud, leads to the formation of the self—Žižek writes that the particular object of attachment "acts as a stand-in for the void of Nothingness (or for the abyss of the impossible Thing)."[102] In a few instances he even calls the abyss "the limit" and "the void" of absolute negativity.[103]

As I have examined in the previous chapters, the abyss, in its Neoplatonic sense, refers neither to a simple limit nor to the mere intersection of lack and plenitude but to the passage from one to the other, which is nonetheless unlocatable and unspeakable. Given the central importance of the parallax/dialectical passage in Žižek's thought, it is ironic that he does not explore the meaning of passage implicated in the abyss. This leads him to translate finitudes as void rather than abyss. This identification is then followed by a celebratory realization—or at least a strong affirmation—of the void (finitude or the death of God) as it also signals the starting point for the inauguration of a new subject. Admittedly, much of Žižek's work is invested in elaborating and dramatizing the painful process of "discovery" and "encounter" with the Real (the death of God) and the recognition that ontological finitude offers a positive ground of possibility. Nevertheless, we are provided with no clues as to *how* the self who goes through the "shattering trauma" of the encounter with the Real manages to reassemble itself and proceed resiliently toward the struggle for self-determination. If the void facilitates for Žižek an easy transition or jump from the ontological limit to the death of God and back into the newly conceived subject, I submit that the "unexplored abyss" in his thought would have provided a more adequate framework for describing the long, ambiguous, and painful process of passage from one stage to the other. Žižek's abyss, in short, leaves much to be desired, especially when we consider that for Hegel the abyss signals the devastating state of "sheer disruption in which, . . . self-identity . . . having become divided against itself, all identity, all existence, is disrupted."[104] Žižek indeed acknowledges that Hegel's night (abyss) involves a violent rupture, an experience of "tearing apart" and "dismemberment." To emphasize the disruptive effect of Hegel's night, Žižek postulates the mystic abyss as a contrasting notion: "It would therefore be too hasty to identify this 'night of the world' with the Void of the mystic experience: it designates, rather, its exact opposite, that is, the primordial Big Bang, the violent self-contrast by means of which the balance and inner peace of the Void of which mystics speak are perturbed, thrown out of joint."[105] Here again we can see how Žižek misidentifies the mystic abyss by conflating it with the void. Any state of peace and harmony that the soul encounters in the mystical abyss is the result of a long and painful process of desperately searching for God in the midst of impossibility. It entails losing the ground of one's being and one's world, including even the original ground that is God. In other words, the ultimate state of unity with the divine that the mystics speak about results from a self-lacerating process of dispossession, displacement, and self-effacement.

Certainly Hegel himself leaves the trope of the abyss underdeveloped. As Judith Butler comments, following Kierkegaard, the infinitely self-replenishing subject of the Hegelian dialectic does not seem wholly engulfed by the negative: "No matter how many times his world dissolves, he remains infinitely capable of reassembling another world."[106] The subject of Žižekian dialectic similarly displays an almost magical power of resilience. The insightful question Butler raises following Kierkegaard as to how often "suffering simply erode[s] whatever ground there is" instead of prompting "the reconstruction of a world on yet firmer ground" is crucially relevant for not only Hegel but Žižek as well. By equating the abyss with the void, a rather simple nothingness, Žižek passes through the traumatic passage of the negative with perhaps too much haste, leaving "little time for grief."[107]

Despite the subtle, yet persisting optimism harbored in Hegel's thought, agonizing despair and grief cast an overwhelming shadow over the account of the Hegelian subject, particularly in Hegel's discussion of the Unhappy Consciousness. The Unhappy Consciousness perhaps represents very well the abyss lurking in the traumatic passage that Žižek attempts to avoid. It refers to the consciousness of the self in its inner disparity and self-contradiction. It points to what Žižek calls the "traumatic encounter," in which one becomes aware of the irreconcilable split between self and other, infinite and finite, universal and particular. In a word, the Unhappy Consciousness represents the principle of self-contradiction that conditions the Hegelian subject. Even though it signals the beginning of the passage from loss to self-discovery, from surrender and dissolution to the reconstruction of the subject, it is the state of a relentless oscillation between these two moments. At this moment we sense grief in the philosopher's reflection on the true meaning and magnitude of "total loss," that is, the loss of substance and self, the loss of the (old) world, and the loss of the Absolute that is the death of God: "Trust in the eternal laws of the gods has vanished, and the Oracles, which pronounced on particular questions, are dumb. The statues are now only stones from which the living soul has flown, just as the hymns are words from which belief has gone. The tables of the gods provide no spiritual food and drink, and in his games and festivals man no longer recovers the joyful consciousness of his unity with the divine."[108] The abyss or passage from a naive consciousness to self-consciousness, from the *in-itself* to *for-itself*, is a "way of despair," a path marked by surrender, loss, and death. What Hegel's Unhappy Consciousness signifies is that consciousness or the subject is structured by some sort of grief, a "grief which expresses itself in the hard saying that God is dead."[109] Such experience of pain and longing enables the inauguration of Spirit, namely the "particular" materializing the universal. What Žižek overlooks is that Hegel, despite his insistence on the indomitable subject and the restless spirit, acknowledges the weight of grief and suffering shadowing the path of the dialectical journey. Nonetheless, to reiterate Butler's comment, Hegel's subject is never fully swept over by the negative, "never devastated beyond repair."[110] The narrative moves on quickly to Spirit and to the next/last chapter: Absolute Knowing. Consequently an in-depth engagement with the Neoplatonic abyss may help us reread the Žižekian-Hegelian abyss. The rich poetic texture of the early mystical abyss was absorbed by the protodialectical system of Boehme and Schelling and was further "sublated" by the "rational" system of the Hegelian dialectic. Nevertheless, the oceanic depth of the mystical tradition and its poetics of abyss that are "remembered" (*erinnert*) and "preserved" (*erhalten*) in sublation (*Aufhebung*) persist in the abyssal crack between the poetic and the dialectic, between theology and politics, and between creaturely finitude and divine potency.

Subjects of Desire

Might Judith Butler's reading of Hegel help convey the dense and rich texture of the abyss in a way that Hegel's and Žižek's works do not? The importance of Butler's work for this chapter is, first, that despite her significant difference from Žižek Butler shares an important common ground with him: like Žižek, she views the subject of the Hegelian dialectic as a failure, marked by an indelible sense of lack. Furthermore, both thinkers are heavily invested not only in psychoanalysis but in a theory of ethics and, ultimately, radical politics. Second, the somewhat vague image of the abyss, which nevertheless persists in the Hegelian dialectic and is misleadingly (under)developed by Žižek, gains a more specific shape in Butler's work. To be clear, Butler does not evoke the term *abyss* in her writings. However, her feminist reading of Hegel with its focus on desire, lack, the body, and particularly the other inscribes a dialectical dynamic structured by a sense of an "irremediable gap" that could not be better described than as "abyssal." In a way, Butler's work may help us address the questions that Žižek's abyss leaves unanswered or unexplored. While Butler does not draw on Neoplatonic sources, her intense engagement with the dense affective elements constituting the path of the dialectic such as pain, despair, desire, and the overall drama of suffering, provides a deep perspective on the unreckonable depth shadowing the trajectory of the Hegelian dialectic. Third and last, Butler's reading of Hegel through desire, recognition, and otherness becomes, via Nietzsche, Freud, and Foucault, the backbone of her critical engagement with melancholia and the "politics of mourning."

Butler views the subject as structurally conditioned by loss and melancholia. The fact that loss constitutes the ontological texture of the self means that an insurmountable otherness is embedded within the structure of the self. Thus Butler reinscribes the ineluctable, opaque, abysslike gap in the structure of both the self and its process of becoming subject. Butler gives a specific shape to the somewhat abstract trope of the abyss by creating an ambiguous link with both the socio-psychic and the historical shape of the other constituting the ground of our social existence. The starting point from which Butler reads Hegel is desire. She views desire as the preliminary and persisting principle sustaining the subject of *Phenomenology*. However, desire has been historically foreclosed from the main trajectory of Western tradition as the other of philosophy. Butler reads desire in Hegel as the "fundamental striving" and "the incessant effort to overcome external difference" by becoming a self-conscious, whole subject.[111] Following Hyppolite, Butler associates desire with negativity. The resemblance between desire and negativity rests on the fact that both are marked by a persisting lack. Butler adds that desire is the mode of externalizing the inner contradictions/differences through which consciousness turns "its own negativity into an explicit object of reflection, something to be labored upon and worked through."[112] Therefore, she suggests a rhetorical reading of *Phenomenology*. She reads the gradual unfolding of the dialectic as the drama of desire, deception, and despair. If, however, the gradual manifestation of the Absolute reveals itself to be only partial and deceptive, and if the magically resilient subject of the dialectic lacks the ground of a historical possibility, what is the significance and relevance of dialectical circularity? Butler answers her own question by claiming that the deceptive cycle is a "progressive cycle" that reveals the "substance," namely the complex and broader reality of the Absolute, as "an all-encompassing web of interrelations, [and] the dynamism of life itself."[113] What makes this cycle progressive is not the promise of a more complete reality/knowledge but the fact that the ingrained "insufficiency of any given relationship to the Absolute is the basis of its interdependence on other relationships, so that the history of deception is, finally, the unity of internal relations which is the Absolute."[114]

The Abyss of the Other

Butler presents the basic formula of the dialectic rather simply by identifying consciousness with partiality (lack) and self-consciousness with mediation or self-reflection. In other words, if consciousness invariably indicates ungraspable negativity, self-consciousness is the result of an attempt to think or mediate the inner difference constituting the object. It also means that the Hegelian subject can know itself only through *mediation*. Butler reasserts Kant's point through the Hegelian lens by pointing out that therefore "object" cannot be separated from "object-as-explained-to-us." Thus mediation or explanation becomes part of the object's actuality.[115] I would argue that an irremediable rift emerges at this juncture—a rift that I would identify as the abyss, if not abyssal—in which an unforeseeable and insurmountable otherness appears to be prefiguring the structure of being in Butler's thought. For it appears that the Hegelian subject can come to self-consciousness only by self-reflection; and coming to self-consciousness involves consciousness's becoming "other" to itself. More simply, the self discovers the other (or the world) in itself and consequently discovers itself in the other. The fact that there is always an inherent otherness imprinted in the texture of the self points to the paradoxical way desire works so that "in desiring something else, we lose ourselves, and in desiring ourselves, we lose the world."[116] Desire is always in contradiction, frustrated and dissatisfied by the mutually exclusive paradox. Nonetheless, this very desire drives the self to a relentless effort to overcome such incongruity. If the Neoplatonic abyss hints at signs of dual—if not multiple—signification by pointing to the restless oscillation (passage) between the finite and the infinite or between the impossible and the possible, the ineluctable trace of the other in Butler's thought evokes the abysslike character of the inscrutable opacity conditioning the self and the other. For Butler, otherness inaugurates self-consciousness, occasioning "its articulation as desire," but at the same time "it is also the source of suffering for this emergent subject."[117]

The place of the other in the journey of self-consciousness, or rather the dialectical relation between self-consciousness and the other, is explored in detail in the section of Butler's early *Subjects of Desire* that examines Hegel's "Lordship and Bondage." The rather vague notion of the other that in its initial stage referred to the external world in general is now, she shows, concretized as another consciousness with reflexivity that is another self-consciousness. This is because, for the self-realization of self-consciousness in/through the other to result in self-discovery (of self-consciousness), this otherness needs to be "an object that mirrors the reflexive structure of desire itself."[118] In other words, self-consciousness can be realized in otherness and yet be absolute *for-itself* because this otherness reveals itself to be "another subject with a structurally identical set of aims."[119] Indeed, as various commentators of Hegel that I have already engaged would concede, mutual recognition is the key to understanding the master-slave dialectic, if not the entire system of the Hegelian dialectic. For Butler too, mutual recognition is the undergirding aim of the journeying self-consciousness and is therefore the only way insatiable desire can achieve satisfaction.[120]

But "discovering" the other should not be understood as an appearance of a reality from nothing. Rather, it is the emergence of a reality that was previously obscure and implicit. Thus otherness or the "other" self-consciousness that the Hegelian subject confronts is not a sheer exteriority irrupting from the outside. Rather, it is the discovery, the affirmation of the inner difference constituted by an ungraspable alterity/exteriority. In this sense, self-realization through the other amounts to consciousness's journey of discovering the trace of alterity that intrinsically structures itself and at the same time discovering itself in alterity. The process of self-discovery or self-realization inevitably entails dealing with this trace, or rather structure, of opacity, the abyss of otherness prefiguring the subject.

It is consequently not surprising that the journey is characterized by despair rather than optimism, for the similarity of the other suggests not "the possibility of reflexivity" but *self-loss*. The subject who was seeking reflexivity in the other finds itself fully absorbed by this other: "It no longer seeks to consume the other . . . *but is instead consumed by the Other*."[121] Traditionally, leftist readers of the master-slave dialectic—whose readings of Hegel are primarily inspired by Marx's reading of the Hegelian dialectic—centered their reading on the paradox around labor and subjection. Represented by Kojève, this view confers on labor an educative role from which revolutionary consciousness and the struggle of the slave begin while rendering the master as a tragic, fixated figure whose subjecthood fails to be recognized by the other. Butler's reading, centered on the paradoxes of subjection through body, desire, and freedom, aims to demonstrate how the almost erotic exchanges of implicit, suppressed, and contradictory desire (as well as their denials) reveal the (self)contradictory and vulnerable nature of self-consciousness. The full extent of the implication for ethics and for a consequential political vision is not developed in Butler's early work on Hegel in *Subjects of Desire*.

Yet one central point seems already clear: otherness and its fundamental bond with the subject.

Loss: Mourning and Melancholia

The subject as the bearer of vulnerability and precariousness is a recurring, or better, central, theme haunting Butler's philosophical works. With her initial reading of Hegel, particularly Hegel's master-slave dialectic, she brings an irremediable sense of breach into the basic contours of her philosophical thinking. Butler's ethical inquiry develops as this abyssal gap results directly in a rift, an ungraspable otherness and loss structuring the self. Such a sense of inner split is well articulated in her exchange with Catherine Malabou.

> Of course, the problem is that the "other" whom I face is in some sense me, and in some sense not "me"—and this means that the redoubling of myself that happens in this initial encounter is one that establishes some "other" who is not me. So I encounter myself at a spatial distance from myself, redoubled; I encounter, at the same time, and in the same figure, the limit to what I can call "myself." . . . So what I have to live with is not just the fact that I have become two, but that I can be found at a distance from myself, and that what I find at that distance is also—and at once—not myself.[122]

The complex question of otherness is further complexified as Butler turns to Freud and Foucault in order to examine the process of subject formation. Central to Butler's claim is the view that agency or the subject is not only born but also sustained by "subjection" to the web of power and discourse that precedes our will and temporality. Her view is profoundly influenced by both Althusser and Foucault, who understand the subject as the product of the power enacted in and through sociopolitical institutions and dominant ideologies. From this, Butler concludes that the subject comes into existence as the result of subordination to power, an act of "passionate attachment" to subjection.

The fact that an unfathomable difference or alterity constitutes an essential part of the self is indicative of the incompleteness and vulnerability of the self, which could also be translated as a certain sense of loss. Meanwhile, another important element that Butler incorporates into the texture of the self is loss caused by prohibition. She concurs with both Nietzsche's and Freud's point that prohibition "turns 'the drive' back on itself, fabricating an internal sphere, the condition for self-inspection and reflexivity."[123] Eventually prohibition leads to subjection, while at the same time it implies that such foreclosed desire constitutes "the subject through a certain kind of preemptive loss," as Freud has remarked.[124] She draws on the example of gender/sexual identification by arguing that heterosexuality is produced by the enforcement of gender norms—that is, by the prohibition of homosexuality. This means that the prohibition and resulting denial of desire or attachment to the same gender produces a melancholia that constitutes the (heterosexual) subject.

Melancholia, as defined by Freud, is the result of an unresolved grief. It becomes the structure of the self as the demand for loss (loss of certain sexual attachments) and the further demand to disavow those losses constitute the social network of power in which the subject is produced. Butler writes in the wake of the many unrecognized and unmourned losses/deaths produced by HIV in the LGBT community, so we find in her writings a contextualized notion of loss, grief, and melancholia. Butler later extends her notion of grief and mourning to the victims of state-sanctioned violence, particularly those whose lives are not deemed as grievable by the rhetoric of war (e.g., the Palestinians and other war victims in the Middle East whose countries are at war with the United States/the West).[125] In this sense, the understated (or unspecified) abyss of Butler's dialectic is already highly political. Going back to the philosophical language framing her theory of the psychic formation of the subject, *loss* refers to the crack opened up between the subject and "the world of others," that is, the web of "social terms that are never fully one's own," yet from which one emerges.[126] The abysslike character of the subject's psychic prefiguration takes a concrete form when Butler points to the paradox of the subject's genesis. Accordingly, agency is not the ability that facilitates one's denial of the social condition constituting the self. Rather, agency is initiated "by the fact that I am constituted by a social world I never chose."[127] We find here the Hegelian passage or what Žižek calls the "parallax shift," which in a way also invokes key attributes of the Neoplatonic abyss: the passage between the finite and the infinite or between the negative and the positive. Butler invokes this passage—a passage in which the negative signifies the condition of possibility—by arguing, "That my agency is riven with paradox does not mean it is impossible. It means only that paradox is the condition of its possibility."[128] In this sense, the negative, namely loss, grief, opacity, and vulnerability, signals a positive condition, "the condition of our existence and survivability," as it also points to the precarious nature of our existence.[129] At the same time it reveals "the way that we are from the start already given over, beyond ourselves, implicated in lives that are not our own."[130] The fact that the other(s) entangled in one's social existence constitute the fabric of one's being signifies that Butler's philosophical inquiry is, inevitably, some sort of ethical inquiry. In Butler, the other bears the traces of the abyss in the form of the unknown site of alterity intrinsic to the structure of being. The ethical significance and the political possibility created by what I call "the abyss of the other" in Butler are further developed with her advancement of the politics of mourning. Here she connects the abiding theme of loss and melancholia with mourning through a revisited reading of Freud.

In Freud's classical 1917 essay "Mourning and Melancholia," mourning is defined as a necessary and healthy process of withdrawing the libidinal projection directed to the lost one.[131] Successful mourning will lead the mourner to find a new object onto which the mourner can project his or her libido again. Butler reflects on the act of mourning as the "opaque self" suffers from loss and the vulnerability of being a part of a socially constituted body, exposed to attachment and the inscrutable trace of the other.[132] Her conception of vulnerability points to the complex web of social relationships lying anterior to and beyond the self, which in turn reveals the incoherence of being a self: a self who is deprived of its agency, a sense of direction, and the ability to foresee who the self is becoming or even to tell who he or she is. At the same time, as Butler's early reading of Hegel indicates, loss entails loss not only of the self but of others. Vulnerability or precarity of the self signifies both the loss of the self's coherence *and* the loss of others who constitute the relationality that enables the self's existence, for there is no way that the "I" will fully know who they are, nor is the "I" able to pay back the price that others paid. Therefore, the self needs to be accountable to the invisible and already passed temporality that constitutes who *we* are. Butler recalibrates loss into an ethical accountability to the concrete others of history from which we emerge. If we take them for granted, Butler warns us, "then our very living depends upon a denial of their historicity, a disavowal of the price we pay."[133] But one may wonder, what is the possible political option that Butler suggests when loss and grief lead us to nothing but mourning? What forms of ethical thought and accountability to others can we derive from mourning that is an act of withdrawing one's libido from the lost object and moving on? To this question about the ethics of mourning Freud himself provides a more refined answer in his later work.

In his 1923 work "The Ego and the Id," Freud revisits his own early position and calls melancholia an inevitable component in the ego's self-formation.[134] Freud argues that the lost object is not completely detached from the mourner but introjected and thus incorporated as a part of the ego. In other words, Freud views narcissistic identification of the ego as a constitutive element of the self. This is where Butler's notion of mourning begins too. She rejects the classical Freudian formula by questioning its alleged goal: "I am not sure I know when mourning is successful, or when one has fully mourned another human being."[135] Rather, mourning reveals the unfathomable depth of our ethical ties to unknown others. As we go through mourning, perhaps we come to terms with our finitude, our vulnerability, and the possible transformation that awaits us. Butler writes, "I'm certain, though, that it does not mean that one has forgotten the person, or that something else comes along to take his or her place. . . . I think instead that one mourns that one accepts the fact that the loss one undergoes will be one that changes you, changes you possibly forever, and that mourning has to do with agreeing to undergo a transformation the full result of which you cannot know in advance."[136] Loss reveals our vulnerability, and vulnerability in turn signals transformation. Then mourning is perhaps the painful process of accepting the volatile nature of our existence. Grief and mourning in this sense are not privatizing or depoliticizing. Rather, they are key for theorizing our dependence and ethical responsibility to one another. They signal the possibility of a "political community of complex order" in which we "make grief itself into a resource for politics." [137] This is not passive inaction or resignation but, as Butler reminds us, "a slow process by which we develop a point of identification with suffering itself."[138] Mourning thus acquires a new political meaning. It signifies the political refusal to conform both to the normative solution of letting go of a completed past and the hasty dissociation from suffering and collective wounds/trauma. To reiterate, Butler's ethico-political concerns are rooted in the specific experience of the political context of the LGBT community (and the victims of state-sanctioned violence) where certain kinds of bodies and desires are unrecognized and this repudiation reproduces an inability to mourn certain kinds of losses. According to the normative account of loss provided by contemporary democracy, certain kinds of lives are ungrievable. These questions around the link between unrecognized (or ungrievable) lives and the act of mourning as the political refusal of unrecognizability lead Butler to identify the problem of (un) recognition in Hegel. The complex intersection between desire and recognition within the Hegelian oeuvre, Butler points out, leads Hegelian scholarship to miss the crucial problem: the failure of recognition. The Hegelian assertion that all desire is a desire for recognition fails to account for the experience of people whose lives are unrecognized by the prevailing social norms.[139] The problem of recognition in Hegel was also taken up by Frantz Fanon several decades before Butler. Fanon reads Hegel's master-slave dialectic from the standpoint of the colonial context, from the site of political struggle in which the Hegelian logic of mutual recognition is expressed in a conflict between the white colonizer (master) and the black slave. Mutual recognition becomes a romanticized ideal in the colonial context. Instead of seeking recognition from the slave, the master finds him laughable.[140] In the colonial reality, the master expects nothing from the slave but labor and servitude. Unlike the Hegelian slave, the black slave finds neither meaning nor self-consciousness in labor: he or she finds no liberation in work.[141] If the Hegelian slave turns away from the master and toward the object, thus objectifying the master, the Fanonian slave turns toward the master by abandoning the object.[142] The slave wants to be *like* the master, so he fails to objectify him: a crucial process for achieving subjectivity in Hegelian dialectic. Therefore, in all these critiques of Hegel, Fanon claims that the existential impasse belongs not to the master but to the slave, who, as I have stated elsewhere, "desires to be recognized as a subject and yet is never granted with such recognition by the master."[143]

Both Fanon and Butler complicate the notion of the other by hinting at the failure of recognition. The otherness at stake therefore is not just about its ungraspability. Rather, there is another side to it: the unrecognized or repudiated other. Butler opens the door for thinking the abyss of the other not only in terms of its "inscrutability" but also in the context of suffering, as the "suffering other." While Butler's notion of the other does not directly derive from the Neoplatonic tradition, the abyssal character of the other in her thought creates a significant tie of resemblance with the abyss of Neoplatonic mysticism, yet with a clearer ethico-political edge. Perhaps the unexplored abyss of Žižekian Hegelianism gazes back upon the impatient subject of dialectical materialism through Butler. Her reading reveals our ties to the countless others of history that perhaps the subject of the Žižekian dialectic fails to acknowledge. She provides the philosophical ground for thinking ethics and politics in such a way that we frame the present and future in conjunction with the missed possibilities and lost temporalities, the inaccessible trace of the other who eludes the grasp of the subject-in-the-becoming. An element of the unknown structures Butler's politics of mourning or politics of recognition. Her unassertive, yet persistent political gesture of recognition and mourning aims at an ethics of becoming in relation to the other: "To ask for recognition . . . is to solicit a becoming, to instigate a transformation, to petition the future always in relation to the Other."[144]

Certainly Žižek's critical assessment of the politics of recognition deserves our attention here. He quotes Butler's repudiation of the prevailing conception of queer politics as a "merely cultural" movement that opposes the economic struggle. He then endorses Butler's claim by stating that the queer politics of recognition is valuable as long as it posits a threat to capitalism. However, he warns at the same time against the potential collusion between cultural politics and the present condition of global capitalism by saying that "in the post-political arena, capital is able to neutralize queer demands, to absorb them as a specific way of life."[145] Žižek's observation resonates with the widely held traditional leftists' critique of the various forms of cultural politics proliferating under the current dominance of postmodern philosophies. These cultural politics find expression in the various form of "critical theory" and play a key role in analyzing the construction and dominance of oppressive social relations. The fact that many such ideas of subversive politics fail to posit a threat to the proliferation of global capitalism disturbingly suggests that they are somehow meeting the partial needs and demands of the all-pervading power of capital. In this context we see the importance and relevance of Žižek's critique.

Žižek similarly critiques Butler's reading of the master-slave dialectic by concluding that politically Butler's reading results in a passive reconfiguration of the hegemonic order rather than a revolutionary displacement of the entire system. In her reading of Hegel's Unhappy Consciousness, Butler examines the doubling effect of the body produced in the process of suppression or renunciation of the body. The lord attempts to negate the precariousness of the body conditioning his existence by suppressing the body and transferring it to the bondsman. As Butler reads, the lord's imperative to the bondsman is then "You be my body for me but do not let me know that the body you are is my body."[146] This dynamic is interesting because the bondsman somehow effectuates his agency by subjecting himself to this imperative and mimicking the lord's body. The main question that arises is whether the bondsman's agency is fully constrained by the negation (or the imperative from which it is generated). The dilemma, for Butler, lies in the fact that "the agency of the subject appears to be an effect of its subordination."[147] The possibility that Butler suggests is that "the attachment required by a regulatory regime" might "prove to be both its constitutive failure and the potential site of resistance."[148] She finds the clue in the paradoxical reversal of the power dynamic produced in the act of renunciation. The paradox lies in that the act of renouncing the body ends up with "doing" or "performing" body, since the act of denial that is the act of showing itself as a "nothing" ends up with a "performing" of nothing, a "doing" of nothing.[149] What Butler reads in Hegel's master-slave dialectic is the fact that the very denial or suppression of the body ends up inadvertently preserving the body. Similarly, Butler argues that just as for Freud prohibition reproduces and intensifies the prohibited desire, every effort and act of renunciation preserves and reasserts the suppressed desire, body, or agency. Then one can say that the power producing the subject does not remain unaltered after it is appropriated by the subject. Rather, "a significant and potentially enabling reversal occurs when power shifts from its status as a condition of agency to the subject's own agency."[150] Butler thus derives the potential for the undoing of subjection in the structure of the same subjection to which the subject is "passionately attached." In short, the political aim that Butler hints at is reconfiguring "the contours of the conditions of life" by the subject whose performative repetition and appropriation of the norm displace, paradoxically, the power structure.[151] Her major point of disagreement with Žižek is that her "performative reconfiguration" is "a subversive displacement which remains *within* the hegemonic field."[152] For Žižek, the political efficiency of such political strategies needs to be questioned because they fail to cut through the "fantasmic core" and indeed may sustain it, just as Butler's "passionate attachment" runs the risk of being conflated with subjection to the symbolic (hegemonic) order.[153] In other words, the risk Žižek finds in Butler's performativity is that its "passive" political gesture may as well end up being absorbed into the all-too-powerful structure of hegemonic power rather than subverting it. Contrastingly, the Lacanian insight points to the "more radical act" of reconfiguring "the entire field which redefines the very conditions of socially sustained performativity."[154] Žižek concludes by calling Butler's move both "too optimistic," in that she overestimates the power of "the marginal gestures of performative displacement," and too pessimistic, in that she does not advance "the radical gesture of the thorough restructuring of the hegemonic symbolic order in its totality."[155]

Žižek's critique of performative reconfiguration points to the important question of political vigilance and the political implications of Butler's account of the subject and subjection. Perhaps we could extend his warning to the broader field of cultural politics that tends to seek the possibility of subversion within the given system of linguistic signification without the "long and painful" process of self-discovery and transformation;[156] at the same time many such theories do not seem to demonstrate the willingness to tackle the all-pervading system of exploitation and violence instigated by capitalism. Thus the dialectical abyss that Žižek brings to the center of his thought indicates the event of the violent "rupture" that, as a result, tears apart the texture of being. Time and again, he emphasizes the painful and traumatic dimension of this process, which consists of traversing the abyss and rediscovering the (missing) subject. But as I have already argued, even as traumatic and dark as his notion of negativity appears, Žižek offers a naively resilient and optimistically successful account of negation, of a finally renewed and rediscovered subject.

To reiterate the question I posited earlier, how does the devastated subject manage to collect its shattered self and proceed forward after countless failures and traumatic encounters with the void? Perhaps we can follow Kierkegaard's and Butler's warning and consider the wider ethico-political landscape of the global context as we reflect on the notion of the abyss, suffering, and the other. The abyss then would no longer be restricted to its narrow metaphysical meanings such as the ground of God (and of the soul) or the "void" lying beneath matter. We could extend its meaning and read it in such a way that the groundlessness of being signifies the symptom of the loss of historical and politico-economic ground within the context of oppression, particularly, (neo)colonial oppression. The question that arises then would be, how does the colonial subject who lives in the deadlock between the memory of unspeakable trauma and the still-absurd present emerge from its all-pervading, all-sinking groundlessness to a new ground? For Hegel too, crossing or passing through the abyss in the dialectical journey is depicted as a painful moment of utter devastation. It is not an abstract notion of suffering, for it "bears not only on knowledge, in the narrow meaning of the word, but also on conceptions of existence."[157] The death of the old consciousness and the birth of the new subject (or the Hegelian passage, as I would call it) takes place at this crossroads in which the demarcation between finitude of the self and the divine spirit is displaced: by reading Hegel with Butler and the postcolonial thinkers (as I will do in the next chapter) we may be able to gaze more deeply at the abyss that is underdeveloped in Hegel. In it, this groundlessness of being, we find not only the death of an ontotheological God but also the gaping wounds of the unmourned histories of unrecognized lives and their sufferings. The underdeveloped trace of the abyss haunting Hegel's dialectic parallels, perhaps, the unrecognized others of (non-European) history upon whom Hegel famously confers Euro-Christian modernity as the culmination of history; the awe-provoking mystery of abyssal otherness is sublated in his philosophy of history so that the other becomes the foil that facilitates the progress of the Absolute Spirit.[158] The pulsating shadow of otherness in the work of the early Hegel haunts the progressive trajectory of his dialectic despite Hegel's denial and the eventual disappearance of that otherness from the system of the mature philosopher of the state. In this sense, like the mystical abyss, which was at least implicitly political, Hegel's abyss is to a certain extent already political. The abyss beneath the Hegelian dialectic is haunted by the cries of unrecognized others that burst out from underneath his Euro-Christian-centric philosophy of history. In this regard, my attempt to politicize the abyss in the Hegelian dialectic is in a way repoliticizing the underdeveloped, yet already political abyss that was harbored in Hegel's thought all along.

Going back to Žižek's critique of Butler, I argue, contra Žižek, that Butler's performative reconfiguration is neither optimistic nor pessimistic. Rather, Butler's reading of Hegel (along with her readings of Freud and Foucault) hints at the political possibility of theorizing the reality of suffering and politicizing the crude reality of vulnerable bodies at the site of extreme violence and oppression. This may not be as "radical" as what Žižek calls a "radical act" of subversion. A radical act requires a sociopolitical ground for self-definition that many oppressed masses, the subalterns of the global world, are dispossessed of. Butler's politics offers a creative channel of resistance for the desperate subject lacking the sociopolitical foundation for enacting radical politics. Her subject politicizes and transforms pain by way of attaching to it "rather than not attach[ing] at all," in contexts where wretchedness and pain "are [the only] sites offered by the regulatory regimes for attachment."[159] She clarifies this political gesture further by saying that negation contradicts "the rhetoric of withdrawal it purports to signify," as the gesture of negation signals a gesture of affirmation (of negation).[160] Therefore, she concludes, rejection/negation is "a site of presence and excitation and, hence, better than no object at all."[161] Perhaps Butler's reading can be seen as "realistic," as her perspective is anchored in the context of communities that are constantly vulnerable and exposed to physical violence.

As I have sketched out my account thus far, we find in Hegel an intrinsic trace of the abyss structuring his entire philosophical system. While it does not make its presence explicit, the abyss nevertheless shadows the Hegelian subject's journey of becoming. In both Hegel and his contemporary readers (Žižek and Butler), the abyss signals an ineluctable otherness constituting the (self-splitting) reality of the subject. This otherness prefiguring the subject inevitably places questions of ethics at the center of being. In Žižek, we find them expressed in the form of an ethics of the revolutionary political subject, while for Butler the other is an invariably present, yet ungraspable source of ethical reflection and political responsibility. In either case, the subject is thrust into the movement of oscillation, and the force behind this movement is what Hegel calls negation or the negative. Negation is the movement of crossing or passing through the abyss. Negation means first negating the self. Then it also signifies negating negation, which points to the act of renunciation, an acceptance of loss that would, paradoxically, defy loss and defeat as the perpetual condition of existence. My interest underlying the current project is this resilient act of passage through which the subject comes to embrace finitude/failure and eventually to transform it into the ground of new possibility.

By reading Hegel, Žižek, and Butler, I have located the indelible and abyssal "trace of the other" in the subject's passage or journey of becoming. The question that arises then regards the possibility of such passage: the shift, act of traversal, transformation, and eventually, reconstruction. The answer to this question will result in varying modalities for thinking ethics and the subsequent political vision regarding the place of the self, the subject, the other, and so on. While the thinkers I have examined above may all maintain a positive perspective on such possibility, their answers as to *how* show significant differences. The answer to these questions varies even more significantly and presents more complications if we extend this ethico-philosophical question to the broader context of the global South, particularly those sites shaped by the contestations of (neo)colonial violence and oppression. I turn to these postcolonial thinkers who strive to find a language for theorizing or politicizing the abyss, a notion that finds its resonances in their concrete experience of violence and suffering. The missing place of grief and the rushed passage of the Žižekian revolutionary subject are partly symptomatic of the fact that the abyss remains underdeveloped and underpoliticized in Hegel's dialectic—even though the palpitating otherness/abyss shadowing the dialectic is already political. It is then in the writings of the post/decolonial thinkers that questions about the abyss and its ethico-political significance give rise to an alternative vision.

The Colonial Abyss

Groundlessness of Being

Nevertheless with all my strength
I refuse to accept that amputation.
I feel in myself a soul as immense as the world,
truly a soul as deep as the deepest of rivers,
my chest has the power to expand without limit.
I am a master and I am advised to adopt
the humility of the cripple.
Yesterday, awakening to the world,
I saw the sky turn upon itself utterly and wholly.
I wanted to rise, but the disemboweled silence
fell back upon me, its wings paralyzed.
Without responsibility, straddling nothingness and infinity,
I began to weep.

—**Frantz Fanon,** *Black Skin, White Masks*

For history is not only absence for us. It is vertigo.
This time that was never ours, we must now possess.

—**Édouard Glissant,** *Caribbean Discourse*

The registers of the abyss shadowing the dialectical unfolding of this book draw different routes of oscillation between multiple points that appear contradictory. One encounters in this restless movement of oscillation a countless number of thresholds that rupture one's horizon and open up newly emerging prospects. Thresholds trouble the boundary between the end and the beginning, between limits and possibilities, thus disrupting the linear trajectory that conditions the movements of crossing, of passage. As such, they testify against any hopeful expectation of the irruption of a radically new reality from nothing. Rather, they designate the radical indeterminacy lurking in the space of the "between." Seen from the threshold, perhaps newness does not enter the world in the form of a violent, radical rupture from the exterior. Rather, it arises from the middle, the middle of the painful horizon of historical reality. The registers of possibility emerge directly from the immanent surface of history, the very site of agony and the painful weight of our existence. Understanding our reality as constituted by thresholds opens room for abyssal thinking, for thresholds lead our steps into the abyss: they indicate the borderless and porous contours shaping the abyss.

Many such encounters spring from unexpected moments and unlikely sites and may plunge us into wonder. But the diverse array of thinkers I have examined thus far take us to the conclusion that the possibility of transformation and passage is the result, not of awe, but of the arduous work of self-reflection and engagement with the bottomless depth of being. A more specific contour of the abyss emerges then as the result of our reflection in the previous chapters to materialize these movements of self-reflection, becoming, and re-creation of the self. The abyss in the writings of mystical thinkers indicates the infinite plenitude and transcendence of God, which, paradoxically, intersects with the ontological finitude of human beings. The human soul agonizes over the limits of its being as its language fails to contain the full experience of the absolute Other. However, the depth of unknowability persisting in both the nature of God and the soul and the relation between them reveals itself to be the threshold of yet another horizon in which the conception of both God and the self is wholly reconfigured. This revelation or discovery is not simply conferred on the soul in a magical instant. Rather, the abyss offers itself as the grounding foundation only as the result of a long and persistent process of self-dispossession that entails submission to the unknown.

The Hegelian dialectic similarly presents a struggling subject whose trajectory of becoming is conditioned by the unrelenting movement of oscillation between opposites. The abyss takes a more concrete form in Hegel as the intractable gap is opened up not only by a mystical/metaphysical abstraction but by *the other*, who exists in the form of concrete flesh and consciousness. The path, therefore, toward the crossing or passage of the abyssal gap is mediated by the other, who in return engraves a sense of ethical responsibility upon the structure of being. With the Hegelian dialectic, we realize that while the abyss elicits the urgency of a political subjectivity in the dialectical journey of becoming and transformation, it also elicits a sense of ethics and responsibility that evokes the trace of the other lying at the threshold of the passage in the subject's journey. Meanwhile, that these tropes of abyss unfold only around speculative languages is perhaps indicative of the regrettable fact that the meaning of the theological/philosophical abyss is molded by its somewhat narrowly defined understanding. The mystical connotations that frame the trope of abyss have, over the course of history, generated an understanding of spirituality that is distant from the political reality of human lives. This tendency has resulted in an unfortunate gap between the spiritual and the political in which the mystical abyss is exclusively associated with a self-absorbed notion of spirituality, characterized by an individualized obsession with the pursuit of the ground for the affirmation of the self and one's God. As a consequence, the abyss as "ontological finitude" becomes *existential* but disconnected from the *reality of existence*.

Therefore, in this chapter I attempt to extend the notion of the abyss by drawing on a wider variety of literatures that endeavor to work through the devastating condition of human reality shaped by political and historical experience. Extending the meaning of the abyss and giving it a concrete historical-political shape may entail thinking the other not only in speculative terms but also as the "suffering other." In what ways does the suffering other alter the texture of the mystical and philosophical abyss that I am exploring here? While previous discussions of the abyss were centered on the experience of negativity and finitude, what is largely missing from those discussions is the living sociopolitical circumstances of human reality. By turning to the work of post/decolonial thinkers I suggest a more politicized or repoliticized understanding of the abyss. In particular, I examine the work of the Afro-Caribbean thinkers whose writings articulate the agonizing experience of their political/historical reality with a language resembling that of mysticism. As the conversation around the affinity between the spiritual and the political unfolds, one notices a strange, yet surprisingly apt parallel between these two seemingly distant discourses. My intention before this unexpected affinity is to explore the intersection between on the one hand the existential chasm of oppressed subjects whose whole existence is conditioned by the reality of suffering and on the other hand the mystical experience of groundlessness in the pursuit of God. Within the matrix of the reconceptualized, or better, repoliticized, abyss, we may find that the theological language alludes to the political gesture while the political vision emerges alongside the theological imagination.

The notion of the suffering other that I suggest along with the Caribbean thinkers, particularly Édouard Glissant, indicates a term that, rather than being reducible to the exclusive category of the other, designates the subject position of the self as well. In other words, what helps us set the parameters of ethical responsibility and political imagination in this chapter is the notion not only of the suffering other but also of the "suffering self." We witness in the writings of the Caribbean thinkers an extended notion of identity rooted in a relational ontology through which the story of the shattered other shapes the contours of the collective history from which the traumatized self emerges. It is then in this middle territory, the groundless site lying between the traumatizing past and the dumbfounded present, between fragmentation and reconstruction, and between suffering and redemption, that we begin to reflect upon the possibility of *passage* that is *beginning* after trauma.

Decolonizing the Abyss: A View from the Antilles

While the swirling convergence of multiple creative resonances within the current constructive dialogue has been leading us through numerous emerging thresholds across different abysses, another crucial threshold has yet to be explored, this one all too literal: that is, the shorelines marking the islands of the Antilles. The geopolitical subjugation of the archipelago to the proliferating forces of neocolonialism parallels, in many ways, the distinctive historical reality of the Caribbean, which is marked by the violence of mass annihilation, transportation, slavery, and colonialism. It is thus not surprising that questions of resistance, national identity, and self-determination occupy a central place in the works of many Caribbean thinkers. For the impasse consists not only of the socioeconomic alienation shaping local societies but also of the impaired collective historical identity breached by the history of colonial violence. It is from this sociohistorical context that Antonio Benitez-Rojo speaks of the "meta-archipelago," the transhistorical experience uniting the "repeating island" of the Caribbean archipelago. He writes, "Beneath the turbulence of *árbol*, *arbre*, tree, etc., there is an island that repeats itself until transforming into a meta-archipelago and reaching the most widely separated transhistorical frontiers of the globe."[1]

The question that arises from reflection on the site manifested by the contesting forces of (neo)colonial violence regards the possibility of passage, that is, the positive register of reconstructing the fragmented self and transforming the devastated ground into the horizon of new possibility. Let me answer this question provisionally in advance: the different interlocutors that I am engaging in this book—including the Caribbean thinkers—all seem to subscribe to such possibility. However, their answers as to *how* to approach such possibility vary significantly. The distance among these answers grows even more significantly when we take into account the social and the geopolitical difference marking the gap between these different contexts. This gap or difference cannot be articulated apart from the black hole of the long history of colonialism and the ongoing reproduction of its violent structure in the global world today. In other words, the abyssal gap between the different answers to the questions regarding the possibility of the passage from trauma to future, from negativity to positivity/possibility, does not just consist of the methodological difference. Rather, this gap emerges out of colonial difference.

As I explained in chapter 1, colonial difference derives from the ongoing effects of coloniality; it points to the irreducible difference of the colonial configuration marked by the spatial articulation of power. In other words, colonial difference signifies the gap opened up by the colonization of the Americas, which, with its racist control of labor and resources, served as a stepping-stone for Europe to consolidate its hegemony at the global level, becoming the axis, as Quijano remarked, "around which all forms of labor were articulated to satisfy the ends of the world market, configuring a new pattern of global control of labor, its resources, and products."[2] It was on the basis of this control over the structure of production and labor that the universalization of Europe at both the epistemic and the political level took place. Under the widely established system of exploitation in America, local systems of meaning making and knowledge production were expropriated, repressed, and excluded. It is in this respect that John Drabinski claims, "The history of the Caribbean is immanent to the meaning of Europe."[3] In the same vein, Benitez-Rojo remarks, "The Atlantic is today the Atlantic (the navel of capitalism) because Europe, in its mercantilist laboratory, conceived the project of inseminating the Caribbean womb with the blood of Africa; the Atlantic is today the Atlantic (NATO, World Bank, New York Stock Exchange, European Economic Community, etc.) because it was the painfully delivered child of the Caribbean."[4] This means that thinking Europe or thinking ethics exclusively on the basis of the North Atlantic experience without considering the reality of its inseparable other, the global South, is not feasible in the age of globalization. This is not only because the global South is an indispensable part of the historical constitution of European identity but also because the current mode of global production and consumption, namely capitalist globalization, makes the bond between the North Atlantic region and the global South tighter than it has ever been before. The new global reality, along with the dark, haunting history of its Atlantic commercial circuit, calls for an ethical response that is accountable to the reality of the colonized.

Decolonizing the abyss or rethinking it in the politicized space shaped by neocolonial globalization eventually provides us with a broader or better, deeper definition of the abyss, reconceptualized and repoliticized upon the base of the concrete historical context. The layers of complexity weaving the fabric of Caribbean historical reality as we encounter it in the works of thinkers such as Aimé Césaire, Frantz Fanon, and Édouard Glissant offer a powerful account of the abyss grounded in the concrete reality of people, an account that extends across culture, economy, and politics. The notion of the abyss encountered in the writings of the post/decolonial Caribbean thinkers suggests an innovative framework for cultivating or creating a new theo-political imagination: one that is capable of discovering future and possibility in an agonizing present reality without failing to acknowledge the full depth and magnitude of suffering caused by colonial violence, and that is able to disentangle God from the white European sovereign, thereby transforming those living in the state of exception into the agents of a new community and new order.

The Colonial Abyss

The work of the French Martinican poet, philosopher, and novelist Édouard Glissant offers a form of thinking that brings together the central topics and questions I have articulated throughout this book: a certain mystical spirituality interwoven with ethics, ontology, poetic imagination, political vision, and most importantly, colonial difference. However, what makes Glissant even more important and relevant for the current project is the fact that the trope of the abyss occupies a central place in his thought. The primary material with which Glissant's thought begins is historical memory. The dilemma that distresses the Caribbean intellectual is about making sense not only of the obliterated past but also of the present: the reality of people and their collective identity that is nevertheless borne or the time/life that *goes on* after trauma. The impasse of the Caribbean writer is that he or she bears the double burden of having to come to terms with both the haunting memory of the traumatic past and the equally ruptured present. The history of the Antilles is characterized, in Glissant's words, by "nonhistory." By this, Glissant is referring to a history of a people whose very birth was given by a violent rupture, a traumatic experience of dislocation, deportation, and mass deaths. "The French Caribbean is the site of a history characterized by ruptures and that began with brutal dislocation. Our historical consciousness could not be deposited gradually and continuously like sediment, as it were, as happened with . . . European peoples, but came together in the context of shock, contraction, painful negation, and explosive forces. This dislocation of the continuum, and the inability of the collective consciousness to absorb it all, characterize what I call a nonhistory."[5] Glissant thus places the horror of the middle passage at the center of his poetic and philosophical vision. The figurative and symbolic meaning of the middle passage serves as one of the central sources of inspiration guiding Glissant's thought. It is also in this middle passage that the figure of the abyss is born. The abyss, as its etymological root of "bottomlessness" indicates, represents the sense of groundlessness constituting the fabric of reality in the colonial world. Loss haunts the horizon of life just as, in Glissant's parlance, the ocean is marked with balls and chains (now gone green) that weighed down the slaves thrown into the water.[6] This is why memory occupies a central place for Glissant. But Glissant does not propose a regressive, melancholic project of mourning the past devoid of an accountable perspective toward the emerging future. Rather, his project gravitates around the paradoxical temporality in which the experience of catastrophe and the middle passage gives birth to a people. This is why the central metaphor for Glissant is neither the sea nor the land but, as Michael Dash comments, "the mediating threshold."[7] In other words, Glissant is interested neither in retrieving the past, like his contemporary Aimé Césaire, nor breaking from it, like Frantz Fanon.[8] Instead, Glissant's main concern lies in "beginning," that is, beginning after catastrophe (the middle passage), which entails affirmation of both the fragmented past and the impaired present.[9] We find imprinted at the heart of Glissant's philosophy a dialectic of dispossession and reconstruction that gives rise to a relational ontology. As Celia Britton remarks, the unbearable pain of "transportation destroys the idealist conception of being as permanent essence. However, this perdition opens up the possibility of relation instead of essence."[10] Glissant finds in the gaping depth of the colonial abyss a womb that gives birth to a new world, a new people whose modes of being find expression in relation and becoming rather than the static terms of essence and being. This is why, in his poetic depiction of the slave ship's voyage across the Atlantic, Glissant names the traumatic abyss of the middle passage (the boat) the "womb abyss."[11] The figurative image of the abyss is translated into the crossing of the middle passage. While it is the source of the indelible memory of death and suffering, the middle passage (and the boat) is at the same time the site where the genesis of the post-traumatic (postabyssal) community takes place.

Glissant's notion of the abyss and the middle passage makes for an interesting resonance and contrast with the accounts of the abyss and passage I have engaged in the previous chapters. While it shares a striking affinity with the mystical abyss and the dialectical abyss, Glissant's abyss carves its own distinctive path with its political contextualization within concrete historical reality. A deep examination of Glissant's colonial abyss, I contend, helps us unveil the hidden or unspecified politics of the mystical-dialectical abyss and thus retrieve the political in the mystical-dialectical tradition. This will eventually invite us to reconsider the politics and possibilities of passage in the abyss. Meanwhile, Glissant's notion of the abyss is closely identical to the Neoplatonic figure of the abyss in many ways. But Glissant's abyss is not born out of a theological or metaphysical project. Rather, the figure of the abyss in his writings emerges from the collective history of suffering and the despairing reality of colonial oppression. While Glissant's thought stands intentionally distant from theological discourse, his writings disclose a strange marriage between the political and the spiritual. His longtime interest lies in articulating the inexhaustible power of the profound solidarity/relation from which the fragile name of the community is born. Riddled with the absurdity of oblivion (of history) and excess (of the landscape), the colonial abyss Glissant locates at the unfathomable bottom of the archipelago's complex history bears striking resemblances to the Neoplatonic abyss. This is because what lies at the heart of Glissant's project is, like that of many other contemporary Caribbean writers of his time, a desire to redeem the fractured historical reality of the archipelago, not by avoiding it or creating a disconnection, but by continuously engaging it. Thus, when the two sets of writers are read alongside each other, there is a strange yet powerful resonance between the Neoplatonists' uncontainable passion to name the unnameable name of God and the Caribbean writers' indomitable desire to name the unnameable trauma of history. The endeavor of working through historical reality requires the difficult task of theorizing the collective wound, that is, affirming the shattered reality and transforming the open wound into the horizon of a new beginning. It is not surprising, then, that this process of transformation or passage in Glissant's writings resembles the theological vision of the mystics. To be clear, and again, Glissant's thought does not directly intersect with theological thinking. His writings are rather concerned with questions of colonial history, collective identity, language, and the political future of the (post)colonial Antilles. Similarly, his notion of the abyss is conceived upon the ruptured horizon of the political impasse and the haunting historical memory that shapes the contours of Caribbean collective consciousness. Nevertheless, despite the absence of explicit allusions to theological ideas in his writings, Glissant offers invaluable insights for the practice of our theological imaginations. He provides a powerful account of reconstructing the self in the colonial abyss, thus hinting at the movement of passage through the abyss. In this sense, the trace of theology in Glissant's thought—if there is any—could be best described as hinting at a form of secular theology. His writings, which employ a secular language of apophaticism and gestures toward the poetic reconstruction of a relational cosmos out of the despairing context of the colonial abyss, open the possibilities for rethinking (political) theology at the crossroads of the complex historical reality of the (post/neo)colonial global world. While it is not my intention to translate Glissant's ideas into a theological language, in the next chapter I read Glissant's poetics alongside the theopoetics of philosophical theologians such as Amos Wilder, Richard Kearney, John Caputo, and Catherine Keller and explore the theological potential that such reading provides for thinking the relation between the spiritual and the political in the middle passage.

The trope of the abyss makes more frequent appearances in the writings of Glissant than in those of Césaire and Fanon. Nevertheless, central to both of the latter authors is the liminal, "in between" space of (post) colonial collective consciousness that is caught in the deadlock of history. At times described as an impasse, at other times as a void, the historico-political context from which Césaire and Fanon think reflects the abyss very suitably. Indeed, mediating this seemingly irremediable gap *is* one of the main concerns in Caribbean literature. As Benitez-Rojo affirms, one finds in Caribbean writers' works "the desire to sublimate social violence" and to "communicate their own turbulence, their own clash, their own void, the swirling black hole of social violence produced by the *encomienda* and the plantation, that is, their otherness, their peripheral asymmetry with regard to the West."[12] In other words, the impasse of colonial difference from which the Caribbean collective consciousness arises may itself rightly be named the abyss, the groundlessness of being upon which the colonized subject constructs meaning and the possibility of a future.

From this perspective, as early as the late 1930s, historical memory became recognized as a crucial political tool propelling the emerging *Négritude* movement.[13] Aimé Césaire, one of the founders of the *Négritude* movement, is perhaps one of the key thinkers whose work played a foundational role in mobilizing a tradition of existentialist decolonial thought tinged with a Marxist class analysis. His *Cahier d'un retour au pays natal* (Notebook of a return to the native land), a celebrated book-length poem influencing the subsequent generation of Caribbean thinkers, captures the excruciating dilemma of the colonial subject whose ontological ground is sunk in the abyssal crack lying between the ruins of colonial oppression and the urgency of a collective self-determination.

We find already in the opening images of the French Caribbean islands in the poem an emerging feature of the abyss, a colonial abyss that I suggest we use as a central framework and figure to read the ontological quandary of the colonial subject: "at the end of daybreak burgeoning with frail coves, the hungry Antilles . . . the Antilles dynamited by alcohol, stranded in the mud of this bay, in the dust of this town sinisterly stranded."[14] Thus the abyss in this chapter is read not only as a metaphysical and existential notion but as an all-pervading ontological groundlessness that involves the absence or loss of material and political ground. In other words, if the political rendering of the abyss in the previous chapter defined it as a metaphysical condition of absence and loss constitutive of the self, this chapter reads the abyss, with the help of Caribbean decolonial imagination, as a symptom of the loss of historical and politico-economic ground within the (colonial) context of oppression.

The figure of the abyss that emerges in Césaire's poem points to the clear difference or gap between the colonizer's culture and the colonized society. Having himself received his education in Europe and adopted the cultural values of the colonizer, Césaire, on returning to his native island of Martinique, sees a dire and impoverished landscape that cries out of its overwhelming sense of misery and devastation: "in this inert town, this desolate throng under the sun, not connected with anything that is expressed, asserted, released in broad earth daylight, its own."[15] At the bottom of Césaire's dramatic narration lies the traumatic memory of colonialism marked by slavery. In his decolonial vision, as in that of many of his contemporary and subsequent generation of Caribbean writers, one of the main images that serves as a source of inspiration is the haunting collective memory of the slave ship and the middle passage: "We, the vomit of slave ships, we the venery of Calabars. . . . I hear coming up from the hold the enchained curses, the gasps of the dying, the noise of someone thrown into the sea . . . the baying of a woman in labor . . . the scrape of fingernails seeking throats . . . the flouts of the whip . . . the seething of the vermin amid the weariness."[16] Césaire's *Cahier* attempts to reconstruct a universal black identity by claiming affinity with the broader pan-African experience of displacement and colonial racism across the Atlantic.

Contrary to the assessment of some critical readers, the *Cahier* is not a simple and blind celebration of black nativism. Rather, as Nigel Gibson suggests, it is a complex work that engages multiple layered issues born with colonialism.[17] Similarly, Gary Wilder notes that *Cahier* reads *Négritude* "as a problematic series of attempts to engage" the impasse of the colonized subject.[18] In this regard, Césaire's epic poem maintains a certain dialectical tension between pessimism and optimism, between despair and hope, which creates the effect of dramatizing the magnitude of agony and anxiety that the colonial subject suffers. For the poet, the only way out, the only possible breakthrough, seems to lie in poetry. However, his view of poetry, while infused with optimism, is enclosed within limitations. Césaire suggests madness over reason, as "an alternative modality of knowing," thus displacing "the very opposition between rationality and irrationality, knowledge and myth, on which colonial order was grounded."[19] But the dialectical tension grows as Césaire recognizes the irremediable abyss lying around the absurdity of claiming a nativist tradition that has been already defiled and devalued by colonial discourse. In other words, as Gary Wilder puts it, "Affirmations of authentic Africanity risk confronting European stereotypes of natives."[20] The narrator is therefore drawn into a deep existential impasse as he finds himself unable to confront colonial racism. His affirmations of African nativism are followed by his pessimism and doubt, a move that eventually leads to a hopeless acceptance: "So be it. So be it. I am of no nationality recognized by the chancelleries."[21] The pessimistic resignation moves, however, from a resentful acceptance of defeat to a gesture of embracing the fissures of imperfection and fragmentation as the painful, yet ineluctable character of the colonial reality:

Oh death your mushy marsh!
I accept!
. . .
. . . the world map made for my own use, not tinted with the arbitrary
colors of scholars, but with the geometry of my spilled blood, I accept
and the determination of my biology . . . and negritude, no longer a
cephalic index, or plasma, or soma, but measured by the compass of
suffering
. . . .
I accept, I accept it all.[22]

We see in this self-lacerating act of surrender and acceptance the movement of dialectical negation or passage, which, as with the interlocutors that I have engaged in the previous chapters, results in the genesis of a new, transformed consciousness. As Césaire writes, "Suddenly now strength and life assail me like a bull and the water of life overwhelms the papilla of the morne."[23] The change of tone and the transition of perspective that happen here are perhaps much too radical, and the poet concludes his long reflection with an affirmation of nativism. Suddenly speech acquires a mystified power, and the speaker stands, as Wilder observes, with a "unified consciousness and unmediated connection with the cosmos."[24] Césaire claims,

And the nigger scum is on its feet
. . . .
standing under the sun
standing in the blood
standing and free.[25]

The long drama of dialectical oscillation that unfolds in Césaire's poem points to the emergence of a new threshold that forms along the fuzzy lines drawing the shores of the repeating islands. The unreckonable wound of the colonial abyss then cracks open on the blurry horizon of the Caribbean shorelines where the sea is not just an indication of the limit of land and history. Rather, the decolonial imaginary of Caribbean philosophy conceives the sea as the continuation of land and its history. This is why Derek Walcott claims in his widely celebrated poem, "The sea is History."[26]

The colonial abyss, therefore, when looked at from the Caribbean standpoint, bears a profound affinity with the figure of the shoreline. For it is the bottom of the sea, from the middle passage of the Atlantic Ocean, where the undying memory and the horrifying history of deaths and drowned names are engraved. The haunting memory of terrifying history seems unfathomable and unending like the bottomless depth of the ocean, yet new history is to be born at the very point where its thin line of demarcation meets the land, the rugged soil of history, just as the end of the ocean marks the beginning of land. Likewise, neither the geography nor the identity of the Caribbean people can be determined by the cartographic confines that separate the islands from the sea, for, as Walcott writes, "There is a territory wider than this—wider than the limits made by the map of an island—which is the illimitable sea and what it remembers."[27] Thus the surface of the colonial abyss that emerges along with Caribbean decolonial thought exposes its complex layers of historicity tied into the most central questions regarding the possibility of dialectical passage that is the possibility of founding the ground upon the groundless horizon of the (post)colonial world. Moreover, their works show that this layered web is also entangled with questions of geography (landscape), political economy, language, and memory. In the work of Glissant we find all of the above-mentioned questions forming together a powerful and persisting body of thought that projects a philosophical and literary imagination toward a decolonizing modality of being-in-the-world. But before we move into an in-depth dialogue with the work of Glissant it is helpful to engage another figure who is Glissant's contemporary and whose work is crucial in contemporary discussions of (post)colonialism, critical race theory, and decolonial politics.

Living in the Zone of Nonbeing: Fanon and the Coloniality of Being

Frantz Fanon's work in postcolonial criticism today is indispensable. The importance of engaging Fanon for the current project is twofold. On the one hand, Fanon develops the existential reflection on the torment of living in the colonial impasse/abyss conceived in the work of Césaire into a full-fledged account of a countercolonial discourse, delving with intensity into the depth of the psychic dimension of the racialized/colonized subject. Fanon's use of both psychoanalytic and phenomenological approaches enables him to scrutinize the embodied experience of living in a colonial order with a particular body. This allows him to further build a compelling account of how the colonial subject's consciousness is formulated through its interaction with the lived experience of the (black) body.

On the other hand, Fanon's political engagement in the Algerian independence movement and his advancement of decolonial political strategy provide an important direction for the articulation of the countercolonial mode of thinking and being that I am seeking in this chapter. But all in all, these features point to the most important reason why Fanon matters for the current conversation: he elaborates one of the most candid and downright painful reflections on the lived experience of the "existence" of the colonized and racialized body. By drawing on multiple aspects of the colonial experience, including not only psychic and sociocultural dimensions but also the economic and particularly the political struggles of the colonial subject, Fanon dramatizes successfully the deathlike experience of the being inhabiting the colonial abyss.

In many ways, Fanon's work can be viewed as a continuation of Césaire's project. This is because the beginning point of Fanon's intellectual trajectory is also *Négritude*. Fanon does not begin with an uncritical celebration of *Négritude*; rather, his departure from *Négritude* marks the genesis of distinctively Fanonian thought. While his initial ideas were molded by *Négritude*, Fanon keeps a critical distance from its central claims by unfolding a countercolonial discourse that overcomes the limitations of *Négritude*'s black essentialism and cultural nationalism. The problem that Fanon identifies in *Négritude* is its "abstract and backward-looking" orientation and its almost exclusive focus on culture "at the expense of urgent social issues and radical political movement."[28]

The problem of essentialism and the uncritical celebration of a transcendental nativism in the *Négritude* movement has been pointed out by many scholars of postcolonial studies. Edward Said, for instance, speaking of another founding figure of the *Négritude* movement, Leopold Senghor, remarks that "to leave the historical world for the metaphysics of essences like negritude . . . is to abandon history for essentializations that have the power to turn human beings against each other."[29] Another big problem of *Négritude* from the perspective of contemporary postcolonial theory is that, as Bill Ashcroft, Gareth Griffiths, and Helen Tiffin put it jointly, "its structure is derivative and replicatory, asserting not its difference, as it would claim, but rather its dependence on the categories . . . of the colonising culture."[30] Valid as these criticisms remain, it is important to acknowledge the internal differences marking the heterogeneous movement labeled as *Négritude*. Césaire's project certainly requires a distinction from Senghor's black essentialism, which proposes the idea of a "black soul." Fanon warns against such a gesture of essentialism, saying, "The black soul is a white man's artifact."[31] The negro construed by such forms of *Négritude*, Fanon adds, is one who "buries himself in the vast black abyss. . . . This attitude . . . renounces the present and future in the name of a mystical past."[32] While Fanon is widely known to challenge *Négritude*, his argument is much too complex to be oversimplified merely as "critical." This is because, as Robert Bernasconi reminds us, while Fanon was critical of thinkers who focused on black history/essentialism such as Cheikh Anta Diop and Leopold Senghor, he showed an ambivalent relation toward Césaire "on the grounds that he was an inspiration for a possible future, even if at times he remained locked in the past."[33] Indeed, Fanon credits Césaire for raising the black consciousness now widespread among the blacks in the Antilles at a time when "no Antillean found it possible to think of himself as a Negro."[34] The importance of Césairean thought for Fanon is further affirmed as Fanon challenges Alioune Diop, another key figure in the *Négritude* movement, whose main thesis is the restoration of black genius over everything else. Dismissing Diop's proposal by remarking that "a true culture cannot come to life under present conditions" and that the talk of the black genius can occur only "when the [black] man has regained his rightful place," Fanon turns to Césaire: "Once again I come back to Césaire; I wish that many black intellectuals would turn to him for their inspiration."[35] To synthesize, Fanon's major disagreement with *Négritude* lies around temporality. The authors of *Négritude* tend to encapsulate the black man in the past, while Fanon holds on to the faint hope of a forward-looking future, a future to be unfolded dialectically through the resilient self who will make itself known, recognized.[36] Even though Césaire seems to make nostalgic gestures at times, he remains a central inspiration for Fanon. We see, somewhere between these two Martinican writers of the twentieth century, a glimpse of the figure of the abyss emerge upon the historical and ontological horizon of coloniality.

As such, the colonial abyss that Fanon gazes upon seems even more despairing than Césaire's abyss. For the whole notion of being and ontology fails in the colonial context, where life, for the native and colonized other, "is already a living death."[37] What lies at the base of Fanon's critical reflections is perhaps the simple fact of living with a black body in a white world or in a world infused with colonial ideology. The basic, fundamental desire, then, is for recognition, a recognition of one's humanity: "All I wanted was to be a man among other men."[38] This is because in the colonial reality "The black man is not a man."[39] The existential impasse of the black person lies, for Fanon, in the fact that his or her existence unfolds in the "zone of nonbeing," a state of perpetual curse.[40] The fractured subject cries for recognition, yet is denied, fixed under the white gaze, and "hated, despised, detested, not only by the neighbor across the street . . . but by an entire race."[41]

The black person's self is structured by a double, or better, triple, consciousness, as self-consciousness is split into the consciousness or image of the self mirrored through the eyes of the other. The encounter with the colonial gaze is also the moment in which inferiority is inscribed in the psyche and the body, the realization of oneself as an object, or rather an *abject*. This encounter is famously captured in Fanon's own traumatic experience of facing the racializing gaze on a train in France: "Look, a Negro! . . . Mama, see the Negro! I'm frightened!"[42] Fanon describes this moment of encounter as an experience where his "corporeal schema crumbled," for the racial, racializing schema defines and conditions his being and existence.

The unfathomable abyss portrayed in Fanon's work is brilliantly caught and explored in Nelson Maldonado-Torres's constructive formulation of the notion of the "coloniality of Being." In his comparative reading of both European (continental) and Latin American decolonial thought, he discusses the meaning of death in Heidegger, for whom only the encounter with one's inescapable death can define the way to authenticity. Maldonado-Torres remarks how the encounter with death is not an extraordinary affair but a constitutive feature of the reality of colonized subjects.[43] In the colonial context, death is not so much individual, as is the case with Heidegger's *Dasein*. Rather, the horizon of collective experience is marked by the threat of death that surrounds colonial subjects in their everyday life experiences. For people who already live with death and are considered as nonbeings, the way of achieving authenticity is different: "The encounter with death always comes too late, as it were, since death is already beside them. For this reason, decolonization, deracialization, and *des-generaccion* (in sum, decoloniality) emerge not only through an encounter with one's own mortality, but from a desire to evade death, one's own but even more fundamentally that of others."[44] Decolonial thinking emerges from this trauma to the very edifice of being: an unending coloniality woven into the fabric of being and the encounter with the omnipresent threat not only of one's own death but of others'. Such an existential reality of racialized/colonized subjects provides context for what Maldonado-Torres calls, following Dussel, the coloniality of being: the miserable situation of a denied existence, the reality of the colonized who "perceives life not as a flowering or a development of an essential productiveness, but as a permanent struggle against an omnipresent death."[45] Examining the black experience in the American South, Abdul JanMohamed also calls the subject whose horizon of existence is bound to death the "death-bound-subject"—that is, "the subject who is formed, from infancy on, by the imminent and ubiquitous threat of death."[46] Living with a black body in the American South, for JanMohamed, is being imbued with a culture that creates permanent states of social death. The idea that the threat of death permeates the structure of subjectivity, as JanMohamed puts it, hints, in many ways, at what Maldonado-Torres attempts to articulate with the coloniality of being. What underlies the horizon of the coloniality of being is colonial difference, which is presupposed by both Cartesian epistemology and Heideggerian ontology, yet never acknowledged by Eurocentric forms of thinking.[47] Given that beneath the logic of Cartesian epistemology, *cogito ergo sum* (I think, therefore I exist), lies the implication that "others do not think," the *damné*, for the European *Dasein*, is the being who is "not there." Therefore, Maldonado-Torres concludes, a reflection on *Dasein* and Being without the awareness of coloniality (colonial difference) "involve[s] the erasure of the *damné* and the coloniality of Being."[48]

Theorizing Decolonial Resistance: From Despair to Countercolonial Politics

The question that arises with Fanon's colonial abyss is whether Fanon leaves us with any sort of hope regarding the possibility of finding a ground for transformation or passage. The abyss that emerges from the body of Fanonian thought seems manifestly hopeless and irrevocable. Is then the colonial impasse in Fanon's thought more a deadly, irredeemable void than a mystical abyss? What hints of hope does one find in the devastating wound and trauma of colonial violence?

Nigel Gibson asks a similar question by reading Fanon's critical engagement with Hegel's master-slave dialectic. As I summarized in the previous chapter, the dialectic of recognition sketched out in Hegel's master-slave dialectic raises important critical questions when viewed from the embodied experience of marginalization. Fanon, among others, points out the impossibility or failure of mutual recognition in a relationship conditioned by absolute power asymmetry (master-slave/colonial context). For Fanon, Hegel's idea of mutual recognition within the structure of the master-slave dynamic is a romanticized ideal. The master—more concretely, the colonial master—does not seek recognition from the slave, as is the case for Hegel. All he expects from the slave is labor. Meanwhile, the black slave fails to negate the master through work or to objectify the master because of his unquenchable desire for recognition. Thus, for Fanon, Gibson writes, "Dialectic becomes motionless."[49] How does the black slave or the colonial subject break free from the insuperable state of nonexistence and nonrecognition? To find the answer to this question, Gibson turns to Fanon's last book, *The Wretched of the Earth*. Certainly the accounts of *Black Skin* do not seem to hint at a clear and compelling conclusion. Fanon maintains a consistently pessimistic view of the colonial relation throughout the entire book. Yet Gibson contends that Fanon, rather than concluding with total pessimism, draws us back to the enduring importance of critical engagement and freedom. While Fanon concludes the last chapter of *Black Skin* by rejecting the trope of mutual recognition in the Hegelian dialectic, he does not give up the power and beauty lying in human beings' critical engagement with reality: "I said in my introduction that man is a *yes*. I will never stop reiterating that. *Yes* to life. *Yes* to love. *Yes* to generosity."[50] This is followed by the remarks in the last few pages of the book, which can be read as an invitation, a call to radical self-reflection and critical engagement. Fanon claims his "self" to be the very foundation of his groundless existence. He refers, not to the self given by the system of social signification, but to the transformed self that emerges from the long, arduous struggle for self-definition and self-discovery.

Therefore, going back to the previously posited question, Gibson observes that for Fanon the only possible way out of the endless cycle of oppression and subjugation lies in the "retreat to a mind of one's own" that is radical self-reflection and the discovery of "Black consciousness as a possible ground for mutual reciprocity."[51] Gibson reads Fanon as quintessentially materializing the dialectic in both his thought and his political actions: that is, Gibson contends that the political thought Fanon formulates in *The Wretched of the Earth* is dialectical particularly when we consider the trajectory of Fanon's life and thought. Thus the master-slave dialectic as depicted in *Black Skin* appears to signal a rupture in the dialectic: the reader is led to a Manichean conception of the world. However, Gibson writes, "Consciousness is, in fact, forced back into self-certainty and the dialectic reappears in Black consciousness which becomes a basis for a new cognition."[52] In *The Wretched of the Earth* Fanon advances a program of decolonial resistance deeply rooted in a firmly self-determined black consciousness. From this, Gibson suggests that Fanon turns to radical self-reflection, a regress into his self-consciousness that results in the birth of a newly acquired sense of self-determination, namely black consciousness. Since mutual recognition is denied by the other encountered in the external world, Fanon turns to the otherness *within*. Only the powerful act of retreating to the painful wound of his own leads Fanon to the possible reconstruction of the shattered self.

This is how the colonial abyss from which Fanon's existential cry is born creates semblances with both the abyss of Neoplatonic mystics and the underdeveloped abyss of the Hegelian dialectic: the very condition of groundlessness becomes, paradoxically, the ground for self-reflection and self-creation. The dialectical subject engages in the journey of continuous becoming, guided by radical self-reflection or what Gibson calls "the method of internalization, or inwardization, [that] gives action its direction."[53] What we see in *The Wretched of the Earth* as a result is, in many ways, a further concretization or complexification of the contours of the colonial abyss sketched out so far. The politico-economic condition of the (post)colonial context that draws us further into its vertiginous depths offers, at the same time, a promising vision of a decolonial movement of resistance. Overall, *The Wretched* is framed by a geopolitical analysis of the decolonial struggle of young nation-states within the international landscape of the postcolonial Cold War atmosphere. Fanon shows us that the life and existence of people in (post)colonial society is marked by a Manichean reality: a society compartmentalized into two different worlds. "The colonized's sector, or at least the 'native' quarters, the shanty town, the Medina, the reservation, is a disreputable place inhabited by disreputable people. You are born anywhere, anyhow. You die anywhere, from anything. It's a world with no space, people are piled one on top of the other, the shacks squeezed tightly together. The colonized's sector is a famished sector, hungry for bread, meat, shoes, coal, and light."[54] The existential quandary of the colonized is attended by the political and economic impasse, which conditions life in the colonial world. Fanon resonates with the Marxist category of base/superstructure by giving it a twist with the claim: "In the colonies the economic infrastructure is also a superstructure."[55] In other words, if the classical Marxist debate of base/structure tends to build a clear binary by viewing one as determining the other, Fanon argues that this distinction loses its meaning in colonial society. For in Fanon's view one's material/economic base is inseparably linked to what species, what race one belongs to. In a way, Fanon stands in the same tradition with Césaire in that he, like Césaire, relies consistently on Marxist class analysis. Just as Césaire advocated the idea of liberation based on proletarian revolution, Fanon understands liberation as the end of racism in which all material means are put into people's hands.[56] Yet above this Manichean reality that splits the colonial subject and devastates colonial society is the reality of Europe positing itself as the absolute subject upon the back of its dialectical other (the colonial world). Here Fanon points rightly at the problem that the young nations in the decolonial struggle are facing. The basic economic structures of most postcolonial nation-states are so deeply dependent on the capital of the colonizer as to be almost inseparable from it. The only way out of the colonial impasse, then, is the dialectical affirmation of black consciousness, that is, national consciousness. However, Fanon's perspective differs clearly from *Négritude*'s essentialism in that the national (black) movement needs to be eventually incorporated into a broader consciousness of sociopolitical needs, namely, "humanism."[57] In other words, Fanon's affirmation of national consciousness needs to be understood in light of his notion of humanism, which entails, in Michael Azar's words, "a specific negation of the Manichean order."[58] This negation, I argue, signals the act of dialectical mediation, which hints at the possibility of a true mutual recognition. Here we witness in Fanon the opening of "the possibility of a national consciousness which may give birth to an 'opening of oneself to the other on a personal level and, on a further scale, to an 'international consciousness.'"[59]

The gesture of passage suggested by Fanon involves the achievement of the universal through the dialectical unfolding of the particular, that is, the colonial subject. The conditions of colonial existence are perhaps another name for the colonial abyss in which the consciousness of the colonized is born.[60] The movement of passage through the colonial abyss is perhaps conceived only when the deathlike abyss is rediscovered as the womb that gives birth to a new consciousness. In this constant dialectic of life and death amid life-in-death a liberating and revolutionary decolonial politics unfolds, thus moving from individual self-consciousness to a collective consciousness, from national consciousness to a broader, pan-African solidarity.

The Limitless Middle? The Eurocentric (Mis)Appropriation of Creolization

The central question Glissant raises in connection with the general direction of the current book is, How to materialize the seeds of new possibility in the abyss of painful history and the inflicted reality of ongoing (neo)colonialism? What are the sociohistorical conditions that enable the passage through the middle passage? Glissant's appeal to the newly conceived postcolonial identity grounded in the creolized notion of multiplicity and relation generates resonances with contemporary critical theorists' advocacy of postmodern/global identity for the age of postcolonial and posthumanist ethics. Glissant's heavy emphasis, particularly in his later works, on nonessentialized identity based on multiplicity, fluidity, eco-poetics, and errantry has strong affinities with the discourse of philosophical no-madism, which is primarily inspired by the philosophical ideas of Gilles Deleuze. Certainly the impact of Deleuze's philosophy on Glissant is sig-nificant, and many of the late Glissant's philosophical ideas are explic-itly affiliated with Deleuze's key philosophical notions. Glissant found in Deleuze creative philosophical ideas that bore surprising affinity to his own philosophy of creolization, and he borrowed several Deleuzean concepts to develop them into important tools for advancing his own theoretical framework of countercolonial poetics.

Among many commentators of the Glissant-Deleuze connection, the Italian-Australian feminist philosopher Rosi Braidotti raises very import-ant questions regarding the dynamics configuring philosophical dialogue that involves two similar, yet different forms of thinking emerging from radically contrasting geopolitical contexts. Braidotti's work points simulta-neously at both the possibility opened up by creative intellectual explora-tions on being, identity, and ethics in the postmodern age of globalization *and* the shadows created by the problematic reading practice that such explorations exercise. My contention is that these forms of reading prac-tices require a careful reexamination of the subtle, yet persisting layers of colonial difference, which often go unnoticed in the dominant forms of intellectual dialogues. Rethinking the dominant forms of European or Eu-rocentric discourse is crucial, since one way Europe's hegemony was able to maintain its status was by producing a universalizing, normative form of reason and subjectivity. In this vein John Drabinski writes, "Thinking from a certain location overturns or 'de-links' the non-located measure of impe-rial reason."[61] It follows then, that while Glissant advocates a deessential-ized mode of being-in-the-world and a unifying vision based on Relation and becoming, we find at the bottom of his thought a relentless effort to root such an approach in the specific context of the archipelago, a socio-historical milieu rifted by colonial difference, namely "the community in its vertigo, the landscape in its excess, [and] time in its uncertainty."[62] In what follows, I present Glissant's decolonial poetics in conjunction with Braidotti's reading of Deleuze. With the end of both delinking the uni-versalizing measure of imperial reason and highlighting Glissant's unique conception of the "groundless middle," I compare Glissant's errantry with philosophical nomadism and suggest, eventually, points of telling disso-nance that open between Deleuze and Glissant.

While the trope of the middle per se does not recurrently appear in the texts of Deleuze, it signifies one of the central structuring principles of his philosophy. Deleuze espouses the logic of multiplicity and difference as opposed to what he believes to be the essentialist tendency of traditional

Western metaphysics and the logic of the One underlying such a metaphysical system.[63] Deleuze's problem with traditional metaphysics is that all basis of the multiple is grounded in Oneness, the root or pivotal center, so that the "many" is multiplied and replicated from the One. What he calls the "rhizomatic multiplicity" is "not the One that becomes Two, or even directly three, four, five, etc."[64] This would make the multiple a mere addition of the One to another One. Instead of a plurality based on a hierarchical or teleological lineage, which represents only quantitative differences, Deleuze argues for a notion of multiplicity that is ontologically nondualistic, open, and fluid. By the same token, the notion of the middle, which has been traditionally repressed by the system of linearity, cancels out the teleological idea of a definite beginning and end. No trajectory reaches a teleological end according to the Deleuzean logic of multiplicity. Rather, each trajectory of becoming consummates at the edge of another middle, which then becomes another beginning point for an ever new process of beginning/becoming. This is, for Deleuze, the very axiom of his idea of multiplicity, as he affirms that the rhizome, a critical metaphor for his logic of multiplicity, "has neither beginning nor end, but always a middle from which it grows and overspills."[65] Refusing an "arboreal" or "treelike" mode of thinking, a linear logic structured by "the alpha and omega, the roots and the pinnacle," he argues for the logic of rhizomatic multiplicity in which beginning takes place *in* and *through* the middle.[66]

Such logic entails an open-ended ontology as the configuration of both the subject and the material reality in the crack of the middle is never self-enclosed but infinitely mutating. When thinking from the middle, one does not *begin* from a timeless sense of origin, *ex nihilo*. In Deleuze's own words, "One never commences; one never has a tabula rasa." Rather, he adds, "One slips in, enters in the middle; one takes up or lays down rhythms."[67] Inspired by Deleuze's endeavor, Rosi Braidotti has been ardently advancing her own brand of nomadic philosophy by bringing feminist theory, continental philosophy, postcolonial theory, and posthumanist discourse into a dialogue with Deleuzean philosophy. As she explains in detail in *Transpositions* (2006), what she envisions is a nonunitary subjectivity, a subject in transit with a "nomadic, dispersed and fragmented vision" that is nonetheless "coherent and accountable mostly because it is embedded and embodied."[68]

In addressing her main target, namely so-called white European/American readers, she urges them to mobilize a new form of identity. Unavoidably, Braidotti claims, the process of detachment from familiar and comfortable forms of identity creates negative emotions such as fear, anxiety, and nostalgia.[69] Certainly, the enriching and positive experience of constructing a new identity entails pain and a sense of loss. Migrants and diasporic subjects are at the center of reference here, as they are the ones who bear the burden of the sense of loss and wound the most. The point for Braidotti is that instead of sinking into the mournful landscape of nostalgic yearning one should move further. One needs to transform such loss into the new material for constructing the ground for multiple belongings or "multilocality." She refers to Glissant as the great example who transformed "the pain of loss into the active production of multiple forms of belonging and complex allegiances."[70]

Despite the radical political aim of her argument and despite her acknowledgment of the conditions of postcoloniality, I find the direction Braidotti takes in order to advance the key principles of her philosophical nomadism troubling. For many racialized/colonized subjects who have experienced slavery, displacement, and diasporization, the pain of loss is neither a mere set of negative feelings nor a historical memory that needs to be overcome or transcended. Rather, such feelings point to a much deeper sense of coloniality inscribed in the fabric of being: an ontological trauma. Likewise, the vision for the beginning of a new world, a new people, in Glissant's reflections is born out of the abyss that parallels the multiply displaced reality of the Caribbean people. Glissant does not endeavor to traverse the bottomless depth of the middle passage in haste. His gestures are, therefore, not ambitious. Neither are they melancholic. Rather, he moves slowly along the path with a murmur or silence, the solitude of the "mute man who stands in the stupor of what remains stupid and unjust, opaque and debilitating."[71]

Braidotti may be right in remarking that Glissant *transformed* the pain of loss into the active production of new and multiple forms of identity. However, her reference to Glissant is problematic, for the simple description of "*overcoming* the sense of loss and fragmentation" does not describe Glissant's agenda properly. Perhaps, to a certain degree, for Braidotti's European/American readers, loss may be perceived as a negative and transitional feeling. But for Glissant loss involves a different level of magnitude and intensity that derives from the "weight" of colonial history and the devastated socioeconomic reality created by it. Braidotti fails to do justice to Glissant by omitting these complex layers that constitute the "groundless horizon" out of which Glissant's decolonial poetics emerges when she affirms that "Glissant captures the productive multiplicity, the resonance of the great vitality of human biodiversity."[72]

Philosophical nomadism privileges freedom as the ultimate liberating state of the subject. Braidotti views freedom as the "capacity to express and explore the subject's ability to affect and be affected."[73] Freedom transcends all boundaries of the classical notion of subjectivity and creates connections, thus facilitating the joyful "lines of flight" of the nomadic subject who is able to embody multiple identities and inhabit multiple locations at the same time. The question that arises is, should not the call for accountability and mourning for the loss and suffering of others precede the joyful celebration of freedom and nomadic ontology? Should not the question of the other be at the center of ethics rather than a preoccupation with the self's endless becoming?

The ethical unaccountability of Braidotti's philosophical vision has been a target of criticism especially within the inner circle of feminist philosophy. Particularly problematic have been notions of mobility, since Braidotti fails to concretize it, as Julie Wuthnow has remarked, in its historic context of colonialization.[74] In other words, Braidotti's affirmation of movement and her model of the all-transcending and unlocatable subject raise questions of accountability to the sociohistoric location of the subject, as Braidotti's erasure of her own subject position, according to Wuthnow, means ignoring "her potential complicity in colonialist discourse."[75] Echoing Irene Gedalof, who problematizes Braidotti's omission of "location" in her discussion of identity construction, Wuthnow concludes that Braidotti's gesture results in solidifying a model of universal subjectivity inscribed with "important features of the unmarked western subject."[76] Braidotti's model represents the ideal of the privileged Western subject who enjoys the freedom to "travel" and "transgress" borders without being marked by class or race. Given the global context of forced displacement and exile, the blind celebration of movement and transgression is a naive romanticization of "rootlessness" for those who cannot afford the privilege of such mobility. As Gedalof has remarked, without a critical examination of its own social location, the nomadic model is "really only available to white western feminists, and only under conditions where our whiteness and our westernness continue to function as the invisible, unmarked norms that do not seem to fix our identity at all."[77]

Admittedly, Braidotti makes visible efforts to take into account the historical experience of slavery and colonialism out of which Glissant's *Poetics of Relation* emerges. Nevertheless, her efforts fall short, as her reading of Glissant leaves out the complex topography of coloniality that gives birth to the constructive dimension of Glissant's work. Braidotti believes that the effects and the power of "transposition" lie in turning what is lost into "an increased desire to belong." She makes it clear that such a gesture is not "the avoidance of pain, but rather about transcending the resignation and passivity that ensue from being hurt, lost, and dispossessed."[78] While this is a valid point and a legitimate reading of Glissant's project, my sense of uneasiness grows as Braidotti appropriates Glissant to advance her "politics of location," which presupposes a universalized vision of a freely moving, nonunitary subject. Following Wuthnow's and Gedalof's voices of warning against Braidotti's overcelebration of movement, I object to the unmarked facileness embedded in Braidotti's account of "transposing the loss" and of constructing a nonunitary subject. Given especially Glissant's context of a social fabric characterized by the omnipresence of loss, discontinuity, and socio-ontological trauma, remembering the past is a crucial move that enables people to come to terms with the present, even before any form of subject position is claimed.

Glissant's poetic vision of relation and the possibility of a Caribbean identity emerges out of the shared memory (knowledge) of suffering and the impossibility of articulating the abyssal experience of coloniality. In the same way, "Relation," the key constructive notion of Glissant's decolonial poetics, is not an empty signifier devoid of any material root. Relation does not emerge from nothing. In Glissant's own words, Relation is "not made up of things that are foreign but of shared knowledge."[79] The generative power behind the poetics of Relation is not merely a memory spelled in past tense but the memory of the abyss depicted in his poetic imageries of the slave boat, which carries the unbearable weight of the innumerable suffering bodies of African slaves. "Imagine two hundred human beings crammed into a space barely capable of containing a third of them. Imagine vomit, naked flesh, swarming lice, the dead slumped, the dying crouched. Imagine, if you can, the swirling red of mounting to the deck, the ramp they climbed, the black sun on the horizon, vertigo, this dizzying sky plastered to the waves. Over the course of more than two centuries, twenty, thirty million people deported. Worn down, in a debasement more eternal than apocalypse."[80] In this crack of the ontological edifice, the overwhelming abyss of suffering, and the terrifying time of the unknown the enigmatic trope of Relation opens up, for, Glissant claims, "Although you are alone in this suffering, you share in the unknown with others whom you have yet to know."[81] The blurry past filled with fractured memories of shock and loss is also at the same time the terrain whereby the mystery of Relation and the indomitable desire to build a ground out of groundlessness are born. This is why Glissant calls the abyss, the weight of the painful history, a "womb," a "womb abyss."[82] The collective memory of suffering is not a mere set of negative emotions that need be overcome and transposed. Rather, the silence of the dead and the cry of the suffering people never cease to haunt "the freeing knowledge of Relation."[83] The enigmatic power of Relation emerges with the knowledge that survives the horror of the middle passage: a knowledge that is born out of the "womb abyss," a "knowledge of the Whole, greater for having been at the abyss and freeing knowledge of Relation within the Whole."[84] The middle passage, however traumatic, gives birth to people. Relation emerges out of this greater knowledge that survives the horrifying experience of terror, as people who were born out of the painful abyss of the middle passage were borne to the shore and "rose up on this unexpected, dumbfounded land."[85] Relation then constitutes the abyssal middle, the groundless ground or soil upon which the future of the Caribbean identity beckons faintly.

The trope of the abyss read in the Neoplatonic and continental tradition acquires a broader meaning in Glissant's thought. Glissant develops his notion of the abyss out of the concrete historical experience of collective suffering that constitutes the sociopolitical texture of Caribbean reality. In both the Neoplatonic context and Glissant's colonial context, the abyss indicates the experience of finitude, the limits of human existence. As I expounded in chapter 2, it is only by submitting to the limits of human existence, to the inscrutable depth of the abyss, that one comes to view the traces of plenitude and possibility harbored in its ocean of bottomlessness. Yet submitting to finitude does not signify renunciation before the impossibility of speaking or naming the absolute Other. Rather, naming the unnameable name (Neoplatonic mysticism) or the traumatic event (Glissant) involves acknowledging or embracing the self's limits. With apophatic theology, we have learned that (un)speaking of God involves acknowledging our creaturely finitude and the vulnerability of incompleteness ingrained in the structure of being. Similarly, Glissant's poetics of Relation seeks to embrace and even to affirm the traumatic wound and the resulting sense of groundlessness conditioning the collective identity of the Martinican/Caribbean people. Nevertheless, speaking of the political trauma must be clearly distinguished from embracing the self's finitude before—as well as speech about—God. Submitting to finitude opens the possibility for reconfiguring the self and the world. Namelessness, likewise, implies a constant renaming and reconstructing of both the self and the name of the Other. The self is undone before the impossibility of naming: all the previously known names and essentialist categories representing the world and the self are dismantled. But what implication does mystical or philosophical namelessness have in a historical context where unspeakability and namelessness are not a mere spiritual and existential condition but the result of a historical and material experience of suffering and survival? There are striking similarities and resonances between the trope of the abyss and the language of mysticism employed in these two different contexts. What remains unnoticed or obscure is the complex difference effectuated when the language and the trope of theological/philosophi-

cal groundlessness are translated into the context conditioned by the sociopolitical impasse. What are the lines of continuity and discontinuity,
challenges, problems, and questions that arise when the tropes of mystical
language are translated from theological text to historico-political context?
What happens when namelessness extends beyond the boundary of the
theological or philosophical impasse and becomes the sociopolitical condition of one's existence? Despite the significant similarity between these
two apophatic discourses, there is an important difference concerning the
nature of the unnameable. The unnameable in both contexts signals a dialectical transformation of the speaking subject; the former aims at empowerment and union with the unnameable, while the latter aims at disentan-
glement (trauma) and empowerment despite (by way of transforming) it.
Apopohatic language, therefore, bears a different kind of ethico-political
responsibility in the political context in which unspeakability and namelessness constitute the conditions of social existence. The parallel between
apophatic discourses in these two distant contexts testifies to the relevance
of the apophatic approach—and the theology implicated in it—in the
political context, while the manifest difference between the two speaks
against the danger of naturalizing political trauma.

In his comparative reading of Glissant and Levinas, John Drabinski
demonstrates how Glissant's thought discloses the colonial difference inherent in his decolonial poetics by offering an account of "beginning after
total catastrophe," that is from the devastating abyss of the middle passage,
which leaves no ruins and no names. Drabinski observes that Emmanuel
Levinas also offers, in a way, an account of beginning after catastrophe.
However, Drabinski writes, "What survives catastrophe, in the context of
the Shoah, *is the name*." This is important because "the fecundity of the
(sur)name gives the future a meaning and continuity that survives loss."[86]
But for Glissant, one of the characteristics marking the abyss of the middle passage is that of the "drowning memory." The countless number of
black bodies buried under the depths of the ocean are the invisible sign-
posts reminding the present of drowned names, bodies, and the obliterated
memory of a traumatic history: "then the sea, never seen from the depths
of the ship's hold, punctuated by drowned bodies that sowed in its depths
explosive seeds of absence."[87] As Drabinski comments, "Drowning memory leaves no ruin," and therefore it "seals namelessness as a condition of
beginning."[88] Unlike the optimistic accounts of philosophical nomadism
or Žižekian political subjectivity, the abyssal beginning for Glissant means
that one "begins without the thin, fragile continuity of the name."[89] From
this we find strange resonances between Glissant's decolonial poetics and
the theological voice of Neoplatonic mystics. In both cases, the writer

aims at the "impossible possibility" of naming the unnameable. For Neo-platonic mystics, the unnameable refers to the radical transcendence of the divine, while the unnameable in Glissant indicates the overwhelming memory of political trauma and the impossibility of tracing a genealogy of the self. Here Jacques Derrida, in his deconstructionist articulation of negative theology, may serve as a helpful interlocutor, since his work on name(lessness) explores the fine line between negative theology and post-modern thought, between Neoplatonic mysticism and the philosophical possibility of ethics. In exploring the *de*-ontotheological possibility of neg-ative theology, Derrida finds an affinity between negative theology and his own deconstructionist project: both aim at the (impossible) possibility of the impossible that is the relentless gesture to name the indestructible, inexhaustible name that lies *beyond* the name. The name of God, then, re-mains as a reference without referents, as the sign of absolute alterity, that is, *namelessness*. For Glissant, on the other hand, namelessness *is* the very condition of beginning—the beginning of a new people, a new future, and a new mode of being/becoming in the world. Might we draw the theolog-ical connection here between "God as namelessness" and "namelessness as the condition of beginning" and thus decolonize the idea of God so that we think of God no longer as the promise of a full form or full presence but as the abyss of namelessness from which we begin? Rather than priv-ileging solid ground and form, we could perhaps envision groundlessness and ruin as the condition from which we build a new cosmopolitan future.

The notion of the other is of paramount importance here, since it serves as the only, actual (yet forever ungraspable) reference to the inexhaustible name. One stands alone in the referentless desert where the only thing one is left with is the unnameable, forever fleeting trace of the other that is *reference*. For Glissant, on the other hand, the trauma of the middle passage gives birth to "*people without reference.*"[90] The question of begin-ning becomes a question of asserting oneself "without reference to what precedes."[91] The problem that Glissant is confronted with is that with the drowned memory/name, all reference, including the name itself, is lost. In this context, the other signifies the only, faint reference to the drowned names and drowned bodies. Drabinski articulates the sense of failure (as well as the possibility that his failure opens) before such loss in strikingly apophatic language: "Originless, beginning begins again. . . . Narrative fails before it begins. The word, and so too the name, is first, wholly new, and always creolized."[92] Might this creolized name and the failure of the word open a creolized and a creolizing cosmopolitan future for us?

On the other hand, what makes survival and passage possible is also the other. This is because the experience of survival in the abyssal bottom of the ocean becomes knowledge *only when it is shared*. Therefore, there are two aspects of the abyss in the other. The other is suggestive of the enigmatic link between the "suffering other" and the survival of the self. The body of the other, moaning and groaning next to my own suffering body, the innumerable bodies of the others buried alive in the bottom of the sea upon which the boat sails, weave the horizon of the painful, yet beautiful ocean. The other, in Glissant's colonial context, is also the reference of the precarity of knowledge and being. The survival through the abyss of the middle passage reveals the cry of the suffering other to be an opacity that nevertheless constitutes and conditions the self.

Perhaps Glissant's notion of opacity and the other finds a strong resonance in Judith Butler's work, as she, too, affirms opacity as the symptom of the irreducible otherness constitutive of the self that indicates the self's implicatedness with unknown others. For Butler, "There is always a dimension of ourselves and our relation to others that we cannot know, and this non-knowing persists with us as a condition of our existence and, indeed, of survivability."[93] The unknown and opacity are privileged in this form of knowing, as they represent both the precarious nature of our finite knowledge and existence *and* the inscrutable depth of our relation to unknown others. For Glissant, the unknown, as one of the central characteristics of the abyss, carries a double meaning: it designates the dizzy, unfathomable density of the unreckonable gap within the texture of the self, which, paradoxically, reveals the horizon of newness emerging from the depth of groundlessness. But the existential finitude that Glissant encounters in the middle passage is more than an existential anxiety caused by the search for meaning and transcendence. The unknown, gazed on from the middle passage, is not a sign of ambiguity from which plenitude and meaning beckon. Rather, it is another name for the experience of indefinite, horrifying terror, and this is why Glissant remarks, "What is terrifying partakes of the abyss, three times linked to the unknown."[94] At the same time, the unknown reveals the greater knowledge that emerges from the shared experience of suffering, a knowledge that reveals one's entanglement in Relation that binds the self to suffering others. This is perhaps why the other marks the sign of survival and the possibility of (the beginning of) a community after traumatic catastrophe. This means that the other *is* the sign of the persistence of time, which carries life on, and which nonetheless gives birth to people, *after trauma*—just as the drowned names (and bodies) mark the "site of multiple converging paths" of connection and relation across the abyss of the dark Atlantic.[95] Therefore, going back to the comparative reading of Glissant's and Derrida's engagement with apophaticism, namelessness is both the condition of beginning *and* the goal (or the beyond) toward which both thinkers are moving. But despite the obvious resonances between Derrida's deconstructionist approach to the name(lessness) and Glissant's idea of Relation and becoming, conspicuous differences mark the distance between them. While Derrida's name is an eternal call or promise always invoking an ethical response/decision, relation is the historically "accumulated" element of exchange or sharing, which one embodies, engages, and lives out in community. In both cases, however, there is a passion for name(lessness). For Derrida, the passion for name(lessness) indicates the passion for the impossible, passion for the unnameable name of God that lies beyond all names, while for Glissant namelessness can be translated as rootlessness, groundlessness, or exile:[96] " For exile did not arise yesterday: it began with the departure of first caravel. It is not a state, but a passion."[97] And this is where the powerful paradox of Glissant's decolonial philosophy of creolization lies: passion for rootlessness, groundlessness, or solitude, driven by an even greater passion for a deeper sense of rootedness grounded in Relation. He quotes the French poet Paul Claudel: "From the steps of exile, he manages a solitude more populated than any empire's land."[98] This is perhaps the moment where the movement of *passage* takes place in the middle passage. What we witness in Glissant's decolonial vision is a twisted account of alternative *passage* born in the middle passage. He shows us how passage might be envisioned in the abyss of the middle passage in which the experience of trauma is transformed into a newly conceived identity rooted in becoming and Relation. In this way the middle passage challenges the somewhat optimistic ideas of agency harbored in the accounts of passage elaborated by the different narratives of (theo)political subjectivity that I have examined in the previous chapters. Glissant's philosophy of creolization also questions the idea of individualized political subjectivity implied in these forms of thought. For in the middle passage the possibility of a new beginning and passage arises, rather, through Relation that emerges out of the unknown, the unfathomable middle of the traumatic ruins.

The notion of the middle opened up by Glissant offers important insights for rethinking the advancement of the postmodern politics of "mobility" and "in-between" as the conceptual tool of empowerment for marginalized communities. Many recent works of critical theorists of gender and race demonstrate their effort to reinvent the traditionally neglected or degraded notions of movement, rootlessness, and fragmentary identity into a positive ground for the creation of new meanings based on the philosophical principles of multiplicity, hybridity, and becoming. As Braidotti's work on "nomadic subjectivity," Kathy Ferguson's notion of "mobile subjectivity," and Chela Sandoval's idea of the "third space" (and her use of Roland Barthes's notion of the "third meaning" and Hayden White's notion of "the middle voice") show, the notion of the middle remains as the site of pure potential and possibility that disrupts the dominant system of signification.

Similarly, as I have already mentioned, for Deleuze the middle is the critical site for his philosophy of multiplicity and becoming, just as the plateau "is always in the middle, not at the beginning or the end."[99] The importance of the middle for Deleuze lies in the fact that the middle never ceases to open new doors to an occasion for an ever-new becoming. This means that the "event" consists, not of a teleological end or a final result of becoming, but of the singular *act* of becoming. In other words, the Deleuzean middle privileges the *act* of becoming itself rather than the *result* of becoming. The middle thus always signals the point of a new beginning at the moment where the previous process of becoming seems to have concluded. This is why, for Deleuze, the middle is not an average but a site in which intensities are negotiated and accumulated. It is not a localizable point. Rather, it is a "perpendicular direction, a transversal movement that sweeps one and the other away, *a stream without beginning or end that undermines its banks and picks up speed in the middle.*"[100] This powerful image of the middle offered by Deleuze finds, in my reading, a striking parallel, with an even more striking twist, in Glissant's imagery of the middle passage, which may help us bracket and refuse the deep-seated ontological privileges presupposed in certain forms of universalized subjectivity. Glissant opens the first chapter of his *Poetics of Relation* with the image of the slave boat in order to evoke the collective memory of the spectral past haunting the present quandary of the Martinican/Caribbean sociopolitical situation. The murky vision of the slave boat is filled with the horrifying images of vomit, naked flesh, and death; the voyage is characterized by the abyss of the unknown. The gape of the abyss opens as the bodies of people are thrown into the boat and as the boat is dragged into the ocean, into the middle of its depths. The middle, in Glissant's poetic vision, is another name for the "petrifying face of the abyss [that] lies far ahead of the slave ship's bow."[101] In the abyssal middle, future does not come in the name of the new. Rather, it comes in the name of the unknown: "a pale murmur; you do not know if it is a storm cloud, rain or drizzle, or smoke from a comforting fire." As the boat keeps sailing into the ocean, murmurs Glissant, "*the banks of the river have vanished on both sides of the boat. What kind of river, then, has no middle?*"[102] This stunning line strikes readers of Deleuzean philosophy with its remarkably disparate view on the middle. If for Deleuze the middle is where the creative flow of the stream picks up its speed, thus finally undermining its banks, for Glissant, the middle is the terrifying abyss of the unknown from which all you can do is to watch the landscape of the familiar land, the banks of the river, *vanish*.

From the middle of colonial groundlessness, Glissant teaches us perhaps an alternative mode of thinking collective identity, ethics, political subjectivity, and the future, *after trauma*. From this, I contend that Braidotti's notion of "transposing" is not the best term to describe Glissant's project. Transposing conveys a sense of reversing and altering a position or form. It implies an active employment of agency to transform the undermined ground into a fertile horizon of becoming. Such movement of passage is far from viable in the middle passage, the groundless middle of the colonial abyss. Alternatively, Drabinski's reading of Glissant proposes a more suitable account of Glissant's project that does justice to the complexity embedded in the soil of the Caribbean history. To describe Glissant's poetics, Drabinski employs the figurative image of "standing at the Caribbean shoreline and speaking the impossible," that is, affirming at one and the same time the tragic sadness and the beauty that the Caribbean landscape embodies.[103] Before the devastating experience of the colonial reality, which is overwhelming and paralyzing, Glissant shows us, in Drabinski's parlance, "how to say yes to ghosts and hauntings, and so how to welcome the memory of terror because it is the constant, if often mute or muted, companion to the excessiveness and profundity of creolized life."[104] Before the sweeping hail of loss, the means of transformation is not sought in assured terms as if one possessed power and control over reality. Rather, with Glissant, we see an unassuming, yet unyielding gesture to name and welcome the weight of the past in order to rise up and begin again.

Glissant begins from the ruins. It is not a glamorous beginning. As Michael Dash remarks, beginnings for Glissant are "lowly, paradoxical, and unspectacular."[105] Beginning here has none of the aura of the romantic and blithe experience that certain philosophical ideas of Western subjectivity suggest. Without the privileged milieu (middle) of time and "without the help of those plateaus in time from which the West has benefited" yet that remain unacknowledged in the Western mode of universal subjectivity, Glissant *begins* from the groundless middle in order to build a *ground* that is a "groundless ground." The middle is the groundless horizon of becoming haunted by the unspeakable past and the unknown future, the "painful notion of time and its full projection forward into the future."[106]

Fragmentation, Duration, and Re-collection

The middle passage, in many ways, is the womb from which the decolonial poetic imagination of the Antilles is conceived. This means that the middle passage epitomizes the colonial impasse or colonial abyss of the Caribbean historical reality. From the ruins of the colonial trauma, one of the most urgent political imperatives emerging in the fuzzy present is that of political subjectivity, or, more specifically, collective identity. As Michael Dash comments in his introduction to Glissant's *Caribbean Discourse*, finding the language for the collective "We" and coming to terms with collective history is crucial in the Martinican context, where history is marked by oblivion and denial.[107] It is easy to imagine that questions regarding the possibility of passage in such a situation take a different form. The colonial subject, as Césaire, Fanon, and Glissant show us, is the one who is dispossessed of a sociopolitical ground from which to envision the "radical act" (*a la* Žižek) of crossing. Before any act of self-determination and bold movement of crossing can take place, the colonial subject needs to be able to come to terms with and reassemble her shattered, fragmented self.

The trope of the abyss lurking in the thought of Hegel and contemporary readers of Hegelian thought (Žižek and Butler) shapes their accounts of the dialectical subject in different ways. Most importantly, the abyss explores the possibility of mediating the position of the subject in the moment of her encounter with the other. The other, here, lends itself to dual meaning: it signifies, on the one hand, the limit, barrier, or finitude of the self; on the other hand, it designates the possibility of the new, reconciled subject. More specifically, the otherness confronting the Hegelian subject implies the *passage* from one side to the other, an act of crossing a seemingly irreconcilable gap. I have examined in the previous chapter how this dialectical movement of reconciliation in Hegel fails to do justice to the unfathomable depth of the abyss with which he has structured his own system of dialectic. Hegel does not fully let his subject immerse him- or herself in the bottomless mystical abyss that he recognizes early in *Phenomenology*. Rather, the infinitely resilient subject of the Hegelian dialectic is able to reassemble him- or herself no matter how many times he or she is crushed. Meanwhile, Žižek also rushes through the valley of the abyss that he has emphasized so much in his own works. Not only does Žižek misidentify the abyss as void or nothing(ness), but, following Hegel, his theory of political subjectivity hints at a sense of certainty in which the vertiginous, devastating abyss of the negative is covered by the infinitely self-replenishing subject. Žižek's Hegelian-Lacanian construction of the subject, in this sense, shares a similar problematic theoretical root with the Deleuzean conception of the "nomadic subject" proposed by contemporary critical theorists in that they both presuppose a certain sense of a "middle ground" that facilitates the radical movement of crossing.[108] Perhaps it is Butler who provides the philosophical possibility of a subject more accountable to the fragility of human social existence, the global reality of marginalized communities, and the overlooked power of residual sociocultural affects that condition the structure of the self. Butler's philosophical positioning, which takes loss and grief as the fundamental condition that prefigures the genesis of the subject, opens the possibility for theorizing the reality of suffering and trauma with the end of constructing an ethico-political vigilance rooted in such "resources." The possibility of passage through the abyss and the subsequent question of *how* such possibility is realized crucially diverge as she suggests that the seed of transformation is found in our vulnerability, which is revealed by loss. In other words, agency, for Butler, emerges from the paradox that my own being is conditioned by a socially constituted web of relations that will always remain opaque and partly unknown to myself. Butler's idea of the self, subjectivity, and the political possibility of an ethical community paves, in my reading, the way for the passage from the Hegelian dialectic to Caribbean decolonial thought. Furthermore, the fact that she articulates her philosophical ideas in the *almost* mystical tone of apophaticism makes Butler's work more relevant for the current conversation. Indeed, one can find in her work multiple resonances with Glissant's decolonial poetics. Her questions directed at the catastrophic effects of suffering and her reservations about the unremittingly resilient subject of the Hegelian dialectic substantially intersect with the central questions that I am raising in this book. Butler adopts the gesture of resignation before the conditions of finitude constituting our human social existence. Yet she affirms that her gestures of negation are not geared toward resignation about the political possibility of the subject. Rather, these signs of the self's vulnerability and her relationality with unknown others *are* the very condition of existence and survivability.[109] Her trope of the unknown resonates with the mystical utterance of negative theology to which both Derrida and Glissant appeal as she elicits the unknown and affirms it as a term of possibility: "We are to an extent driven by what we do not know."[110] The recognition of the self's limit and the absolute alterity (inscrutability) of the other—which, in return, is projected back to the opaque structure of the self—renders the unknown a crucial element that enables the existence of the self. If the other first inscribes signs of limit, despair, and resignation in our selves, it also means that this other opens us, at the same time, to the unknown. In this respect, the act of mourning for loss implicated in the unknown helps us examine "the relational ties that have implications for theorizing fundamental dependency and ethical responsibility."[111] But despite these junctures of creative resonances, there lies, in Glissant's Caribbean context, an immediate historical urgency to affirm the collective identity that has been largely absent throughout history. The imperative of breaking from the all-destructive dominion of colonial violence necessitates a political vision and a social imagination capable of constructing a more politically engaging and constructive model of subjecthood. While Butler offers profound insights on the groundlessness of the self and ethics, the creolized selves arising in the colonial abyss demand a more affirming, more risky, and perhaps more adventurous mode of mobilizing the politics of becoming even when at times that means our shared vulnerabilities are at stake. Glissant's philosophy of creolization addresses the problem of historical loss and trauma deriving from the atrocious and frightening events of violence that leave the self dumbfounded, speechless, completely fragmented, and *without a name*. The imperative to "name the unnameable" and take over the impossible task of re-*collecting* the collective identity is even more pressing in the ruins, since the abyss of suffering, the horror of the traumatic middle passage, gestates, nonetheless, a *future*. As Drabinski writes, "Glissant sees the opening of the future as a break from catastrophe—not as redemption, but rather, and simply, *as the persistence of time*."[112] Before the irrevocable gap lying between namelessness and the urgency to name the unnameable, between the haunting past and the impossible future, Glissant turns to the notion of persistence, the indestructible continuity of time, that is, *duration*. Drabinski adds: "It is not just that descendants survive. Descendants become a people." This is because "memory of pain persists, without ruin, as drown memory, but so too does future."[113] The abyss, the middle passage, therefore, inaugurates a future, a future sealed with namelessness, yet still carrying life on: "that womb which bequeaths no name, yet *still bequeaths time*."[114]

Duration refers to the persistence of time, the endurance of life that survives death and goes on after catastrophe. Duration does not connote any sign of ambition or triumphalistic hope. Yet, as its literal meaning indicates, duration is that which endures and persists. This is one of the reasons why the tragic landscape of the Caribbean islands and the history that accompanies it remains, at the same time, beautiful. Despite pain, life marked with fragmentation endures, survives, and *inaugurates* a future. While the enigmatic power of Relation is that which emerges in the groundless middle, beyond one's control and knowledge, the freeing knowledge of the greater Whole, that is Relation, is not something that can be grasped freely. Rather, the possibility of future and Relation emerges only in the relentless effort to name the unnameable, that is, in the poetics and politics of decolonization. Duration, in this sense, must contain or hint at the gestures of recollection. Fragmentation, duration, and recollection are, then, part of the whole process of decolonial poetics/

politics. Derek Walcott's Nobel lecture expresses these ideas magnificently as he writes:

> Break a vase, and the love that reassembles the fragments is stronger than that love which took its symmetry for granted when it was whole. The glue that fits the pieces is the sealing of its original shape. It is such a love that reassembles our African and Asiatic fragments, the cracked heirlooms whose restoration shows its white scars. This gathering of broken pieces is the care and pain of the Antilles, and if the pieces are disparate, ill-fitting, they contain more pain than their original sculpture, those icons and sacred vessels taken for granted in their ancestral places. Antillean art is this restoration of our shattered histories, our shards of vocabulary, our archipelago becoming a synonym for pieces broken off from the original continent.[115]

The key to survival, the possibility of regathering the shattered collective identity, Glissant shows us, lies in duration. Subsequently, the "freeing knowledge of Relation within the Whole" also arises from it, for duration is neither an individual endeavor nor an apolitical notion. Rather, Glissant writes, "Duration is share. It is the house of the We."[116] Duration opens the door to Relation, and it is only when the self is submitted to the power of Relation that the possibility of future beckons. Glissant's notion of multiplicity arises out of this topographical matrix composed of relations: the bottomless middle where finitude and vulnerability found the ground for new relations and new beginnings. The underdeveloped trope of relation in Deleuze (Braidotti) and Hegel (Žižek) becomes, in Glissant, the very material with which he transposes the void of loss, the painful middle of fragmented history. We could say that one important difference between the boundless freedom of nomadic ontology and creolized freedom lies in relation. The creolized self and her freedom are conditioned—and enabled—by relation. A limitless horizon of being opens up in the inexhaustible mystery of the other—and in the illimitable webs of solidarity with unknown others. The creolized being is therefore a being in freedom, a self who is engaged in "an ongoing practice of liberation."[117] Michael Monahan effectively describes the way creolization works as a practice of relation, and eventually liberation, as "the maintenance of a *relation* that affirms and builds upon human agency, understood as constitutively social." This perspective differs markedly from the traditional liberal view that equates freedom (liberation) with having control over external elements that interfere with the "unfettered exercise of the individual (understood in an atomistic way) will."[118] Relation elicits and solicits the unexplored possibility of both the self and the other, and this is why the relational being, the creolized self, rejects the notion of being as a complete and finalized state. In the same way, creolization—and the idea of relational becoming behind it—does not designate a particular state, mode, or form, but passion: the unending desire to welcome the always ongoing process of change and exchange, forming and re/trans-forming, giving, receiving and everything in between that exceeds the economy of onto(theo)logy. In her compelling reading of Heidegger, Malabou tells us that the truth of being lies in its mutability: "Ontology is therefore the name of an originary migratory and metamorphic tendency, the aptitude to give change. . . . Everything announced is changed at the origin."[119]

Ethically (and therefore theologically), the relation of the other to the self in Glissant's thought reveals the complexity that defies the simple dynamic of relation or the disruption of the self-other binary. On the one hand, the other is the constitutive element of the self who offers the possibility of the self's survival. The other evokes an endless passion in the self: a passion for the impossible; passion for alterity; passion for the creolized life and for the landscape in excess; passion for the name or, perhaps, for God. At the same time, passion for the other is not indicative of a desire to fully grasp and master the other. Neither does it signify a mere lack of hope (to comprehend the other). Beyond its given appearance, the other signals an alterity that eludes our totalitarian attempt to grasp her while invoking an unending passion (for the other) in us at the same time. Here name and relation evoked passionately in Glissant's writings signal the point where the theological endeavor of naming God and the ethical quest for the other intersect. While the other imprints the precarity of self in Glissant's thought, it is not an absolute exteriority in the Levinasian or Derridean sense.[120] The other in Glissant does not invariably signify the outside, nor does it serve as the mere limit of the self. Rather, the other is indicative of the very conditions of possibility, the sign of the self's survival and of the future. The self, submerged in the groundless middle, finds in it the other *within*. Might not this Glissantian notion of the other attest to something like the Neoplatonic idea of the abyss, the porous boundary lying at the threshold between God and creation in which one finds him- or herself only as entangled with the other? Furthermore, in what way does the other as "the suffering other" reconfigure the texture of the self and the fabric of this self's ethical responsibility? What are the ethical questions that the suffering other raises in the theological space of the mystical abyss? Might this convergence of the ethical and the mystical in the abyss, the encounter between "the relational and the apophatic," according to Keller, help us reset the parameters of the political struggle for building a creolized, cosmopolitan future?[121]

The political potential of Glissant's poetics needs a full examination, which I offer in the next chapter. For now, suffice it to say that he makes crucial contributions to the politicizing of memory and trauma. Glissant suggests a mode of thinking, being, and resisting that is rooted in and instigated by the abyssal wound of the historical reality. What the decolonized abyss reveals at the bottomless bottom of its depths is not a void that needs to be a-voided. Rather, it reveals the fleeting, yet corporeal traces of the other—and so of relation—that make survival and passage possible. Thus the movement of passage through the abyss is not solely dependent on the self's radical act and decision but also dependent on the other, and so on the ties of relation and solidarity that survived the terrifying depths of the traumatic middle. It is in this groundless horizon of the middle that the intersection between Glissant's decolonial poetics and theopoetics emerges.

Creolizing Cosmopolitics

Poetics from the Deep

> For every poet it is always morning in the world.
> History a forgotten, insomniac night;
> History and elemental awe are always our early beginning,
> because the fate of poetry is to fall in love with the world,
> in spite of History.
> —**Derek Walcott, "The Antilles: Fragments of Epic Memory"**

With the help of Caribbean decolonial imagination, we are able to read the abyss as the space in which spiritual and political experiences converge. The figure of the abyss, reconceptualized by the (post)*Négritude* thinkers, particularly by Glissant, points to some crucial considerations for thinking theologically about the self, political urgency, and the possibility of passage. Reflecting theologically about such questions, then, leads to rethinking the very notion of God at the crossroads of neocolonial, capitalist globalization. First, the abyss becomes the critical site for gathering or reconstructing the self and for thinking about the future. The abyss is a crucial constituent in the metaphysical tradition of both negative theology and Hegelian scholarship. But the trope of the abyss in the colonial world exceeds its metaphysical contours; as viewed from the middle passage, it takes on the shape of the historical continuum. The primary material weaving of its physical texture is altered by the lived experiences and the reality of the community. The urgent, pressing needs for political reconfiguration of the sociocultural order arise from its open and haunting historical wound. This groundlessness grounds the new consciousness, the creolized self. It is a groundless ground, a groundless middle that in the spirit of Glissant's decolonial poetic we might inscribe as the unde(te)rmined ground. Second, the groundless ground, the abyssal middle, is constituted by relation. The notion of passage, as the political possibility offered to the undetermined self, takes, from Glissant's writings, the form of duration: that is, the collective endeavor of enduring, surviving, and becoming by transforming loss and pain into the womb of possibility and a future. The question that arises, then, is how to reconstruct the groundless ground that has been undermined and obliterated.[1] Reconstructing the new ground is about more than reconstructing the self. It is about reinventing a new idiom for rethinking the very framework that structures the mode of thinking and inhabiting the world. It amounts to what Glissant calls—drawing upon the marine imagery of an island perspective—the "submarine roots: floating free, not fixed in one position in some primordial spot."[2]

This chapter explores the possibilities of reconstructing the groundless ground by way of what Glissant calls poetics. Poetics occupies a central place in the works of Glissant not because it is the only way to resist colonial ideology and reconstruct a collective identity but because it *is* the mode of being in the world. In this chapter, I present a comparative reading of contemporary philosophical theologians' "theopoetics" and Glissant's notion of "counterpoetics." If the tradition of contemporary theopoetics developed by American theologians and philosophers of religion evokes the passion for the traces of the divine in the poetic rearticulation of the world, Glissant's counterpoetics seeks for a new root and a center of gravity in the poetic reconstruction of the world. There is, in both cases, a passion for the ground amid groundlessness. But despite the shared goal of theopoetics and counterpoetics, the colonial difference from which Glissant's decolonial counterpoetic emerges opens a wider horizon of meaning for poetics in which the spiritual potential immanent in poetics leads to liberation and solidarity. This is followed by my reading of Glissant's counterpoetics in juxtaposition to feminist theologian Catherine Keller's theopoetics, whose *tehomic* theology of becoming and relationality shows intriguing parallels with Glissant's poetics. Keller's endeavor of divinizing beginning, as an act of decision that is born *ex profundis*, provides key language with which to build a theology of the middle (passage), a theology of beginning after loss. Finally, I examine theopoetic narratives on the grounds of political theology. As I have argued in chapter 1 and throughout this book, political theology in the age of capitalist, neocolonial globalization needs to take a decolonial direction, thus assuming the critical-cosmopolitan agenda. This will allow us to explore both the theological significance and the political possibility that (theo)poetics offers for the decolonial, critical-cosmopolitan project emerging from the groundless middle.

Theopoetics: Passion for God

For the philosophical theologians and for Glissant, poetics is the only, if not the best, way to set truth free from its metaphysical and ontological constraints. The poetic deconstructs the dogmatic shell enfolding the event of truth. It indicates the impossibility of spelling out the full name of truth. But such an impossibility is not conducive to resignation; instead, it cultivates the capacity for the passion for truth. Both the name of God and the profound intensity of creolized existence repudiate the notion of certainty framing the traditional metaphysical mode of knowledge. The unspeakable nature of these events makes poetics, grounded in the mystery of everyday reality and the power of imagination, a crucial instrument for recreating and reconstructing the self and the notion of the divine.

While the claims of negative theology point to the impossibility of containing the divine name in the limited capacity of human language and logic, they evoke, at the same time, a burning passion for (the name of) God. Theopoetics begins at this juncture of impossibility, as a theological movement that arises from the abyss of the death of God. That is, it was first born in reaction to the "death of God" theology of the 1960s. For this reason, both Stanley Hopper and David Miller suggest that the first step of theopoetics is a "step back," which, subsequently, prompts a "step down."[3] The darkness experienced in the bottom, "and its concomitant bottomlessness," Miller explains, "is requisite to and requires a third step, one which Hopper called step through."[4] He goes on to add that the step through is "a repoeticizing of existence," an act that is distinct from reading poetry since it refers to "reading everything in life and work poetically."[5] As the way to begin and rise up from the abyss, theopoetics aims at restoring the missing power of imagination and affect in theo-logic. Amos Wilder affirms that the works of great theologians were instigated by imagination and filled with "plastic and dynamic elements."[6] Having recourse to imagination does not mean walking away from the reality of human experience. Rather, it is about engaging life deeply by repossessing the mystery of everyday experience. Wilder writes, "It is a question rather of heightened sensitivity for which the ordinary transactions of life are shot through with meaning, with moving charities, and with providence. "[7]

In resonance with the early proponents of theopoetics, the philosopher John Caputo, who joined the tradition of theopoetics several decades after Amos Wilder and Stanley Hopper, presents his theopoetic of the "weakness of God" by reinterpreting Derrida's deconstructive reading of negative theology. By following Derrida's rejection of the "metaphysics of presence," Caputo aims to set the "event" (of God) free from the name of God. In other words, Caputo contends that the name of God does not contain truth (or the event) in the form of an immutable essence. Rather, he proposes that the uncontainable event is harbored in the name of God in the form of "a promise to be kept, a call or solicitation to be responded to, a prayer to be answered, a hope to be fulfilled."[8] Theology then, is not the search for a certain *logos*, a logic that contains the full presence of the eternal God. Rather, it is about the passion and prayer for the "event to come," for the event that solicits, promises, and calls us to the unknown future. Caputo's theological claim is grounded in the philosophical ideas of Jacques Derrida, for whom the "event" of "truth" (if there is such a thing) is not an essence but always a future and a promise—to come. Derrida's idea of the "messianic," for instance, differs from historical "messianism" in the sense that the messianic is an absolute and indeterminate future that elides and defers any claim absolutizing the present form of messianism. Caputo clarifies, "The messianic future is not a future-present and is not sparked by a determinate Messiah; it is not future simply in the sense that it has not as a matter of fact shown up yet, but futural in the sense of the very structure of the future. The messianic future is an absolute future, the very structure of the to-come that cannot in principle come about, the very open-endedness of the present that makes it impossible for the present to draw itself into a circle, to close in and gather around itself."[9] Caputo insists on the significance of poetics by juxtaposing and contrasting logic with poetics. While logic interprets the world on the basis of real occurrences, "a poetic addresses the event of being addressed, not by what actually is but by what is promising."[10] Caputo writes further, "Poetics interrupts the workings of the real by evoking another possibility, the possibility of the event. In the logic of impossibility, the impossible is something that cannot be, whereas in a poetics, we are hailing an event that is otherwise than being. Poetics is a discourse with a heart, supplying the heart of a heartless world, a discourse with passion and desire (passion ignited by the impossible)."[11] The other pillar that sustains the ontotheological God of metaphysics besides logic is the obsessive notion of power married with the idea of God in Western metaphysics. Over and against the omnipotent God of the traditional religion, Caputo follows contemporary theologians and philosophers of religion by proposing the idea of God as a weak force. At the unfathomable edge of our ephemeral language and powerlessness, theopoetics is perhaps an attempt to insist on the "impossible possibility": an evocation emerging from the darkness of the abyss.[12] In his more recent work, Caputo develops his theopoetics further by extending the definition of theopoetics into the wider discourse of radical theology. He argues that as radical theology uproots classical theology, the *logos* of old theology is pulled up and replaced by poetics.[13] If what matters for classical theology and metaphysics is what something *is*, what matters for Caputo is what it *promises*. In this sense, theopoetics evokes the name of God who is a *call* and a *promise* rather than a God who *is*. It is then passion and desire that keep the theopoetic hope alive. Caputo suggests the constructive theological notion of "perhaps." "Perhaps" refers neither to a guaranteed hope nor to resignation. In this sense, it is a groundless ground. It does not *do* anything. "It does not pray or weep; it does not desire anything."[14] Rather, it is "what makes it possible for what exists to take place—or to lose its place."[15] As the groundless ground, "perhaps" exposes the brokenness and the contingency of our existence. But instead of leading us into despair and resignation, "it calls for what is coming, strange and unforeseen though it be."[16] Caputo's notion of "perhaps" is based on the understanding of the self as emerging from the bottomless abyss. In a way, Caputo's theopoetics shows significant resemblances with Glissant's vision, as what Caputo envisages is a poetic response to an "impossible future" from the groundless ground. What makes Caputo's argument compelling is that he strives to "insist" on the seemingly impossible project of saying yes to the future without disregarding the uncertainty and contingency surrounding our existence. Nevertheless, I wonder if Caputo's tendency to place the event as an absolutely irreducible alterity beyond name and image risks a certain danger of fostering a transcendence perhaps all too familiar to traditional theology and metaphysics. On this point, Catherine Keller questions the event's capacity for reciprocity and relationality: "Does he [Caputo] want the event, as with a Moltmann and a Levinas, of a transcendent coming that trumps any *emergent* becoming; what comes from an exterior, a sheer alterity[?]"[17] The radical exteriority of Caputo's event might invite skepticism about the potential sense of transcendence implicated in such an event, as it purports to be completely "unpredictable," "shattering" the horizon of our expectation. Caputo writes: "Metanoetic time is more discontinuous and abrupt, more shocking and surprising . . . one that is continually disturbed by the shock of the impossible."[18] He adds, "To wait for the event is to be completely surprised and overtaken, that which you are not prepared to."[19] Again, to move further with Keller's questions, might not this event be a bit too powerful (rather than weak, as Caputo suggests), too unilateral to account for the web of relations constituting both the fabric of the event itself and the horizon of our messy creaturely existence? A striking line of comparison is born at this juncture between Caputo and Glissant, as the colonial abyss from which Glissant writes is composed of the very elements that constitute Caputo's event, namely shock, surprise, abruptness, and discontinuity. Might this strange and twisted parallel between the two contexts of poetics hint at the colonial difference between them? While I turn to Glissant's decolonial poetic later, Caputo's theopoetics is highly important for the inquiry that I am pursing here. Caputo's theopoetics shows us very well not only how poetics always arises out of the abyss but how it is a powerful—if not the only—way of constructing the future, of gesturing toward the impossible, *ex profundis*.[20] Theopoetics, for Caputo, is the prayer for help, a prayer born in the bottomless depths. Prayer as the work of theology, as the act of evoking the name of God (and being called by God), does not suggest an appealing step marked with excitement and promise. Rather, for Caputo, the impossibility of prayer *is* the very condition of prayer. Prayer or theology arises out of the abyss, as he brilliantly puts it: "I'm praying where it is impossible to pray. . . . Being left without a prayer is the true beginning of prayer."[21] The question that arises at the intersection between Caputo's theopoetics and the poetics of decolonial resistance (which I will examine soon) emerging in the colonial abyss is, Does theopoetic prayer offer the ethical and political accountability that the contextualized abyss of the community-in-despair demands? What would theopoetics look like in a context where poetics is the means of resistance and survival? Would the desperate reality of the community alter the politics of this (theo)poetics? Perhaps evoking Caputo's theopoetic prayer in the contextualized abyss of the middle passage requires forging a notion of the event and self that defies the Western liberal conception of the event/self as an individualized entity.

Another important voice in the continental philosophy of religion, Richard Kearney, working in close dialogue with Derrida and Caputo, also alludes to theopoetics by appealing somewhat more explicitly to transcendence. Against the traditional theological understanding that views God only in terms of actuality, Kearney suggests God as *posse*, a possibility. God is a possible God, a God who may be. Ontotheology fails to accommodate the theology that Kearney proposes. In his work, as in Caputo's, being yields its place to becoming, while essence loses its privilege over possibility. God contains a meaning larger than a mere spiritual significance, as Kearney contends that God, as a possibility and promise, "remains powerless until and unless we respond to it."[22] Kearney's theopoetics, therefore, renders theology and God an ethical call to action and responsibility. It is the passion of our desire, response, and action that makes God possible. Thus the human pursuit of God is, in a way, a theopoetic of the possible. In his more recent work *Anatheism*, Kearney gestures toward a post-a/theist direction by advancing his theopoetics of the possible further. Faith in God (or in the absence of this God) is not a fixed object of possession that can be either gained or lost. Rather, faith in God is a question of a wager, of the drama of encounter characterized with invitation, embrace, welcome, or repudiation. The somewhat disembodied notion of God as *posse* is incarnated in *Anatheism* into the fleshier figure of the Stranger. But the palpability of this figure does not make the Stranger reducible to his or her materiality or representability. Rather, the Stranger remains an "irreducible transcendence and alterity" before the I.[23] What Kearney proposes as anatheism—that is, the seeking of faith after the death of God—is a wager on our responsibility to either welcome or repudiate the Stranger: "Compassion or murder. You either welcome or refuse the stranger."[24]

To counter ontotheology theologically, Kearney suggests an eschatological approach by placing the kingdom at the forefront of his theopoetics. Theopoetics is the human response that makes the possibility of the kingdom happen in the world: "The kingdom is possible but we may decide not to accept the invitation."[25] That is, Kearney's theopoetic is a response to a God who calls us beyond our present to a promise, a future of possibility. As with Caputo, part of Kearney's agenda is to deconstruct the duality separating the sacred and the mundane, the immanence of everyday experience and the transcendence of revelation. He accomplishes this by arguing that the kingdom is realized by our participating and being transfigured by the power of God's transcendence.[26] Yet this is not an appeal to a form of transcendence as an escapist move that leads one away from the embodied experience of our existence. Rather, Kearney shares the same ground with other proponents of theopoetics in that he views the goal of theopoetics as restoring the sacred embedded in the mystery of the mundane experience. If the ontotheological dialectics of the theo-*logic* has enclosed the theo-*logos* in the meta-physical (disembodied) discourse of language and representation, theopoetics, Kearney argues, humbly surrenders the *logic* of the *logos* to the unrepresentable presence of the divine surrounding the embodied experience of the mundane life, the "epiphanies of the everyday."[27]

Despite his shared aim with Derrida and Caputo to reject the ontotheological God of Being and seek a notion of divine that lies beyond language and representation, Kearney ultimately disagrees with Derrida's and Caputo's deconstructionist direction. He finds problematic their radically transcendent idea of God beyond God, beyond any form or name without name (desire beyond desire or religion without religion).[28] In a way, Kearney's critique of Caputo is similar to mine in that Kearney is also uneasy with the radically abrupt and transcendently indeterminate nature of deconstructionism—or of what (the openness to whatever) "comes" in deconstruction. The problem for Kearney is that such a gesture takes the risk of indiscriminateness. He writes, "If every other is wholly other [as Derrida claims], does it still *matter* who or what exactly the other is?"[29] With his famous claim "Tout autre est tout autre" (Every other is wholly other), Derrida has made a remarkable turn to ethics and politics. The exclusive nature of the absolute alterity attributed to God, or *différance*, in Derrida's parlance, is now extended to a broader horizon: a transition from wholly *other* to *every* other. For Kearney, the problem is that we need to be able to distinguish God from monster, good from evil: "God needs to be *recognized* for us to be able to say that it is indeed God we desire."[30] A faith that says yes to the coming event without recognizing what it actually is may turn into a blind faith that loses "something of the God of love who takes on very definite names, shapes, and actions at specific points in time."[31] I am, however, less concerned about the indiscernibility that deconstruction's radical alterity and undecidability risk than about the unilateral way that "transcendental" alterity breaks radically and almost invasively into the horizon of the I. Caputo's event or God might indeed be the God who solicits us. But, following Keller again, might not the absolute transcendence of this alterity keep itself a little distant—if not indifferent—from the web of relations and collective work that precedes and enables our response (prayer)? In this regard, Kearney's skepticism about the absolutely "undecidable" and abrupt nature of the event is effectively sound. Nevertheless, I keep some skepticism regarding a certain facileness—if not a subtle form of optimism, to be harsh—driving faith in the "possibility" of realizing God's kingdom that Kearney's proposal—the poetic of the possible—leads us to. He urges us to take on the ethical responsibility of responding to God that is cocreating the world with God. What is perhaps missing in this poetics is the discussion of *how* to say yes to the call in the ruins of despair and devastation. Might we not be concerned about the horrendous reality of human experience that impedes us from saying "yes" to the call and making the *posse* (possibility) of God a reality? What *enables* the person or community that is crushed by violence and catastrophe to say yes to the call? Does the subject or the community born in the colonial abyss enjoy the "free[dom] to choose between faith or nonfaith," and to "perform the drama of decision [between hospitality and hostility] whenever humans encounter the stranger," as Kearney's anatheism proposes?[32] I am by no means charging Kearney with being inconsiderate of the human condition of agony and despair. He takes the historical context of suffering (the Holocaust) as one of the primary conditions that solicits the anatheist turn. Atrocious conditions of human suffering, for Kearney, testify to the death of God, to the need to turn to the figure of the Stranger in order to seek the trace of the divine. But despite the ethical gesture that Kearney's insistence on a hearty faith signals, I wonder if his poetics (of saying yes to the kingdom and to the Stranger) is not a bit too sanitized to mediate the messiness of the fleshy fissures that crack open the ruins of atrocious historical violence. For how do you utter yes when language (and politics) fail? And how do you keep this apophatic "yes" political? Such poetics addresses actively the event of the encounter with the coming other/Stranger but is perhaps a bit passive in responding to the actual event of encounter with the evil taking place in the present. But like his fellow adherents of theopoetics, for Kearney (theo)poetics emerges from the depths, the dark night of the abyss. He writes, "But to return after nocturnal not-knowing, after the abandonment of old Master Gods, to a second light, to a second faith, we must first traverse the dark."[33] By suggesting traversal through the dark, Kearney, in a way, points to the movement of passage in which the self, once having been split and lost from itself, returns to itself, to a "second light," with a renewed "second faith."

Nevertheless, the poetics of the abyss is not merely an abstract, speculative notion. Just as both Caputo and Kearney are well aware that one of the primary principles of theopoetics is to be rooted in the actual reality of our embodied existence, the early proponent of theopoetics Amos Wilder already suggests that theopoetics be grounded in "creaturehood, [and] embodied humanness."[34] Wilder warns us that theopoetics is neither an escape from the experience of corporeal existence nor a recourse to imagination for its own sake, "the cult of imagination for itself alone; vision, phantasy, ecstasy for their own sakes; creativity, spontaneity on their own, without roots, without tradition, without discipline."[35] Rather, theopoetics emerges out of the struggles of creaturely existence, from the abyss opening between finitude and the potential witnessed in solitude, "solidarity, and involvement in life-struggles."[36]

The Cry of Poetry: Forced/Counterpoetics

> The other is not others but my consenting difference.
> Others are but of morality;
> in the Other everything is a poetics.
>
> **—Édouard Glissant, *Poetics of Intention***

What would a poetics arising from the abyss, particularly from the ruins of the colonial abyss, look like? In what ways can poetics materialize a form of ontology that encourages solidarity, resistance, and transformation of the wound of the community living in despair and pain? If theopoetics shows that poetics can offer one—if not the only—compelling way of speaking about God and the future from the abyss of our precarious existence,

Glissant's decolonial poetics shows how the poetic, in the colonial abyss, is both a new mode of inhabiting the creolized landscape—opening the creolized future—and a way of resistance. In Glissant's decolonial poetics, the unreckonable wound of the colonial abyss cracks open on the blurry horizon of the Caribbean shoreline where the sea is not just an indication of the limits of land and history. Rather, the decolonial imaginary of Caribbean thought conceives the sea as the continuation of land and its history. The impasse and the solitude of inhabiting the abyssal shoreline between lack (of language) and excess (of the landscape), between the haunting past and the elusive present, between suffering and redemption, mark the entire trajectory of Glissant's writings.

More concretely, two critical layers of significance weave Glissant's poetics. First, Glissant's poetics can be understood as an attempt to rebuild the aesthetic of the Caribbean. The creolized aesthetic, however, requires further explanation, as it signifies more than mere beauty. Rebuilding the creolized aesthetic signifies the search for or reconstruction of a landscape to fit the newly conceptualized being, namely the be(com)ing in *relation* (creolized being)—in relation with others, the larger whole, composed of historical memory, political vision, spirituality, and cultural identity. Poetics, in Glissant's vision, is neither a choice nor a practice restricted to the linguistic and epistemological realm. Rather, poetics in the Caribbean is the act of gathering the shards of the fragmented cultural heritage, the exploration of the landscape in excess, the weaving and creating of an entire cosmos for the community in vertigo. Poetics comes before resistance, before any act of agency takes place. In other words, poetics *is* the mode of being in the world. At the same time, poetics reveals the self's relation to the other as the primordial condition of existence, "for the poetics of relation assumes that to each is proposed the density (the opacity) of the other."[37] What its multiply branching root reveals are the scars holding together the broken pieces of the Caribbean cultural history, the failure of language and of being articulated in terms of essence. This is, perhaps, why the Glissantian passage of the colonial abyss bears a surprising similarity to the Hegelian passage of the dialectical abyss. For what lies at the center of both of these accounts of passage is the place of the other and its implication for the self. Also, however, poetics is resistance. Glissant's poetics is born at the intersection of the complexities of colonial history and the ongoing reality of (neo)coloniality shaping the present of the Caribbean. The abyss of the middle passage and the slave ship, the central historical symbol framing Glissant's philosophical imagination, is not only the site of trauma and loss but the generative matrix and womb that inaugurates the future. Time persists despite loss, just as people who survived the middle passage continue to inhabit the creolized landscape. Glissant's primary concern, therefore, involves articulating the paradoxical possibility of identifying the future and its beauty in the groundless middle while constantly remembering and honoring the terrifying memory of the haunting past.

The trope of the abyss in Glissant's writing has a multifaceted character, as it is the groundless ground in which his poetic imagination is contained. In *Poetics of Relation*, Glissant links the image of the slave ship and the middle passage three times to the unknown. One experiences the first abyss on being thrown into the belly of the boat: "A boat has no belly; a boat does not swallow up, does not devour; a boat is steered by open skies. Yet, the belly of this boat dissolves you, precipitates you into a non-world from which you cry out."[38] The next abyss surges from the depths of the sea, the unfathomable depths of the ocean marked by the balls and chains tied to the bodies thrown into the water. The third and the last manifestation of the abyss lies in the fading memory "of all that had been left behind . . . in the blue savannas of memory and imagination."[39] These powerful figurative characteristics of the abyss are supplemented by a more comprehensive and concrete account of the abyss presented in *Caribbean Discourse*. Consequently the trope of the abyss carries a broader meaning, for it is linked to questions of history, political reality, language, and cultural identity. The first and foremost question Glissant is grappling with concerns collective identity. The major obstacle is oblivion. Glissant calls Martinican history a nonhistory, characterized by radical rupture and discontinuity, while the collective consciousness refuses to remember its history.[40] The question becomes further complicated as the Martinican community lacks the language to speak from its own collective consciousness. This is because the complexity and the intensity of the traumatic historical reality of the Caribbean (Martinique) cannot find expression in language and because, from the Martinican perspective, French is a contaminated means of communication and Creole is equally debased. Michael Dash comments that with the reduction of production in Martinique, Creole becomes less functional, "no longer, the language of responsibility nor of production."[41] Glissant extends his analysis to the socioeconomic structure in claiming that the lack of an appropriate language in Martinique is partly attributable to economic circumstances (production).[42]

However, Creole represents the potential for resistance. Creole works as a form of poetics, what Glissant calls a "counterpoetics" or "forced poetics," in a situation where "a need for expression confronts an inability to achieve expression."[43] He contrasts forced poetics with "free or natural poetics," a collective yearning for expression that is not opposed either in its content (what people wish) or in its language (their means of expression). Forced poetics (counterpoetics), on the other hand, is the "collective desire for expression that, when it manifests itself, is negated at the same time because of the deficiency that stifles it."[44] While all poetics emerge, to a certain extent, from the abyss and strive to speak the unspeakable, forced poetics is born in the very specific abyss of coloniality. The sense of failure is not restricted to language and being; the collective consciousness itself fails, and the sociocultural reality of the community is "marked by a kind of impotence, a sense of futility."[45] In introducing the concept of forced poetics, Glissant warns us against the optimism that glamorizes poetics. Forced poetics, as represented in Creole folktales, "leaves no room for quiet rest. No time to gaze at things . . . it hardly concerns itself with appreciating the world. . . . The world is ravaged, entire peoples die of famine or are exterminated."[46] Poetics, in this context, is the inevitable means of resistance and survival. And this is the everyday reality with which counterpoetics, emerging from the colonial abyss, struggles.

In counter/forced poetics, the recourse to opacity and relation is key to survival. Glissant claims opacity to be the site of resistance, the right of people born amid suffering. As such, the unknown is the central characteristic of the abyss. The unknown, in Glissant's colonial context, is not merely a mystical site filled with plenitude and surprises. To open up room for a cross-cultural reading and cross-contextual comparison, Caputo and Glissant share a similar ground in that they evoke a poetic response that insists on the "impossible" or the unspeakable from the depths. Caputo's "theopoetic event" belongs to the realm of absolute surprise, beyond name, as a discontinuous, abrupt, and shocking event to come. Such attributes of Caputo's event resemble those of the "historical event" of the middle passage. In other words, the poetic response Caputo reinvents from the abyss bears striking resemblances to the abyssal trauma with which Glissant is struggling. For the colonial subject standing at the shoreline of the archipelago, newness does not erupt in a glamorous or abrupt way. Beginning, for Glissant, is neither glamorous nor pure. Rather, it is lowly, slow, and relational. This is why opacity is the key characteristic of counterpoetics. Opacity uncovers both the precarious finitude of our existence and the inscrutable depth of our entanglement with unknown others.[47] For this reason, relation—nurtured by opacity and born in the groundless middle (passage)—is the matrix of being/becoming in the Caribbean. The site of loss becomes the womb for the genesis of new being and metamorphosis. The insularity of the island carries another meaning, as Glissant puts it: "Ordinarily, insularity is isolation. In the Caribbean, each island embodies openness. The dialectic between inside and outside is reflected in the relationship of land and sea."[48]

To go back to Kearney's question regarding the indeterminate nature of Caputo's event, perhaps the event that Kearney yearns to be able to distinguish might take the burden of discernability off our shoulders, not through a more recognizable face, but through our ties of relation and solidarity with the suffering of many nameless others. Perhaps the "ethical handrail" for which Kearney is searching—before saying yes to the event—finds a hint in Glissant's reinvention of multiplicity and relationality: "For the poetic of abyss, the depths are not only the abyss of neurosis but primarily the site of multiple converging paths."[49]

Tehomic Reverberations

In many ways, reconstructing the groundless ground amounts to reconfiguring the notion of the divine, as the trope of the abyss carries strong theological implications. But the theological connection imprinted in the intertextual reading between theopoetics and Glissant's counterpoetics remains obscure. What kind of theological implications can we draw from Glissant's counterpoetics? How do we draw the connection between the secular form of mystical philosophy—entangled with the complex knot of historical reality—and the theological (re)construction of the abyss?

Glissant's poetics finds, in my reading, a surprising parallel and resonance in Catherine Keller's theopoetics. Drawing on the Hebrew word *tehom*, the depth or the primordial water of creation in Genesis 1:2, Keller presents in *The Face of the Deep* a constructive theology of creation that redefines creation as becoming in the multiplicity of beginning. She traces not only the theological tradition but also the Western literary and philosophical traditions that have fostered a strong abomination of depth (*tehom*ophobia) and its associated image of darkness. The theological consequence of this, according to Keller, is the establishment of an unquestionable doctrine that "everything is created not from some formless and bottomless something (abyss) but from nothing: an omnipotent God could have created the world only *ex nihilo*."[50] Keller's tehomic theology of becoming suggests the abyssal "Deep" beneath the water of creation as the womb or "the site of becoming as *genesis*."[51] In other words, the abyss, for Keller, is the womb and matrix where each and every new act of becoming takes place (begins) in/with God. By deconstructing the linear notion of origin that inscribes a cosmology with a clear beginning and end, Keller proposes the idea of beginning as the new imagery of creation. Therefore—and this is where the similarity between Glissant and Keller opens up—every beginning is abyssal: "*Tehom* is inscribed . . . not before the beginning, but *in* it."[52] Common to both authors is the metaphor of the depth of the sea as it denotes the abyss, which for both authors signifies the middle space of becoming: the womb that gives life to a new beginning/becoming that, at the same time, is the horizon haunted by the innumerable number of deaths (Glissant) or "missed possibilities" (Keller). Creation—of the cosmos, including the creation of a new (creolized) race and of the self—in this sense, refuses to belong to a pure timeless origin of "before." Rather, creation belongs to the time- and relation-bound flow of ever new beginnings. But just as, for Glissant, every beginning is haunted by irretrievable loss, for Keller too each beginning "is a beginning that is always haunted by a cloud of missed possibilities."[53] This is because any beginning, every actualization of possibility, entails decision/choice and therefore a sense of loss. At the moment of beginning/creating/becoming in which certain possibilities are chosen, other possibilities are excluded and missed. *Tehom* is the depth, the difference that enfolds and unfolds those possibilities. Keller writes, "A cloud of missed possibilities envelops every beginning: it is always *this* beginning, *this* universe and *not* some other. Decision lacks innocence. Around its narrations gather histories of grievance: what possibilities were excluded? The darkness over the deep precedes the beginning. The cries of loss—*de profundis*—disrupt the confidence of total origin in a secure end. A wound to the text, *vulnus, vulva* of the text, gapes open, *ginan*, at the beginning of the canon."[54] Keller's tehomic theopoetics emerges, like any other (theo)poetics, from the abyss preceding creation/beginning. Like Caputo and Kearney, she in a way insists on the seemingly impossible task of speaking of that which surpasses image and speech, of setting the divine free from the metaphysical constraints of the *logos*. But instead of appealing to decisions for ethical actions or to prayer for the event, Keller seeks the trace of the divine in the grace of relations that emerge, endure, and survive each loss, thus leading us to ever new beginnings at the site where previous acts of becoming ended. The burden of impossibility is lightened, and thus the gap between human and divine since the abyss enclosing each act of new beginning/creation reveals "this self-organizing relation" to be the very possibility of God. Even this abyss (*tehom*) cannot be identified with "God nor with the All." She writes: "It signifies rather their relation: the *topos* of Creation."[55] *Tehom*, therefore, "remains neither God nor not-God, but the depth of God."[56] For both Keller and Glissant, relation is self-organizational and born in the abyss, the depth of the ocean. Relation signifies the sign and the means of survival in the bottomless ocean of the middle. In its mystery of the unknown, we transform the unfathomable bottom of the ocean filled with loss into the womb of possibility and of new beginnings.

Beginning . . . and the Theology from the Middle

Tehomic theopoetics turns our attention to the surface of immanence, to the web of myriad relations constituting the known and the unknown, what precedes, what is there, and what is to come. But the self-organizing matrix of relation necessitates "decision." And this is why in a way (theo) poetics *is* decision. As Keller writes, becoming requires the political act of decision: "Any form of actualization takes the form of a decision."[57] While acknowledging that the womb and matrix of our becoming emerges from the web of relations, she claims that the difference, the possibility of salvation out of the ceaseless continuation of becoming—which may end up in meaningless death—lies in *decision*.[58] Likewise, for Glissant, beginning is an act of decision, a political act of searching for a new center of gravity and founding a new ground (groundless ground)—for the new world to emerge. Commenting on Glissant's poetics of relation, Stanka Radovic asserts, "To begin is an act of gravity and an act of responsibility, especially if a new world is about to begin."[59] Poetics, in this sense, is an act of politics—especially if this poetics is a forced poetic emerging from the context of political struggle. All (ethno)poetics, Glissant argues, "must face up to the political situation."[60] For a poetics born as a response to the urgent experience of collective struggle, it is not enough to set "saving language" as its only goal. Rather, "It will be necessary to transform the *conditions of production* and release thereby the potential for total, technical control by the Martinican of his country, so that the language may truly develop."[61] Counterpoetics is more than transforming language and symbol. Its transformative imagination is rooted in and geared toward the concrete material conditions that determine the survival of the community.

The poetics of/about God, theopoetics finds its theological possibility at this juncture. Its horizon is the abyss; its first step always takes place from the ruins, from the countless losses haunting the new possibility; its goal is beginning, beginning in the groundless middle. Beginning is an ethical act and a political move. Beginning is the founding of the new ground in the ruins. It signals the (re)construction of the groundless ground as the soil for a new mode of being, in which both the self and the divine *become*. Perhaps, to take one step further, with the theopoetic imagination we might be able to envision the notion of the divine itself differently. Keller provides the key insight here as she brings Derrida's reading of the medieval mystic Angelus Silesius into conjunction with the Jewish mystical tradition. She intertwines Silesius's claim that "the place is the word," and "the place and the word is one" with the Jewish mysticism that views God as place.[62] According to Keller, the medieval rabbi Jacob ben Sheshet associates the Hebrew word *bet* of *bereshit* (beginning), at the opening of the verse of Genesis 1:1, with "house" (*bayit*): "The Holy One, blessed be He, is the abode of the universe, and the universe is not His abode. Do not read [the letter bet], but rather 'house,' as is said 'With Wisdom the house will be built' (Proverbs 24:3)."[63] This way, Keller builds the metonymic connection among three seemingly different notions: God is not only revealed as place and house but also as *beginning*. In other words, beginning is an act of founding the place/house, an act of grounding, which is, at the same time, *divine*. Certainly, as David Miller reminds us, the ancient root of theopoetics, poeticizing of the divinity, comes from *theopoiesis*, "a term meaning 'deification,' 'making God,' 'making Divine.'"[64] Might we not, then, view the inaugurating of the ground, the place/house for the creolized self from the colonial abyss, as divine in itself?

The various thinkers examined in this chapter point out that poetics may be one way of carrying out the impossible task of reconstructing the self in the abyss. Seen from the colonial abyss, poetics is the mode of being in the world, a mode of differently inhabiting the land(scape) and time that in return opens the creolized future. In the colonial abyss, every poetics is a forced poetics, a counterpoetics, that binds the spiritual and the political, history and future, the sacred and the mundane. The middle passage marks the path woven with the invisible presence of drowned bodies. Not only bodies, but memories, and names too, are drowned in the depths of the ocean, and so is the name of God, the ontotheological deity of metaphysics. Beginning, therefore, takes namelessness "as a condition of beginning."[65] The bottomless depth of this terrifying ocean, is, however, a "womb abyss" that gestates people and the life that goes on and persists after catastrophe. The trauma of the middle passage gives birth to people without reference. Nevertheless, and paradoxically, this suffering, the suffering self and her shared experience with suffering others, reveals the possibility of survival and transformation. And it is poetics that discloses the self's entanglement with others by opening oneself to the other, by revealing "that this [illimitable] sea exists within us with its weights of now revealed islands."[66] The insularity of the island reveals one's separation from others, yet just as each island embodies an openness, this insularity shows one's unbreakable tie to others. This is how poetics enables the passage from loss to life, from death to womb. It discovers in the ties of relation and solidarity the potential for transforming the unde(te)rmined middle into the root of new possibility: "The creativity and solidarity that will make rootlessness more tolerable, make the present void more negotiable."[67] Might this poetics of the abyss and the opening of the door to relation and solidarity invite us to take on the cosmopolitan political project or cosmopolitical struggle in which we envision a theology where both the name of God and the name of the shattered self (and the dismantled community) find their future in each other? In what ways might poetics from the ruins of the abyss inform our cosmopolitical consciousness in the age of neocolonial globalization?

Toward a Decolonial, (Cosmo)Political Theology

As I outlined in chapter 1, cosmopolitanism is a social/political idea based on the Stoic notion of the "citizen of the world." To this is added the Kantian idea of "hospitality," thus making cosmopolitanism one of the most important political discourses for advocating the equal rights of transnational/dislocated subjects in the age of globalization. Situating cosmopolitanism within the ongoing sociopolitical processes of globalization, Ulrich Beck contends that the question to be asked in an age where the traditional notion of nation-state is no longer able to give definition to the global order "is not how to revive solidarity, but how solidarity with strangers, among non-equals can be made possible."[68] Beck provides a helpful definition of political cosmopolitanism that repudiates the traditional political framework of the nation-state for thinking about the ethical questions of human rights, migration, and ethnicity. Lying behind his investment in political cosmopolitanism is a philosophical and ethical concern for the "otherness" of the other. The discourse of cosmopolitanism arises, Beck writes, out of the question of "how to handle otherness and boundaries during the present crisis of global interdependency."[69] Beck rightly points out the tension in the idea of cosmopolitanism with regard to universalism and relativism, that setting up a universal principle of respect for others may lead to the erasure of particularity/difference. Therefore, the main question is how to find the delicate balance of founding a universal principle of equality while not falling into the trap of imperialism/colonialism. Beck contends that cosmopolitanism, or what he calls "realistic cosmopolitanism," rejects the either/or proposition, which is a false set of alternatives.[70] Instead, it seeks a contextualized universalism. What are these basic universal norms that transcend the complex boundaries of contextual/cultural differences? Beck gives us a specific list of what such principles look like by telling us what cosmopolitanism rejects: "dictatorial standardization, violation of human dignity, and of course, crimes against humanity such as genocide, slavery, and torture."[71] Beck's influential work on cosmopolitanism, however, fails to address the crucial question of structural violence, the all-encompassing web of coloniality underlying modernity and the contemporary phenomenon of globalization. As I emphasized in chapter 1 following the warning of Mignolo, critical cosmopolitanism must by necessity take a decolonial direction. In other words, cosmopolitan conviviality and solidarity cannot be envisioned unless we address the deep-seated structure of violence configuring the global order of Euro-American hegemony and capitalist dominion; the violence practiced by the history of colonialism and the ongoing reality of neocolonialism; violence effectuated by the ever-spreading force of capitalist globalization. Put differently, as is the case with many other contemporary discussions of cosmopolitanism, it is not clear whether Beck's cosmopolitanism takes a critical stance toward the "cosmopolitanism of capitalism."[72] It is worthwhile to remember David Harvey's point that sometimes it is not clear whether cosmopolitanism is a counternarrative to globalization or a mere reflection of it. We might also benefit from reiterating Mignolo's point that modern (Kantian) discourse of cosmopolitanism continues the age-old Western Christian agenda of *Orbis Christianus* (the Christian cosmos), which dates back to the ancient Roman Empire. Without a serious engagement with coloniality, cosmopolitanism can easily fall into the trap of imperialism and triumphalism that extends the rationally advanced ideal of equality to "inferior" others.[73]

In the final chapter of this book, after having articulated the abyss from the standpoint of coloniality and the suffering caused by political trauma and violence, we may take a different approach to political theology in light of cosmopolitanism and decolonial poetics. With the insights drawn from the Neoplatonic mystics, Hegel, Butler, Fanon, Glissant, Caputo, and Keller, among many others, we witness a decolonial (cosmo)political theology emerge from the (theo)poetics of the abyss. Cosmopolitics requires a distinction from the kind of cosmopolitanism that assumes "one cosmos" as something that already exists out there and as something that serves as the ground of conviviality. Cosmopolitics grounds itself on the understanding that the common world is not something to be "discovered," or taken for granted. The ground of cosmopolitics is not a noun, a mere description of the given ground, but a verb, an action in process, a process in action. It *grounds*. It refuses, therefore, to be a mere description of the cosmopolitan state of globalized capital or the elitist ideal of neonomadic transnationalism accompanying it. Rather, as Bruno Latour suggests in his comment on Beck's cosmopolitanism, cosmopolitics seeks to build the common world from below, "from scratch."[74] Just as counterpoetics begins in the middle of the abyss, cosmopolitics emerging from the colonial abyss begins from the ruins, from below, by cocreating the world of cosmopolitan justice and solidarity with others. Cosmopolitical theology as a countercolonial narrative would refuse any utopic understanding of the "common cosmos" as a given, realized, and finalized notion. The process of its construction is perennially accompanied by deconstruction. Its making is also its unmaking in that it is an open project, always becoming, always creolized.

In many ways, Glissant's passage, his counterpoetics, points inescapably to cosmopolitics. The openness of both the ocean and the archipelago hints at the cosmopolitan visions inherently framing a creolized ontology. His philosophy of creolization consists of mediating the dialectical tension constituting the exilic state of living in permanent displacement: the tension between the withdrawal to solitude and the arduous engagement in the politics of home-making, between solitude and solidarity, between self and other. And this is precisely what cosmopolitics emerging in the colonial abyss comes to: refining rootlessness, the constant state of exile, into a new groundless ground for the cosmopolitical struggle for global justice and relational solidarity that aims at dismantling the powerful sovereign of coloniality. In this sense, I argue, cosmopolitics requires a certain sense of exilic consciousness, a sense of groundlessness, of the abyss. Glissant tells us how the creole folktale describes the Caribbean landscape not as a place to be permanently inhabited but as "a place you pass through. So the land is never possessed."[75] This groundless cosmopolitics grounds itself in the ontology of multiplicity and errantry, a mode of be(com)ing that allows "each person to be there and elsewhere, rooted and open, lost in the mountains and free beneath the sea, in harmony and errantry."[76] This is not a glamorous, poetic errantry but "the search for a new center of gravity, for a new point of equilibrium."[77] If Keller tells us that beginning as an act of grounding is itself divine, we may perhaps be able to say that the inaugurating of the ground, the place/house for the creolized self in the colonial abyss, is divine in itself. But since I want to avoid the risk of making grand constructive claims about "God"—as this book is interested in engaging theology to the extent that it attempts to explore the (post)secular possibility of the theological—I would only go as far as to say that beginning and the act of grounding are theological. In this regard, Glissant's errantry, his search for a new center of gravity, is also in a way theological. Glissant himself—who rarely makes any reference to the theological/spiritual— once referred to errantry as the postulation of the sacred: "The founding books have taught us that the sacred dimension consists always of going deeper into the mystery of the root, shaded with variations of errantry. In reality errant thinking is the postulation of an unyielding and unfading sacred."[78] Similarly, in an interview he had in his last year that was published posthumously, Glissant refers to creolization as a battle—not a military but a spiritual one.[79]

Exile or groundlessness does not merely signify loss of origin, loss of the self and the pure, no longer retrievable past. The movement of passage that Glissant takes in the middle passage does not gesture toward a solid ground. Beginning and founding the ground in colonial groundlessness are not synonymous with conquering, crossing, and overcoming. This is why Glissant tells us that the seer, having no place (no ground on which to stand), "founds exile." Exile is not a state "but a passion."[80] Creolization points to this passion for exile. This is not a normalization of displacement "but an active cosmopolitical engagement and reappropriation—a passionate exploration—of its unmaterialized possibilities."[81] It is the inexhaustible praxis of resisting the violent sovereign regime and its regulatory distribution of identities, of life and death by creating new, creative forms of identities and solidarity across borders. Like passage, which does not designate a teleological one-time event, creolization is always a *creolizing* force, a nonteleological movement, an always ongoing process without closure.

The poetics of resistance, counterpoetics as cosmopolitics, calls us from the abyss, from its own abyss and our own abysses. It invites us back to the abyss again, teaching us how to live with this groundlessness, to live in rootlessness, in exile: with contradictions, loss, ambiguities, trauma; always creolizing and in constant dialectical oscillation (passage) between two, three, multiple points of signification; and with an openness to the mystery and the abyss of the other. Cosmopolitics solicits the ethical responsibility that is the ability and the openness to embrace the loss of one's own self before the other—to do, undo, and be undone by this other. Cosmopolitical theology affirms the power of the people who, however fractured, fragmented, traumatized, or displaced, gather themselves and begin, and thus (re)build the cosmos (and the *polis*) from the ruin. Within this cosmopolitical scheme, the name of the divine cannot be restricted to the realm of the unnameable divorced from the political struggle of the community. Rather, as Keller elucidates, God may be the "name for the precarious life of all who are entangled in it."[82] The unnameable name of the divine then denotes the very condition of abyssal ruin from which we construct a decolonized cosmopolitan future and a new, creolized name of God.

Every beginning is an act of *theopoiesis*, a divine act. This is because every beginning is a new beginning, *creating* the self and founding the ground from the ruins of the groundless middle. Life or the self is born in this middle: the groundless horizon of becoming in which the hope of new life and new becoming is conceived right where the previous act of becoming ended. Each loss is singular, therefore irredeemable. Death and suffering might seem to prevail. Nevertheless, the irreparability of loss need not lead to resignation about the possibility of justice and of restoring the fractured name of the self and of the community. For the abyssal middle is also the womb in which the shared experience of suffering gives rise to a sense of collective identity pregnant with a futural vision of cosmopolitical solidarity. The theological resounds in the political work of the community to create, uncreate, and recreate its own ground. There we may envision the cosmopolitical possibility of reconstructing or re-*collect*-ing the self and the community in the collective work of bearing the weight of the unbearable past and gazing upon the unknown future.

Conclusion

In *Beyond Good and Evil*, Friedrich Nietzsche writes, "When you stare for a long time into an abyss, the abyss stares back into you."[1] The journey that I have taken in this book can be read, perhaps, as an act of staring into the abyss. Perhaps, to be more accurate, the path that my inquiry has taken through the chapters of this book might be better described as "plunging into" the abyss rather than just gazing on it. As I have been consistently arguing, the abyss, after all, cannot be restricted to matters of epistemology. Rather, it signals an ontological question. What, then, does the abyss that stares back at us look like? What happens to us as we gaze upon the abyss and as it gazes back upon us?

My answer, to echo the central argument of this book, is that the self is reconstructed, assembled anew, as she walks through the unfathomable valley of the abyss. This is not, as I hope has become evident, some refreshed version of the all-too-familiar story of a triumphalistic theology. Rather, my reading of the abyss points to the ceaseless movement of the dialectical tension lurking at the heart of the indeterminacy structuring the self. This implies, first, that the self and her world are not constituted by an immutable, prefigured substance but by an open-ended process made of the relentless unfolding of a dialectical oscillation. The self emerges through the process of becoming, always in *relation* to the other. Second, the *dialectical* movement does not indicate resignation or passive surrender to the unknown. Rather, it points to the self's arduous labor and commitment to take on the movement of passage from the negative to the positive, from limit to possibility, from death to life. It is to this resilience of the self and her act of the passage that the accounts of the abyss in both Neoplatonic mysticism and the Hegelian dialectic testify.

Nevertheless, the question that is somewhat overlooked in these accounts is what happens when the self is not just a metaphysical notion of a disembodied self but a contextualized self, a racialized and gendered/sexualized self. Do the modes and forms of the passage take the same shape or trajectory for the different selves entangled and conditioned by various forms of power relations infused with violence and foreclosure? Is the passage or the reconstruction of the self even possible at all for certain subjects? These questions become crucial for thinking about theology, philosophy, and politics in the era of capitalist, neocolonial globalization. By staring at the abyss of the traumatic historical womb of modernity/coloniality, namely, the middle passage, I am proposing the possibility of a decolonial cosmopolitics conceived upon the horizon of colonial difference. The long journey of conversation with multiple intersecting voices in this book leaves us with a complex idea of the self, the subject, and God through which our previous understanding of the self and of the world is undone. The theological and political potential of the overlooked figure of the abyss has then been lurking all along in the theological thought of the mystics in which ontotheology yields to a relational understanding of God, just as the apophatic gesture of mystical theology hints at the failure of ontology. The Neoplatonic abyss, a constitutive element structuring the self and its relation to God, becomes in the Hegelian dialectic the ethical threshold that opens and mediates the self's place in relation to its exteriority ingrained at the heart of itself, namely the other. If the Hegelian dialectic unveils the ethico-political significance of the passage in the abyss, Caribbean decolonial thought shows us that any actual such passage for the contextualized self is possible only through counterpoetics, a poetics of resistance that invokes the theological, and through the persistent force of Relation that survives the terrifying depth of the middle passage. Thus reconceived, the political promise of the creolized self inaugurated in the middle passage lies in that it comes to be itself through the restless struggle to found the ground.

As we stare at the abyss and as the abyss stares back at us, we lose ourselves for a creolized self yet to be created on the ever-unfolding horizon of the groundless middle. In the colonial abyss, passage implies plunging not only into the abyss of the self and the other but also into the abyss of becoming—sinking into the unknown mystery and thus the generosity of becoming, and of the other, that solicits a future; generosity that fosters the original (ex)change—an exchange that takes place at the very outset of being—which therefore exceeds the capitalist economy of exchange. A gift: the gift of becoming and creolization, the exchange before being; the sacred. Being, Malabou teaches us, is a site of change and exchange. It points to nothing but its mutability: "Being is from the outset changeable and changed. It substitutes for itself and is exchanged—in exchange for nothing; it loses its name."[2] It is perhaps here that the boundary between the human and the divine or between the spiritual and political dissolves, at this juncture of exile in the groundless middle, between absolute solitude and the inexhaustible ties of our solidarity with suffering others.

Acknowledgments

First of all, I would like to thank the dean and the colleagues in the Department of Religion and Philosophy at Lebanon Valley College for their generous support that made the publication of this book possible. I'm particularly indebted to Jeffrey Robbins, who provided invaluable advice and support during the initial stage of the review process. I also want to thank John Caputo, the series editor, and the editorial staff of Fordham University Press, particularly Tom Lay and Richard Morrison

This book is the result of conversations and friendship nurtured by many people. I can't ever find the right words to express my gratitude for Catherine Keller, without whose unparalleled guidance, support, and friendship I would have not been able to become a scholar that I am today. From the inception of the project to its full development, Catherine's mentorship and encouragement were key. I also want to thank Hyo-dong Lee, who provided a critical, yet encouraging reading throughout the process. It was thanks to my conversation with him that I was able to explore the daunting territory of Hegelian scholarship. Mayra Rivera has always provided me with inspiring ideas and directions, from my seminary years back in Berkeley to the completion of this manuscript. Most importantly, she holds the responsibility for igniting my interest in Édouard Glissant and the Caribbean intellectual tradition. I also want to thank Stephen Moore from whom I have learned so much about Derrida in my early years at Drew. Many friends and colleagues have nurtured my academic journey and life along the way. I want to thank Anna Blaedel, Beatrice Marovich,

Benjamin Goldman, Joya Colon-Berezin, Michael Campos, Cristian de la Rosa, Karen Bray, Carl Fisher, Santiago Slabodsky, Jennifer Harford Vargas, Hugo Cordoba Quero, SungUk Lim, Alexis Rognehaugh, Patricia Bonilla, Charon Hribar, Rajeev Yemeni, Retu Singlar, and Nancy Noguera-Maduro. Karen Bray and Kathy Brown have read parts of the manuscript and given me invaluable feedback. I want to thank Kayla Zimmerman for helping me with the index. Mary-Jane Rubenstein read the full manuscript thoroughly and provided tremendously helpful feedback at the last stage of its completion. The many conversations I had with Eric Trozzo and Erika Murphy helped me shape my own understanding of the notion of the abyss. I am also indebted to Unhey Kim for her continuous mentorship and support since my undergraduate years in Seoul. My parents and my cousins Joohan and Betty have a special place. A very special thanks goes to Almudena Toral, whose love and presence encourage me every day to stare into my own abyss without fear. For the last, I am eternally grateful to my irreplaceable friend, mentor, and father figure, the late Otto Maduro.

Notes

Introduction

The epigraph reads, in English, "It's sunny outside / It's only a sun / Yet men look at it and sing / I don't know about the sun / I know about the melody of angels and the heated sermon of the last wind / I know how to scream until dawn when death settles naked on my shadow / I cry beneath my name / I wave handkerchiefs in the night and boats thirsty for reality dance with me / I hide my nails to mock my sickly dream / It's sunny outside / I dress in ashes" ("The Cage"). See Frank Graziano, *Alejandra Pizarnik: A Profile*, trans. Maria Rosa Fort, Frank Graziano, and Suzanne Jill Levine (Durango, CO: Logbridge-Rhodes, 1987).

1. The sun and the word are metaphors that occur concurrently in the works of Pizarnik. Contrary to the night and the void, both sun and word are viewed as the deceptive or futile attempts that try to fill in the void of meaning, the darkness of the night.

2. "Si Alguien puede . . . comprender a Artaud, soy yo. Todo su combate con su silencio, con su abismo absoluto, con su vacío, con su cuerpo enajenado, ¿como no asocio con el mío?" (If there is anyone who can . . . understand Artaud, that's me. All his struggles with his silence, his absolute abyss, his void, and his alienated body. How would I not associate it with mine?). See Alejandra Pizarnik, *Diarios* (Buenos Aires: Lumen, 2003), 159.

3. This term, originally coined by the poet John Keats, was later adopted by the philosopher of religion John Hick, a twentieth-century advocate of the Irenaean theodicy. See John Hick, *Evil and the God of Love* (New York: Macmillan, 1966).

4. Bonaventura de Sousa Santos, "Beyond Abyssal Thinking: From Global Lines to Ecologies of Knowledge," *Review* 30, no. 1 (2007): 45–46.

Chapter 1: Situating the Self in the Abyss

1. David K. Coe, *Angst and the Abyss: The Hermeneutics of Nothingness* (Chico, CA: Scholars Press, 1985), 31.

2. Robert Barnhart, ed., *The Barnhart Dictionary of Etymology* (Oxford: Oxford University Press, 1988); *Greek-English Lexicon* (Oxford: Oxford University Press, 1968).

3. David Sedley, "The Two Conceptions of Vacuum," *Phronesis* 27, no. 2 (1982): 177.

4. Brad Inwood, "The Origin of Epicurus' Concept of Void," *Classical Philology* 76, no. 4 (October 1981): 275.

5. Sedley, "Two Conceptions of Vacuum," 183.

6. Catherine Keller, *The Face of the Deep: A Theology of Becoming* (London: Routledge, 2003), 7.

7. Ibid., xv.

8. Grace Jantzen rightly points out the term that, in modern times, became predominantly associated with the negative connotations of nihilistic groundlessness (*abgrund*) and loss of meaning. Grace Jantzen, "Eros and the Abyss: Reading Medieval Mystics in Postmodernity," *Literature and Theology* 17, no. 3 (2003): 250–55.

9. Ludovicus Blosius, *A Book of Spiritual Instruction (Institutio spiritualis)*, trans. Bertrand A. Wilberforce, ed. Benedictine of Standbrook Abbey (Westminster, MD: Newman Press, 1955), 84–85.

10. Here self-discovery does not always–and necessarily—indicate a reconstructed self. The discovered "truth" of the self in the mystical tradition can often be the realization of the annihilation or extinction of the self in the union with God.

11. Hadewijch, letter 5, "False Brethren," in *The Complete Works*, trans. C. Hart (New York: Paulist Press, 1980), 56.

12. Hadewijch, "The New Path," in *Complete Works*, 145.

13. Ivone Gebara, *Out of the Depths: Women's Experience of Evil and Salvation* (Minneapolis: Augsburg Fortress Press, 2002), 58.

14. Elie Wiesel, *Night*, trans. Marion Wiesel (New York: Hill and Wang, 2006), 25.

15. Edouard Glissant, *Poetics of Relation*, trans. Betsy Wing (Ann Arbor: University of Michigan Press, 1997), 7.

16. Ibid., 8.

17. Frantz Fanon, *The Wretched of the Earth*, trans. Richard Philcox (New York: Grove, 2005), 48.

18. My own personal social location is by no means representative of the reality of people living at the edge of globalization. After all, the "illegal" period of my family's immigration status lasted for only a few years, as we managed to get the green card for "legal" residency. Neither has my family ever gone through "extreme poverty." Rather, I situate myself here with the hope to show where the geographic trans-spatiality of my arguments originates.

19. Derek Walcott, "The Antilles: Fragments of Epic Memory" (Nobel Prize Lecture, December 7, 1992), repr. in *The Routledge Reader in Caribbean Literature*, ed. Alison Donnell and Sarah Lawson Welsh (London: Routledge, 1996), 506.

20. Judith Butler, *Undoing Gender* (New York: Routledge, 2004), 15.

21. Martha Nussbaum, *Therapy of Desire: Theory and Practice in Hellenistic Ethics* (Princeton, NJ: Princeton University Press, 1996), chap. 9.

22. Marcus Aurelius, *Meditations* 10.15, quoted in Martha Nussbaum, "Kant and Stoic Cosmopolitanism," *Journal of Political Philosophy* 5, no. 1 (1997): 7.

23. Immanuel Kant, *Toward Perpetual Peace and Other Writings on Politics, Peace, and History*, ed. Pauline Kelingeld (New Haven, CT: Yale University Press, 2006), 82.

24. Immanuel Kant, *Political Writings* (Cambridge: Cambridge University Press, 1991), 107–8.

25. David Harvey, *Cosmopolitanism and the Geographies of Freedom* (New York: Columbia University Press, 2009), 25.

26. Immanuel Kant, "The Difference between the Races," in *The Portable Enlightenment Reader*, edited by Isaac Kramnick (New York: Penguin Books, 1995), 637–38.

27. Harvey, *Cosmopolitanism*, 33.

28. Ibid., 37.

29. Ibid., 81.

30. Ibid., 84.

31. Walter Mignolo, *The Darker Side of Western Modernity: Global Futures, Decolonial Options* (Durham, NC: Duke University Press, 2011), 271.

32. Ibid., 277.

33. Ibid.

34. Walter Mignolo distinguishes between the moment of the "elaboration" of postcolonial criticism and its "introduction" to the First World academy. Addressing Arif Dirlik's critique that the postcolonial begins with Third World intellectuals' arrival in the First World academy, Mignolo makes it clear that the history of postcolonial criticism dates back much further than that. Mignolo argues that while postcolonial criticism has been introduced, if not commodified, in the First World academy, it has always coexisted with colonialism itself. See Walter Mignolo, *Local Histories/Global Designs: Coloniality, Subalternity, and Border Thinking* (Durham, NC: Duke University Press, 2000).

35. Certainly some generalizations are presupposed in this claim made by the decolonial thinkers. Some of the foundational figures of decolonial thought, for instance, draw on European thinkers (Fanon and Dussel), while some postcolonial thinkers, such as Gayatri Spivak, include non-European/Western thought in their counterhegemonic narrative. Like some Latin American/Caribbean decolonial thinkers, Spivak is an adamant critic of migrant intellectual elites.

36. Arturo Escobar, *Mas allá del Tercer Mundo: Globalización y diferencia* (Bogotá: Instituto Colombiano de Antropología e Historia, 2005), 71.

37. Mabel Moraña, Enrique Dussel, and Carlos Jáuregui, "Colonialism and Its Replicants," in *Coloniality at Large: Latin America and the Postcolonial Debate*, ed. Mabel Moraña, Enrique Dussel, and Carlos Jáuregui (Durham, NC: Duke University Press, 2008), 6.

38. Walter Mignolo, "Philosophy and the Colonial Difference," in *Latin American Philosophy: Currents, Issues, Debates*, ed. Eduardo Mendieta (Bloomington: Indiana University Press, 2003), 85.

39. Moraña, Dussel, and Jáuaregui, "Colonialism and Its Replicants," 9.

40. Mignolo, "Philosophy," 81–82.

41. Emmanuel Levinas, *Totality and Infinity* (Dordrecht: Kluwer Academic Publishing, 1991), 172.

42. Ibid., 36, 39.

43. Enrique Dussel, *The Underside of Modernity: Apel, Ricoeur, Rorty, Taylor, and the Philosophy of Liberation*, ed. and trans. Eduardo Mendieta (Atlantic Highlands, NJ: Humanity Press, 1996), 3.

44. Ibid., 7.

45. Frantz Fanon, *A Dying Colonialism* (1965; repr., New York: Grove Press, 1994), 94.

46. One of the recent publications from the Drew TTC series at Fordham University Press marks an exceptional turn in the field by creating a channel of constructive dialogue among Latina/Latin American philosophy, decolonial thinking, and theology. See Ada Maria Isasi-Diaz and Eduardo Mendieta, eds., *Decolonizing Epistemologies: Latina/o Theology and Philosophy* (New York: Fordham University Press, 2012).

47. While a significant number of voices in political theology address issues related to coloniality and neocolonialism in terms such as *empire, capitalist globalization,* and *cosmopolitanism,* most of them lack interest in carrying on a comprehensive analysis that ties race and history with the political/economic/epistemological dimension of coloniality.

48. Édouard Glissant, *Caribbean Discourse: Selected Essays*, trans. J. Michael Dash (Charlottesville: University of Virginia Press, 1989), 131.

49. Catherine Keller, *Cloud of the Impossible: Negative Theology and Planetary Entanglement* (New York: Columbia University Press, 2014), 37.

Chapter 2: The Mystical Abyss: *Via Negativa*

1. William Franke, *On What Cannot Be Said: Apophatic Discourses in Philosophy, Religion, Literature, and the Arts*, vol. 1, *Classic Formulations* (Notre Dame, IN: University of Notre Dame Press, 2007), 37.

2. Derrida points out the similarity between deconstruction and negative theology. Nonetheless, he claims in the same passage that, however these two notions resemble each other, his project is "different" from negative theology. Jacques Derrida, *Margins of Philosophy*, trans. Alan Bass (Chicago: University of Chicago Press, 1982), 6.

3. Jacques Derrida, *On the Name* (Stanford, CA: Stanford University Press, 1995), 36.

4. Jantzen, *Eros and the Abyss*, 252.

5. As I will explore more in the next chapter, Augustine's view of the abyss and freedom finds an interesting resonance in the works of modern and contemporary thinkers such as Kierkegaard, Hannah Arendt, and particularly Slavoj Žižek, whose reading of the Hegelian dialectic through the abyss will be an important component of the next chapter.

6. Sigridur Gudmarsdottir, "Abyss of God: Flesh, Love, and Language in Paul Tillich," PhD diss., Drew University, 2007, 64.

7. Catherine Malabou, *The Heidegger Change: On the Fantastic in Philosophy* (Albany: SUNY Press, 2011), 123.

8. Baine Harris, *The Significance of Neoplatonism* (Albany: SUNY Press, 1976), 3.

9. Plotinus, *Enneads* 5.4.1, in *Plotinus, The Six Enneads*, trans. Stephen MacKenna and B. S. Page (Blacksburg, VA: Virginia Tech Press, 2001), 357.

10. Plotinus, *Enneads* 6.9.6, trans. MacKenna and Page, 559.

11. Harris, *Significance of Neoplatonism*, 7.

12. Franke, *On What Cannot Be Said*, 50.

13. Ibid., 51.

14. Plotinus, *Enneads* 6.9.3, trans. MacKenna and Page, 556–57.

15. Philippus Villiers Pistorius, *Plotinus and Neoplatonism: An Introductory Study* (Cambridge: Bowes and Bowes, 1952), 2.

16. Ibid., 30.

17. Plotinus, *Enneads* 5.3.13, trans. MacKenna and Page, 352.

18. Plotinus, *Enneads* 5.3.14, trans. Mackenna and Page, 162.

19. Robert Arp, "Plotinus, Mysticism, and Mediation," *Religious Studies* 40, no. 2 (June 2004): 145–63.

20. Plotinus, *Enneads* 5.3.14, trans. Mackenna and Page, 162.

21. Harris, *Significance of Neoplatonism*, 28.

22. John W. Cooper, *Panentheism, the Other God of the Philosophers: From Plato to the Present* (Grand Rapids, MI: Baker Academic, 2006), 43.

23. Even though such participation generates the possibility of a relational framework, it may not be yet a form of interrelation.

24. Plotinus, *Enneads* 6.9.3, trans. MacKenna and Page, 557.

25. Harris, *Significance of Neoplatonism*, 7, 28.

26. Franke, *On What Cannot Be Said*, 161.

27. John M. Dillon and Sarah Klitenic, *Dionysius the Areopagite and the Neoplatonist Tradition: Despoiling the Hellenes* (Aldershot: Ashgate, 2007), 23–24.

28. Pseudo-Dionysius, *The Divine Names* 977C, in Pseudo-Dionysius, *The Complete Works*, trans. Colm Luibheid (Mahwah, NJ: Paulist Press, 1987), 128. Subsequently cited as *DN*.

29. *DN* 588B, trans. Luibheid, 50.

30. *DN* 593B, trans. Luibheid, 53.

31. *DN* 593B, trans. Luibheid, 54.

32. *DN* 593C, trans. Luibheid, 54.

33. *DN* 872A, trans. Luibheid, 109.

34. Pseudo-Dionysius, *Mystical Theology* 1000A, in Pseudo-Dionysius, *The Complete Works*, trans. Colm Luibheid (Mahwah, NJ: Paulist Press, 1987), 135. Subsequently cited as *MT*.

35. *DN* 589B, trans. Luibheid, 50.

36. *DN* 816B, trans. Luibheid, 96.

37. *MT* 1000A, trans. Luibheid, 135.

38. *MT* 1001A, trans. Luibheid, 137.

39. *MT* 1025A, trans. Luibheid, 138.

40. *MT* 1001A, trans. Luibheid, 137.

41. Jean-Luc Marion, *Idol and Distance: Five Studies*, trans. Thomas A. Carlson (New York: Fordham University Press, 2001); Thomas Carlson, *Indiscretion: Finitude and the Naming of God* (Chicago: University of Chicago Press, 1999), 217.

42. Carlson, *Indiscretion*, 217.

43. Ibid., 215; Jacques Derrida, "How to Avoid Speaking: Denials," in *Derrida and Negative Theology*, ed. Harold Coward and Toby Forshay (Albany: SUNY Press, 1992), 77.

44. Carlson, *Indiscretion*, 215.

45. Jacques Derrida, "How to Avoid Speaking," 137.

46. The tie between negative theology and negative anthropology is one of Carlson's central assertions in *Indiscretion*. See, for example, Carlson, *Indiscretion*, 4, 7, 239, 260.

47. Ibid., 168.

48. Pseudo-Dionysius, *Complete Works*, 138.

49. Meister Eckhart, "German Sermon 10," in *Meister Eckhart: Teacher and Preacher*, ed. Bernard McGinn (Mahwah, NJ: Paulist Press, 1986), 261.

50. Meister Eckhart, Sermon 230, in *The Essential Sermons*, trans. Edmund Colledge and Bernard McGinn (Mahwah, NJ: Paulist Press, 1981).

51. Gudmarsdottir, "Abyss of God," 64.

52. Meister Eckhart, "German Sermon 76," in *Meister Eckhart*, 329.

53. Ibid., 290.

54. Charlotte Radler, "Living from the Divine Ground: Meister Eckhart's Praxis of Detachment," *Spiritus* 6, no. 1 (Spring 2006): 33.

55. Meister Eckhart, "German Sermon 4," in Meister Eckhart, *Meister Eckhart*, 250.

56. Slavoj Žižek and John Milbank, *The Monstrosity of Christ: Paradox or Dialectic?* ed. Creston Davis (Cambridge: MIT Press, 2009), 33.

57. Ibid.

58. Reiner Schurmann, *Wandering Joy: Meister Eckhart's Mystical Philosophy* (Great Barrington: Lindisfarne Books, 2001), 70.

59. Žižek and Milbank, *Monstrosity of Christ*, 33.

60. Ibid., 34.

61. Ibid.

62. Ibid., 38.

63. Meister Eckhart, "Commentary on Exodus" 15.72, in Meister Eckhart, *Meister Eckhart*, 67.

64. Franke, *On What Cannot Be Said*, 290.

65. Ibid.

66. Slavoj Žižek, *The Sublime Object of Ideology* (London: Verso, 1989), 192.

67. Slavoj Žižek, *The Parallax View* (Cambridge, MA: MIT Press, 2009), 206.

Chapter 3: The Dialectical Abyss: The Restless Negative of Hegel

1. Jon Mills, *The Unconscious Abyss: Hegel's Anticipation of Psychoanalysis* (Albany: SUNY Press, 2002), 22.

2. Jean Hyppolite, *Genesis and Structure of Hegel's Phenomenology of Spirit* (Evanston, IL: Northwestern University Press, 1974), 167.

3. In translating *Schaft* as "abyss," Mills argues that Hegel's use of *Schaft* in describing the abundance of images deposited in the pit of the soul is very unusual. Thus Mills sees Hegel as taking an idiosyncratic, poetic liberty in his use of the term. Furthermore, Mills adds, *Schaft* and *Abgrund* overlap in their meaning in multiple instances, particularly when referring to the depths of the human soul. See Mills, *Unconscious Abyss*, xiv.

4. G. W. F. Hegel, *Phenomenology of Spirit* (Oxford: Oxford University Press, 1977), 313.

5. Ibid., 315.

6. Ibid.

7. See Hyppolite, *Genesis and Structure*; Judith Butler, *Subjects of Desire: Hegelian Reflections in Twentieth-Century France* (New York: Columbia University Press, 1987); Žižek, *Sublime Object of Ideology*; Slavoj Žižek, *The Ticklish Subject: The Absent Centre of Political Ontology* (London: Verso, 1999); Catherine Malabou, *The Future of Hegel: Plasticity, Temporality, and Dialectic* (London: Routledge, 2004); Katrin Pahl, *Tropes of Transport: Hegel and Emotion* (Evanston, IL: Northwestern University Press, 2012).

8. Butler, *Subjects of Desire*, 22. See also Katrin Pahl, "The Way of Despair," in *Hegel and the Infinite*, ed. Slavoj Žižek, Clayton Crockett, and Creston Davis (New York: Columbia University Press, 2011), 142.

9. Žižek, *Sublime Object of Ideology*, 199.

10. Butler, *Undoing Gender*, 19.

11. Glenn Magee provides a clear and historically comprehensive review of Hegelian scholarship that focuses on the relation between Hegel and Boehme. See Glenn Magee, *Hegel and the Hermetic Tradition* (Ithaca, NY: Cornell University Press, 2008), 38–50.

12. Despite the significant impact of Boehme's theosophy on his thought, Hegel rejects the "sensual" approach of Boehme, which precludes the "free representation of the Idea." See ibid., 49.

13. Eric Trozzo, *Rupturing Eschatology: Divine Glory and the Silence of the Cross* (Minneapolis: Fortress Press, 2014), 85.

14. Mills, *Unconscious Abyss*, 23.

15. Trozzo, *Rupturing Eschatology*, 90.

16. Mills, *Unconscious Abyss*, 25.

17. Quoted in ibid., 26.

18. Quoted in ibid.

19. Ibid., 28.

20. Robert Brown, *The Later Philosophy of Schelling: The Influence of Boehme on the Works of 1809–1815* (Lewisburg, PA: Bucknell University Press, 1977), 55.

21. Cooper, *Panentheism*, 97.

22. Adrian Johnston, *Žižek's Ontology: A Transcendental Materialist Theory of Subjectivity* (Evanston, IL: Northwestern University Press, 2008), 92.

23. Jacob Boehme, *Of the Election of Grace, or Of God's Will toward Man*, ed. Martin Euser, trans. John Sparrow (San Rafael, CA: Hermetica Press, 2008), cited in Trozzo, *Rupturing Eschatology*, 86.

24. R. Brown, *Later Philosophy of Schelling*, 54.

25. Cooper, *Panentheism*, 100.

26. Slavoj Žižek, *The Abyss of Freedom/Ages of the Word, F. W. J. von Schelling* (Ann Arbor: University of Michigan Press, 1997), 93.

27. For the place of reason (being) and nonbeing in Schelling, see James Lindsay, "The Philosophy of Schelling," *Philosophical Review* 19, no. 3 (May 1910): 259–75.

28. Jean Hyppolite, *Logic and Existence*, trans. Leonard Lawlor and Amit Sen (Albany: SUNY Press, 1997), 105.

29. Alexandre Kojeve, *Introduction to the Reading of Hegel: Lectures on the Phenomenology of Spirit* (Ithaca, NY: Cornell University Press, 1980), 4, 38.

30. Butler, *Subjects of Desire*, 81.

31. Hyppolite, *Genesis and Structure*, 14, 18.

32. Jean Wahl, *Le malheur de la conscience dans la philosophie de Hegel* (Paris, 1929), 29, cited in Hyppolite, *Genesis and Structure*, xxx.

33. Karl Popper, *Open Society and Its Enemies*, vol. 2, *Hegel, Marx, and the Aftermath* (Princeton, NJ: Princeton University Press, 1966), chap. 12.

34. Robert Solomon, *In the Spirit of Hegel* (Oxford: Oxford University Press, 1983), 277.

35. Kojeve, *Introduction*, 201.

36. Hyppolite, *Genesis and Structure*, 14.

37. Ibid., 12–13, 18.

38. Hegel, *Phenomenology of Spirit*, 49.

39. Robert Williams, *Recognition: Fichte and Hegel on the Other* (Albany: SUNY Press, 1992), 150.

40. Kojeve, *Introduction*, 3.

41. Hyppolite, *Genesis and Structure*, 124.

42. Ibid., 64.

43. Hegel, *Phenomenology of Spirit*, 104 [second emphasis mine].

44. Ibid.

45. R. Williams, *Recognition*, 146.

46. Hegel, *Phenomenology of Spirit*, 113.

47. Kojeve, *Introduction*, 3.

48. Butler, *Subjects of Desire*, 48

49. Hegel, *Phenomenology of Spirit*, 18.

50. Jean Luc Nancy, *Hegel: The Restlessness of the Negative*, trans. Jason Smith and Steven Miller (Minneapolis: University of Minnesota Press, 2002), 5.

51. Ibid., 14.

52. Ibid., 15.

53. Solomon, *In the Spirit*, 180.

54. Morris Cohen, "Hegel's Rationalism," *Philosophical Review* 41, no. 3 (1932): 285.

55. Hyppolite, *Genesis and Structure*, 221.

56. Christopher Lauer, *The Suspension of Logic in Hegel and Schelling* (New York: Continuum, 2010), 108.

57. Ibid., 111.

58. Butler, *Subjects of Desire*, 81.

59. Kojeve, *Introduction*, 180.

60. Ibid., 194. However, Judith Butler notes, following the consensus in Hegelian scholarship, that Kojeve is still not free from teleological reading, as he equates the movement of spirit with human action (ontology). In Kojeve, teleology remains as a potential feature of an individual life. See Butler, *Subjects of Desire*, 81.

61. Hegel, *Phenomenology of Spirit*, 10.

62. Hyppolite, *Genesis and Structure*, 31.

63. R. Williams, *Recognition*, 204.

64. Hyppolite, *Genesis and Structure*, 167.

65. Kojeve, *Introduction*, 49.

66. Hegel, *Phenomenology of Spirit*, 17, 19.

67. R. Williams, *Recognition*, 170.

68. Hegel, Jena *Logic*, 31, cited in Hyppolite, *Genesis and Structure*, 151.

69. Nancy, *Hegel*, 31.

70. Ibid., 5.

71. Ibid.

72. Johnston, *Žižek's Ontology*, 19.

73. Žižek, *Ticklish Subject*, 55.

74. Johnston, *Žižek's Ontology*, 128–30.

75. Žižek, *Parallax View*, 27.

76. Žižek, *Ticklish Subject*, 25–27.

77. Ibid., 158.

78. Slavoj Žižek, *Tarrying with the Negative: Kant, Hegel, and the Critique of Ideology* (Durham, NC: Duke University Press, 1993), 88.

79. Žižek, *Sublime Object of Ideology*, 190.

80. Ibid., 192.

81. Johnston, *Žižek's Ontology*, 70.

82. Slavoj Žižek, *The Indivisible Remainder: An Essay on Schelling and Related Matters* (London: Verso, 1996), 74.

83. Johnston, *Žižek's Ontology*, 75.

84. Žižek, *Abyss of Freedom*, 76.

85. Ibid., 92.

86. Johnston, *Žižek's Ontology*, 80.

87. F. W. J. von Schelling, *The Ages of the World*, trans. Jason Wirth (Albany: SUNY Press, 2000), 22–23.

88. Žižek, *Indivisible Remainder*, 13.

89. Johnston, *Žižek's Ontology*, 95.

90. Ibid., 96.

91. Slavoj Žižek, *The Fragile Absolute: Or Why Is the Christian Legacy Worth Fighting For* (London: Verso, 2000), 73.

92. Johnston, *Žižek's Ontology*, 106.

93. Žižek, *Sublime Object of Ideology*, 195.

94. Žižek, *Tarrying with the Negative*, 31.

95. Žižek, *Ticklish Subject*, 31.

96. Ibid., 212.

97. Žižek and Milbank, *Monstrosity of Christ*, 61.

98. Johnston, *Žižek's Ontology*, 139.

99. Žižek, *Tarrying with the Negative*, 26.

100. Dominick LaCapra, "Trauma, Absence, Loss," *Critical Inquiry* 25, no. 4 (Summer 1999): 700–701, 727.

101. "The point of these paradoxes is that what we call 'subjectivization' (recognizing oneself in interpellation, assuming an imposed symbolic mandate) is a kind of defense mechanism against an abyss, a gap, which 'is' the subject." See Žižek *Tarrying with the Negative*, 171.

102. Žižek, *Ticklish Subject*, 107.

103. Žižek, *Tarrying with the Negative*, 27, 116.

104. Hegel, *Phenomenology of Spirit*, 315.

105. Žižek, *Ticklish Subject*, 31.

106. Butler, *Subjects of Desire*, 22.

107. Ibid.

108. Hegel, *Phenomenology of Spirit*, 455.

109. Ibid.

110. Butler, *Subjects of Desire*, 22.

111. Ibid., 6.

112. Ibid., 9.

113. Ibid., 23.

114. Ibid.

115. Ibid., 27.

116. Ibid., 34.

117. Ibid.

118. Ibid., 40.

119. Ibid., 46.

120. Ibid.

121. Ibid., 47–48.

122. Catherine Malabou and Judith Butler, "You Be My Body for Me: Body, Shape, and Plasticity in Hegel's Phenomenology of Spirit," in *A Companion to Hegel*, ed. Stephen Houlgate and Michael Baur (Malden, MA: Blackwell, 2011), 625.

123. Judith Butler, *The Psychic Life of Power* (Stanford, CA: Stanford University Press, 1997), 22.

124. Ibid., 23.

125. For Butler's work on mourning in the context of war and violence, see Judith Butler, *Precarious Life: The Powers of Mourning and Violence* (London: Verso, 2004), *Frames of War: When Is Life Grievable?* (New York: Verso, 2010), and *Parting Ways: Jewishness and the Critique of Zionism* (New York: Columbia University Press, 2013).

126. Butler, *Psychic Life*, 28.

127. Butler, *Undoing Gender*, 15.

128. Ibid.

129. Ibid.

130. Ibid., 22.

131. Peter Sacks, *The English Elegy: Studies in the Genre from Spenser to Yeats* (Baltimore: John's Hopkins University Press, 1987), 6.

132. Butler, *Precarious Life*, 20.

133. Judith Butler, *Giving an Account of Oneself* (New York: Fordham University Press, 2005), 121.

134. Sigmund Freud, *The Ego and the Id* (New York: W. W. Norton, 1990), 51.

135. Butler, *Undoing Gender*, 18.

136. Ibid.

137. Ibid., 19.

138. Butler, *Precarious Life*, 30.

139. Butler, *Undoing Gender*, 2–3.

140. Frantz Fanon, *Black Skin, White Masks*, trans. Charles Lam Markmann (New York: Grove Press, 1968), 201.

141. Charles Villet, "Hegel and Fanon on the Question of Mutual Recognition: A Comparative Analysis," *Journal of Pan African Studies* 4, no. 7 (November 2011): 43.

142. Ibid.

143. An Yountae, "Breaking from Within: The Dialectic of Labor and the Death of God," in *Common Goods: Economy, Ecology, and Political Theology*, ed. Melanie Johnson-DeBeaufre, Catherine Keller, and Elias Ortega-Aponte (New York: Fordham University Press, 2015), 256.

144. Butler, *Precarious Self*, 44.

145. Žižek, *Ticklish Subject*, 225.

146. Butler, *Psychic Life*, 35.

147. Ibid., 12.

148. Ibid., 62.

149. Ibid., 49.

150. Ibid., 12.

151. Ibid., 28–29.

152. Ibid., 264.

153. Ibid., 266–67.

154. Ibid., 264.

155. Ibid.

156. In commenting on Hegel's master-slave dialectic, Kojeve also points out that the process of education and transformation by labor in which the worker surmounts the terror of death and rises up is long and painful. See Kojeve, *Introduction*, 53.

157. Hyppolite, *Genesis and Structure*, 13.

158. The Argentinian-Mexican philosopher Enrique Dussel charges Hegel for championing the totalitarian metaphysics and the Eurocentric geopolitics underlying European modernity. Dussel calls modernity a European phenomenon that was established in a dialectical relation with non-European alterity. Enrique Dussel, "Eurocentrism and Modernity (Introduction to the Frankfurt Lectures)," *Boundary 2* 20, no. 3 (Autumn 1993): 65.

159. Butler, *Psychic Life*, 61.

160. Ibid.

161. Ibid.

Chapter 4: The Colonial Abyss: Groundlessness of Being

1. Antonio Benitez-Rojo, *The Repeating Island: The Caribbean and the Postmodern Perspective* (Durham, NC: Duke University Press, 1997), 24.

2. Anibal Quijano, "Coloniality of Power, Eurocentrism, and Latin America," *Nepantla: Views from South* 1, no. 3 (2000): 550–51.

3. John Drabinski, *Levinas and the Postcolonial: Race, Nation, Other* (Edinburgh: Edinburgh University Press, 2013), 161.

4. Benitez-Rojo, *Repeating Island*, 5.

5. Glissant, *Caribbean Discourse*, 62.

6. Glissant, *Poetics of Relation*, 6.

7. Michael Dash, *Edouard Glissant* (Cambridge: Cambridge University Press, 1995), 35.

8. John Drabinski, introduction to *Abyssal Beginnings*, unpublished manuscript.

9. John Drabinski articulates eloquently the question of beginning (after catastrophe) in Glissant in comparison to Levinas. See Drabinski, *Levinas and the Postcolonial*, 141–62.

10. Celia Britton, *Edouard Glissant and Postcolonial Theory: Strategies of Language and Resistance* (Charlottesville: University of Virginia Press, 1999), 15.

11. Glissant, *Poetics of Relation*, 6.

12. Benitez-Rojo, *Repeating Island*, 17, 27.

13. Gary Wilder, "Race, Reason, Impasse: Césaire, Fanon, and the Legacy of Emancipation," *Radical History Review*, no. 90 (Fall 2004): 33.

14. Aimé Césaire, *Notebook of a Return to the Native Land*, trans. Clayton Eshlemann (Middletown, CT: Wesleyan University Press, 2001), 1.

15. Ibid., 3.

16. Ibid., 28.

17. Nigel Gibson, *Fanon: The Postcolonial Imagination* (Cambridge: Polity Press, 2003), chap. 3.

18. G. Wilder, "Race," 39.

19. Ibid., 40.

20. Ibid., 41.

21. Césaire, *Notebook of a Return*, 29.

22. Ibid., 42–43.

23. Ibid., 43–44.

24. "There still remains one sea to cross . . . that I may invent my lungs . . . the master of laughter? / The master of ominous silence? / The master of hope and despair? / The master of laziness? Master of the dance? / It is I!" Césaire, *Notebook of a Return*, 83; G. Wilder, "Race," 44.

25. Césaire, *Notebook of a Return*, 47–48.

26. Derek Walcott, "The Sea Is History," in *The Poetry of Derek Walcott, 1948–2013* (New York: Farrar, Strauss and Giroux, 2014), 253–56.

27. Walcott, "Antilles."

28. G. Wilder, "Race," 36.

29. Edward Said, *Culture and Imperialism* (New York: Vintage, 1993), 228–29.

30. Bill Ashcroft, Gareth Griffiths, and Helen Tiffin, *The Empire Writes Back: Theory and Practice in Post-colonial Literatures* (London: Routledge, 2004), 124.

31. Fanon, *Black Skin*, 16.

32. Ibid.

33. Robert Bernasconi, "The Assumption of Negritude: Aimé Césaire, Frantz Fanon, and the Vicious Circle of Racial Politics," *Parallax* 8, no. 2 (2002): 79.

34. Fanon, *Black Skin*, 153.

35. Ibid., 187.

36. "Since the other hesitates to recognize me, there remains only one solution: to make myself known." Fanon, *Black Skin*, 115.

37. Gibson, *Fanon*, 14.

38. Fanon, *Black Skin*, 112.

39. Ibid., 8.

40. Ibid.

41. Ibid., 118.

42. Ibid., 112.

43. Nelson Maldonado-Torres, "On the Coloniality of Being: Contributions to the Development of a Concept," *Cultural Studies* 21, nos. 2–3 (2007): 251.

44. Ibid.

45. Frantz Fanon, *A Dying Colonialism* (New York: Grove Press, 1994), 128.

46. Abdul JanMohamed, *The Death-Bound-Subject: Richard Wright's Archaeology of Death* (Durham, NC: Duke University Press, 2005), 2.

47. Maldonado-Torres, "On the Coloniality of Being," 252.

48. Ibid., 253.

49. Gibson, *Fanon*, 33.

50. Fanon, *Black Skin*, 222.

51. Gibson, *Fanon*, 37.

52. Ibid., 40.

53. Ibid.

54. Fanon, *Wretched of the Earth*, 4.

55. Ibid., 5.

56. Nigel Gibson, *Rethinking Fanon: The Continuing Dialogue* (Amherst: Humanity Books, 1999), 11.

57. Michael Azar, "In the Name of Algeria," in *Frantz Fanon: Critical Perspectives,* ed. Anthony Alessandrini (London: Routledge, 1999), 30.

58. Ibid., 31.

59. Ibid.

60. Fanon seldom uses the word *abyss* in his writings. But his articulation of the colonial conditions of existence exemplifies or evokes the abyss in sociopolitical terms.

61. Drabinski, *Levinas and the Postcolonial*, 13.

62. Edouard Glissant, *Poetic Intention*, trans. Nathalie Stephens (Callicoon: Nightboat, 1997), 166.

63. Deleuze's relation to the One and the many has been subject to controversy ever since Alain Badiou suggested that Deleuze, in fact, does not reverse Platonism but instead promotes a "Platonism of the virtual." Badiou maintains that Deleuze is not a thinker of multiplicity since Deleuze relentlessly underscores that everything exists on one ontological level alone. However, Badiou's reading of Deleuze has become itself the subject of disagreement among many commentators, as his interpretation of Spinoza's Univocity of Being can be seen as problematic and thus the source of his misinterpretation of Deleuze. See Nathan Widder, "The Rights of Simulacra: Deleuze and the Univocity of Being," *Continental Philosophy Review* 34 (2001): 437–53; Todd May, "Badiou and Deleuze on the One and Many," in *Think Again: Alain Badiou and the Future of Philosophy*, ed. Peter Hallward (London: Continuum, 2004); Clayton Crockett, *Deleuze beyond Badiou: Ontology, Multiplicity, and Event* (New York: Columbia University Press, 2013).

64. Gilles Deleuze and Felix Guattari, *A Thousand Plateaus*, trans. Brian Massumi (Minneapolis: University of Minnesota Press, 1980), 21.

65. Ibid., 23.

66. Gilles Deleuze and Claire Parnet, *Dialogues II* (London: Continuum, 1987), 39.

67. Gilles Deleuze, *Spinoza: Practical Philosophy* (San Francisco: City Lights Books, 1988), 123.

68. Rosi Braidotti, *Transpositions: On Nomadic Ethics* (Cambridge: Polity Press, 2006), 4.

69. Ibid., 83.

70. Ibid., 84.

71. Avita Ronnell, endorsement of Glissant's *Poetics of Intention*.

72. Braidotti, *Transpositions*, 68.

73. Ibid., 148.

74. Julie Wuthnow, "Deleuze in the Postcolonial: On Nomads and Indigenous Politics," *Feminist Theory* 3, no. 2, (2002): 187.

75. Ibid., 190.

76. Irene Gedalof, "Can Nomads Learn to Count to Four? Rosi Braidotti and the Space for Difference in Feminist Theory," *Women: A Cultural Review* 7, no. 2 (1996): 192; Wuthnow, "Deleuze in the Postcolonial," 181.

77. Irene Gedalof, "Identity in Transit: Nomads, Cyborgs and Women," *European Journal of Women's Studies* 7 (2000): 337–54, 343.

78. Braidotti, *Transpositions*, 84.

79. Glissant, *Poetics of Relation*, 6.

80. Ibid., 5–6.

81. Ibid., 6.

82. Ibid.

83. Ibid., 8.

84. Ibid.

85. Ibid., 7.

86. Drabinski, *Levinas and the Postcolonial*, 135, 144.

87. Glissant, *Caribbean Discourse*, 9.

88. Drabinski, *Levinas and the Postcolonial*, 148.

89. Ibid.

90. "What is referred to here as order is the terrifying nothingness in which a stained illiterate society attempts to maintain a people without reference. Every poetics is a search for reference." Glissant, *Poetic Intention*, 176.

91. Drabinski, *Levinas and the Postcolonial*, 153.

92. Ibid., 154.

93. Butler, *Undoing Gender*, 15.

94. Glissant, *Poetics of Relation*, 6–7.

95. Glissant, *Caribbean Discourse,* 66.

96. Again, there are important differences between namelessness in Derrida and in Glissant. Derrida's is utterly negative, alluding to the impossible, and constantly deferred, while Glissant's is located in the material reality of creolized life. Both thinkers, however, evoke the passion for that which constantly disavows the myth of being/presence, that which deconstructs the metaphysical illusion from *within*.

97. Glissant, *Poetic Intention*, 106.

98. Ibid., 108.

99. Deleuze and Guattari, *Thousand Plateaus*, 24.

100. Ibid., 28.

101. Glissant, *Poetics of Relation*, 6.

102. Ibid., 6–7.

103. John Drabinski, "Shorelines: In Memory of Edouard Glissant," *Journal of French and Francophone Philosophy* 19, no. 1 (2011): 6.

104. Ibid.

105. Glissant, *Caribbean Discourse*, vii.

106. Ibid., 63–64.

107. Michael Dash, introduction to Glissant, *Caribbean Discourse*.

108. Clearly, the Hegelian-Žižekian account of the subject, like Deleuze's and Braidotti's, does not reference the notion of a "middle ground." But there seems to be an unmarked, latent ground, an originary synthesis in the interval between death and life, absence and presence, within the structure of the dialectic, especially if we remember Butler's Kierkegaardian remarks that often "suffering simply erode[s] whatever ground there is" instead of "prompt[ing] the reconstruction of a world on yet firmer ground." See Butler, *Subjects of Desire*, 22.

109. Butler, *Undoing Gender*, 15.

110. Ibid.

111. Butler, *Precarious Life*, 22.

112. Drabinski, *Levinas and the Postcolonial*, 153 (emphasis mine).

113. Ibid., 160.

114. Ibid., 153 (emphasis mine).

115. Walcott, "Antilles," 506.

116. Glissant, *Poetic Intention*, 201.

117. Michael Monahan, *The Creolizing Subject: Race, Reason, and the Politics of Purity* (New York: Fordham University Press, 2011), 202.

118. Ibid.

119. Malabou, *Heidegger Change*, 270. Changes (*Wandeln*), along with transformations (*Wandlungen*) and metamorphoses (*Verwandlungen*), occupy an important place in Heidegger. For Heidegger, metamorphosis predicates man's relation to *Dasein*: "This requires that we actively complete the transformation of the human being into the Da-sein that every instance of anxiety occasions in us." See Martin Heidegger, "What Is Metaphysics?," in *Pathmarks*, ed. William McNeill (Cambridge University Press, 1998), 89.

120. Glissant's philosophy of creolization is an ethical call that makes us gravitate toward "being oneself to be the other, forever and without hope." One opens toward the other not by giving up oneself, but by fully becoming oneself. Thus being oneself is equated with being "for the other." On the other hand, the contradicting juxtaposition of "forever" and "without hope" might be understood as evoking passion (forever) for the evanescent truth that disappears at the moment one grasps it (without hope). See *Poetic Intention*, 201.

121. Keller, *Cloud of the Impossible*, 6.

Chapter 5: Creolizing Cosmopolitics: Poetics from the Deep

1. It needs to be clarified that what has been undermined is the "ground"; its "other," the "groundless," is never fully obliterated or eliminated.

2. Glissant, *Caribbean Discourse*, 66.

3. David Miller, "Theopoiesis: A Perspective of the Work of Stanley Romaine Hopper," in Stanley Romaine Hopper, *Why Persimmons and Other Poems* (Atlanta, GA: Scholars Press, 1987), 4.

4. Ibid.

5. Ibid., 4.

6. Amos Wilder, *Theopoetic: Theology and the Religious Imagination* (Philadelphia: Fortress Press, 1976), 25.

7. Ibid., 106.

8. John Caputo, *The Weakness of God: A Theology of the Event* (Bloomington: Indiana University Press, 2006), 5.

9. John Caputo, *Deconstruction in a Nutshell: A Conversation with Jacques Derrida* (New York: Fordham University Press, 1997), 162.

10. Caputo, *Weakness of God*, 103.

11. Ibid.

12. For Derrida, the "impossible" is not an antithetical concept of possibility but an "impossible possibility," an impossibility that always "continues to haunt the possibility." See Jacques Derrida, "A Certain Impossible Possibility of Saying the Event," in *The Late Derrida*, ed. W. J. Mitchell and Arnold I. Davidson (Chicago: University of Chicago Press, 2008), 234.

13. John Caputo, *The Insistence of God: A Theology of Perhaps* (Bloomington: Indiana University Press, 2013), 63.

14. Ibid., 260.

15. Ibid.

16. Ibid., 261.

17. Catherine Keller, book review of *The Weakness of God: A Theology of the Event*, by John Caputo, *Cross Currents* 56, no. 4 (Winter 2007): 138.

18. Caputo, *Weakness of God*, 150.

19. Ibid., 110.

20. Caputo's root in the "depths" is partly indebted to his reading of Catherine Keller, whose *Face of the Deep* provides an important theological (and theopoetic) structure for Caputo's *Weakness of God*.

21. Ibid., 286.

22. Richard Kearney, *The God Who May Be: A Hermeneutics of Religion* (Bloomington: Indiana University Press, 2001), 4.

23. Richard Kearney, *Anatheism: Returning to God after God* (New York: Columbia University Press, 2011), 40.

24. Ibid., 20.

25. Ibid., 110.

26. Ibid., 5.

27. Richard Kearney, "Epiphanies of the Everyday: Toward a Micro-eschatology," in *After God: Richard Kearney and the Religious Turn in Continental Philosophy*, ed. John Panteleimon Manoussakes (New York: Fordham University Press, 2006).

28. While Kearney's critique targets the deconstructionist foundations laid out by Derrida, his major disagreement is with Caputo. This is because Derrida acknowledges in many other instances the danger in the radical "undecidability" of the event to come. See Kearney, *God Who May Be*, 75–77.

29. Ibid., 73.

30. Ibid., 75.

31. Ibid., 74.

32. Kearney, *Anatheism*, 7, 14.

33. Ibid., 38.

34. A. Wilder, *Theopoetic*, 19.

35. Ibid., 57.

36. Ibid., 29.

37. Glissant, *Poetic Intention*, 18.

38. Glissant, *Poetics of Relation*, 6.

39. Ibid., 7.

40. Glissant, *Caribbean Discourse*, xxxii.

41. Dash, introduction to ibid., xxii.

42. Ibid., 173.

43. Ibid., 120.

44. Ibid, 120.

45. Ibid, 121.

46. Ibid, 131, 254.

47. Another important aspect of Glissant's opacity derives from the lack of hinterland in Martinique. Literally speaking, there is no hinterland in Martinique where slaves who fled from the plantation could hide. Historically, there is no local, indigenous culture to which the fugitives can retreat. In other words, there is no cultural hinterland that provides protection for the colonized. See Britton, *Edouard Glissant*, 25.

48. Glissant, *Caribbean Discourse*, 139.

49. Ibid., 66.

50. Keller, *Face of the Deep*, xvi.

51. Ibid., 12.

52. Ibid., 158.

53. Ibid., 160.

54. Ibid.

55. Ibid, 227.

56. Ibid.

57. Ibid., 226.

58. Ibid., 227.

59. Stanka Radovic, "The Birthplace of Relation in Edouard Glissant's *Poetique de la Relation*," *Callaloo* 30, no. 2 (Spring 2007): 475.

60. Glissant, *Caribbean Discourse*, 133.

61. Ibid. (emphasis mine).

62. Keller, *Face of the Deep*, 167. Originally cited in Derrida, *On the Name*, 104.

63. Jacob ben Sheshet of Gerona, "The Books of Faith and Reliance," in *The Early Kabbalah*, 126, cited in Keller, *Face of the Deep*, 167.

64. Miller, *Theopoiesis*, 8.

65. Drabinski, *Levinas and the Postcolonial*, 148.

66. Glissant, *Caribbean Discourse*, 139.

67. Ibid., 112.

68. Ulrich Beck, "The Cosmopolitical Perspective: Sociology of the Second Age of Modernity," *British Journal of Sociology* 1, no. 1 (January 2000): 92.

69. Ulrich Beck, "The Truth of Others: A Cosmopolitan Approach," *Common Knowledge* 10, no. 3 (Fall 2004): 430.

70. Ibid., 438.

71. Ibid., 439.

72. Paul Gilroy, "Planetarity and Cosmopolitics," *British Journal of Sociology* 61, no. 3 (2010),: 622.

73. Similarly, Sheldon Pollock, Homi Bhabha, Carol Breckenridge, and Dipesh Chakrabarty also warn against this danger as they write, in their introduction to the special issue on "cosmopolitanisms" in *Public Culture*, that cosmopolitanism needs to be clearly distinguished from "other more triumphalistic notions of cosmopolitan existence" because "modernity has never fallen short of making universalist claims to world citizenship." See Sheldon Pollock et al., "Introduction: Cosmopolitanisms," *Public Culture* 12, no. 3 (Fall 2000): 581.

74. Bruno Latour, "Whose Cosmos, Which Cosmopolitics: Comments on the Peace Terms of Ulrich Beck," *Common Knowledge* 10, no. 3, (2004): 462.

75. Glissant, *Caribbean Discourse*, 128.

76. Glissant, *Poetics of Relation*, 34.

77. Yanick Lahens, "Exile: Between Writing and Place," *Callaloo* 15, no. 3 (Summer 1992): 737.

78. Glissant, *Poetics of Relation*, 22.

79. Manthia Diawara, "One World in Relation: Edouard Glissant in Conversation with Manthia Diawara," *Journal of Contemporary African Art* 28 (Spring 2011): 6.

80. Glissant, *Poetic Intention*, 106.

81. An Yountae, "From Exile to Cosmopolitics: Creolizing the Spiritual after Trauma," *Horizontes Decoloniales* 1, no. 1 (2015): 161.

82. Keller, *Cloud of the Impossible*, 264.

Conclusion

1. Friedrich Nietzsche, *Beyond Good and Evil: Prelude to a Philosophy of the Future*, ed. Rolf Peter and Judith Norman Horstmann, trans. Judith Norman (Cambridge: Cambridge University Press, 2002), 69.

2. Malabou, *Heidegger Change*, 135.

Bibliography

Alves, Rubem. *The Poet, the Warrior, the Prophet.* London: SMC Press, 1990.

An Yountae. "Breaking from Within: The Dialectic of Labor and the Death of God." In *Common Goods: Economy, Ecology, and Political Theology*, edited by Melanie Johnson-DeBeaufre, Catherine Keller, and Elias Ortega-Aponte. New York: Fordham University Press, 2015.

———. "From Exile to Cosmopolitics: Creolizing the Spiritual after Trauma." *Horizontes Decoloniales* 1, no. 1 (2015): 143–63.

Anzaldúa, Gloria. *Borderlands/La Frontera: The New Mestiza.* San Francisco: Aunt Lute Books, 1999.

Arp, Robert. "Plotinus, Mysticism, and Mediation." *Religious Studies* 40, no. 2 (June 2004): 145–63.

Ashcroft, Bill, Gareth Griffiths, and Helen Tiffin. *The Empire Writes Back: Theory and Practice in Post-colonial Literatures.* London: Routledge, 2004.

Azar, Michael. "In the Name of Algeria." In *Frantz Fanon: Critical Perspectives*, edited by Anthony Alessandrini, 21–33. London: Routledge, 1999.

Barnhart, Robert. *The Barnhart Dictionary of Etymology.* Oxford: Oxford University Press, 1988.

Beach, Edward Allen. *The Potencies of God(s): Schelling's Philosophy of Mythology.* Albany: SUNY Press, 1994.

Beck, Ulrich. "The Cosmopolitical Perspective: Sociology of the Second Age of Modernity." *British Journal of Sociology* 1, no. 1 (January 2000): 79–105.

———. "The Truth of Others: A Cosmopolitan Approach." *Common Knowledge* 10, no. 3 (Fall 2004): 430–49.

Benhabib, Seyla. *The Rights of Others: Aliens, Residents, and Citizens.* Cambridge: Cambridge University Press, 2004.

Benitez-Rojo, Antonio. *The Repeating Island: The Caribbean and the Postmodern Perspective*. Durham, NC: Duke University Press, 1997.

Bernasconi, Robert. "The Assumption of Negritude: Aimé Césaire, Frantz Fanon, and the Vicious Circle of Racial Politics." *Parallax* 8, no. 2 (2002): 69–83.

Blosius, Ludovicus. *A Book of Spiritual Instruction (Institutio spiritualis)*. Translated from the Latin by Bertrand A. Wilberforce. Edited by Benedictine of Standbrook Abbey. Westminster, MD: Newman Press, 1955.

Boehme, Jacob. *Mysterium Magnum: An Exposition of the First Book of Moses Called Genesis*. Translated by John Spanow. San Rafael, CA: Hermetica Press, 2008.

———. *Works of Jacob Behmen: The Teutonic Philosopher*. Part 4. London: Kessinger, 2003.

Braidotti, Rosi. *Transpositions: On Nomadic Ethics*. Cambridge: Polity Press, 2006.

Britton, Celia. *Edouard Glissant and Postcolonial Theory: Strategies of Language and Resistance*. Charlottesville: University Press of Virginia, 1999.

———. "Transnational Languages in Glissant's Tout-Monde." In *World Writing: Poetics, Ethics, Globalization*, edited by Mary Gallagher, 62–85. Toronto: Toronto University Press, 2008.

Brown, Robert F. *The Later Philosophy of Schelling: The Influence of Boehme on the Works of 1809–1815*. Lewisburg, PA: Bucknell University Press, 1977.

Brown, Wallace, and David Held, eds. *The Cosmopolitanism Reader*. Cambridge: Polity Press, 2010.

Butler, Judith. *Frames of War: When Is Life Grievable?* New York: Verso, 2010.

———. *Giving an Account of Oneself*. New York: Fordham University Press, 2005.

———. *Parting Ways: Jewishness and the Critique of Zionism*. New York: Columbia University Press, 2013.

———. *Precarious Life: The Powers of Mourning and Violence*. London: Verso, 2004.

———. *The Psychic Life of Power*. Stanford, CA: Stanford University Press, 1997.

———. *Subjects of Desire: Hegelian Reflections in Twentieth-Century France*. New York: Columbia University Press, 1987.

———. *Undoing Gender*. New York: Routledge, 2004.

Caputo, John. *Against Ethics: Contributions to a Poetics of Obligation with a Constant Reference to Deconstruction*. Bloomington: Indiana University Press, 1988.

———. *Deconstruction in a Nutshell: A Conversation with Jacques Derrida*. New York: Fordham University Press, 1997.

———. *The Insistence of God: A Theology of Perhaps*. Bloomington: Indiana University Press, 2013.

———. *On Religion*. London: Routledge, 2001.

———. *The Weakness of God: A Theology of the Event*. Bloomington: Indiana University Press, 2006.

Caputo, John, and Catherine Keller. "Theopoetic/Theopolitic." *Cross-Currents* 56, no. 4 (Winter 2007): 105–11.

Carabine, Deirdre. *The Unknown God: Negative Theology in the Platonic Tradition—Plato to Eurigena*. Gran Rapids, MI: Eerdman, 1995.

Carlson, Thomas. *Indiscretion: Finitude and the Naming of God*. Chicago: University of Chicago Press, 1999.

Césaire, Aimé. *Discourse on Colonialism*. Translated by Joan Pinkham. New York: Monthly Review Press, 2000.

———. *Notebook of a Return to the Native Land*. Translated by Clayton Eshlemann. Middletown, CT: Wesleyan University Press, 2001.

Cetinic, Marija. "Sympathetic Conditions: Toward a New Ontology of Trauma." *Discourse* 32, no. 3 (Fall 2010): 285–301.

Chaning-Pearce, Melville. "Boehme and the Ungrund." *Church Quarterly Review* 149, no. 297 (1949): 15–26.

Coe, David K. *Angst and the Abyss: The Hermeneutics of Nothingness*. Chico, CA: Scholars Press, 1985.

Cohen, Morris. "Hegel's Rationalism." *Philosophical Review* 41, no. 3 (1932): 283–301.

Cooper, John W. *Panentheism, the Other God of the Philosophers: From Plato to the Present*. Grand Rapids, MI: Baker Academic, 2006.

Critchley, Simon. *Ethics, Politics, Subjectivity: Essays on Derrida, Levinas, and Contemporary French Thought*. London: Verso, 1999.

Crockett, Clayton. *Deleuze beyond Badiou: Ontology, Multiplicity, and Event*. New York: Columbia University Press, 2013.

———. *Radical Political Theology*. New York: Columbia University Press, 2011.

Dash, Michael. *Edouard Glissant*. Cambridge: Cambridge University Press, 1995.

———. Introduction to *Caribbean Discourse: Selected Essays*, by Edouard Glissant, translated by Michael Dash. Charlottesville: University Press of Virginia, 1989.

Deleuze, Gilles. *Spinoza: Practical Philosophy*. San Francisco: City Lights Books, 1988.

Deleuze, Gilles, and Felix Guattari. *Anti-Oedipus: Capitalism and Schizophrenia*. Minneapolis: University of Minnesota Press, 1983.

———. *A Thousand Plateaus*. Translated by Brian Massumi. Minneapolis: University of Minnesota Press, 1980.

Deleuze, Gilles, and Claire Parnet. *Dialogues II*. London: Continuum, 1987.

Derrida, Jacques. "A Certain Impossible Possibility of Saying the Event." In *The Late Derrida*, edited by W. J. Mitchell and Arnold I. Davidson, 223–43. Chicago: University of Chicago Press, 2008.

———. "How to Avoid Speaking: Denials." In *Derrida and Negative Theology*, edited by Harold Coward and Toby Forshay, 73–142. Albany: SUNY Press, 1992.

———. *Margins of Philosophy*. Translated by Alan Bass. Chicago: University of Chicago Press, 1982.

———. *On the Name*. Stanford, CA: Stanford University Press, 1995.

Diawara, Manthia. "One World in Relation: Edouard Glissant in Conversation with Manthia Diawara." *Journal of Contemporary African Art* 28 (Spring 2011): 4–19.

Dillon, John M., and Sarah Klitenic. *Dionysius the Areopagite and the Neoplatonist Tradition: Despoiling the Hellenes*. Aldershot: Ashgate, 2007.

Dooley, Mark, ed. *A Passion for the Impossible: John Caputo in Focus*. Albany: SUNY Press, 2003.

Drabinski, John E. Introduction to *Abyssal Beginnings*, unpublished manuscript.

———. *Levinas and the Postcolonial: Race, Nation, Other*. Edinburgh: Edinburgh University Press, 2013.

———. "Shorelines: In Memory of Edouard Glissant." *Journal of French and Francophone Philosophy* 19, no. 1 (2011): 1–10.

———. "What Is Trauma to the Future? On Glissant's Poetics." *Qui Parle* 30 (2010): 31–47.

Dussel, Enrique. "Eurocentrism and Modernity (Introduction to the Frankfurt Lectures)." *Boundary 2* 20, no. 3 (Autumn 1993): 65–76.

———. *The Underside of Modernity: Apel, Ricoeur, Rorty, Taylor, and the Philosophy of Liberation*. Translated and edited by Eduardo Mendieta. Atlantic Highlands, NJ: Humanities Press, 1996.

Escobar, Arturo. *Mas allá del Tercer Mundo: Globalización y diferencia*. Bogotá: Instituto Colombiano de Antropología e Historia, 2005.

Fanon, Frantz. *Black Skin, White Masks*. Translated by Charles Lam Markmann. New York: Grove Press, 1968.

———. *A Dying Colonialism*. 1965. Reprint, New York: Grove Press, 1994.

———. *The Wretched of the Earth*. Translated by Richard Philcox. New York: Grove Press, 2005.

Franke, William. "Apophasis and the Turn of Philosophy to Religion: From Neoplatonic Negative Theology to Postmodern Negation of Theology." *International Journal of Philosophy of Religion* 60 (2006): 61–76.

———. *On What Cannot Be Said: Apophatic Discourses in Philosophy, Religion, Literature, and the Arts*. Vol. 1. *Classic Formulations*. Notre Dame, IN: University of Notre Dame Press, 2007.

Freud, Sigmund. *The Ego and the Id*. New York: W. W. Norton, 1990.

Gebara, Ivone. *Out of the Depths: Women's Experience of Evil and Salvation*. Minneapolis: Augsburg Fortress Press, 2002.

Gedalof, Irene. "Can Nomads Learn to Count to Four? Rosi Braidotti and the Space for Difference in Feminist Theory." *Women: A Cultural Review* 7, no. 2 (1996): 189– 201.

———. "Identity in Transit: Nomads, Cyborgs and Women." *European Journal of Women's Studies* 7 (2000): 337–54.

Gibson, Nigel. *Fanon: The Postcolonial Imagination*. Cambridge: Polity Press, 2003.

———. *Rethinking Fanon: The Continuing Dialogue*. Amherst, MA: Humanity Books, 1999.

Gilroy, Paul. "Planetarity and Cosmopolitics." *British Journal of Sociology* 61, no. 3 (2010): 620–26.

Glissant, Édouard. *Caribbean Discourse: Selected Essays*. Translated by Michael Dash. Charlottesville: University Press of Virginia, 1989.

———. *Poetic Intention*. Translated by Nathalie Stephens. Callicoon, NY: Nightboat, 1997.

———. *Poetics of Relation*. Translated by Betsy Wing. Ann Arbor: University of Michigan Press, 1997.

Gordon, Lewis. *Fanon and the Crisis of European Man: An Essay on Philosophy and Human Sciences*. New York: Routledge, 1995.

Graziano, Frank. *Alejandra Pizarnik: A Profile*. Translated by Maria Rosa Fort, Frank Graziano, and Suzanne Jill Levine. Durango, CO: Logbridge-Rhodes, 1987.

Gudmarsdottir, Sigridur. "Abyss of God: Flesh, Love, and Language in Paul Tillich." PhD diss., Drew University, 2007.

Hadewijch. *The Complete Works*. Translated by C. Hart. Mahwah, NJ: Paulist Press, 1981.

Hantel, Max. "Errant Notes on a Caribbean Rhizome." *Rhizomes*, no. 24 (2012). www.rhizomes.net/issue24/hantel.html.

Harris, Baine. *The Significance of Neoplatonism*. Albany: SUNY Press, 1976.

Harvey, David. *Cosmopolitanism and the Geographies of Freedom*. New York: Columbia University Press, 2009.

Hegel, G. W. F. *Lectures on the Philosophy of Religion: The Lectures of 1827*. Edited by Peter C. Hodgson. Translated by R. F. Brown. Berkeley: University of California Press, 1988.

———. *Phenomenology of Spirit*. Edited by John N. Findlay. Translated by Arnold Vincent Miller. Oxford: Oxford University Press, 1977.

Heidegger, Martin. "What Is Metaphysics?" In *Pathmarks*, edited by William McNeill, 82–96. Cambridge University Press, 1998.

Herman, Judith. *Trauma and Recovery*. New York: Basic Books, 1992.

Hick, John. *Evil and the God of Love*. New York: Macmillan, 1966.

Hoppe, Elizabeth, and Tracey Nicholls, eds. *Fanon and the Decolonialization of Philosophy*. Lanham, MD: Lexington Books, 2010.

Hyppolite, Jean. *Genesis and Structure of Hegel's Phenomenology of Spirit*. Evanston, IL: Northwestern University Press, 1974.

———. *Logic and Existence*. Translated by Leonard Lawlor and Amit Sen. Albany: SUNY Press, 1997.

Inwood, Brad. "The Origin of Epicurus' Concept of Void." *Classical Philology* 76, no. 4 (October 1981): 273–85.

Isasi-Diaz, Ada Maria, and Eduardo Mendieta, eds. *Decolonizing Epistemologies: Latina/o Theology and Philosophy*. New York: Fordham University Press, 2012.

JanMohamed, Abdul. *The Death-Bound-Subject: Richard Wright's Archaeology of Death*. Durham, NC: Duke University Press, 2005.

Jantzen, Grace. "Eros and the Abyss: Reading Medieval Mystics in Postmodernity." *Literature and Theology* 17, no. 3 (2003): 244–64.

Johnston, Adrian. *Žižek's Ontology: A Transcendental Materialist Theory of Subjectivity*. Evanston, IL: Northwestern University Press, 2008.

Kant, Immanuel. "The Difference between the Races." In *The Portable Enlightenment Reader*, edited by Isaac Kramnick, 637–39. New York: Penguin Books, 1995.

———. *Political Writings*. Cambridge: Cambridge University Press, 1991.

———. *Toward Perpetual Peace and Other Writings on Politics, Peace, and History*. Edited by Pauline Kelingeld. New Haven, CT: Yale University Press, 2006.

Kearney, Richard. *Anatheism: Returning to God after God*. New York: Columbia University Press, 2011.

———. "Epiphanies of the Everyday: Toward a Micro-eschatology." In *After God: Richard Kearney and the Religious Turn in Continental Philosophy*, edited by John Panteleimon Manoussakes, 3–20. New York: Fordham University Press, 2006.

———. *The God Who May Be: A Hermeneutics of Religion*. Bloomington: Indiana University Press, 2001.

———. *Poetics of Modernity: Toward a Hermeneutic Imagination*. Amherst, MA: Humanity Books, 1999.

Keller, Catherine. Book review *The Weakness of God: A Theology of the Event*, by John Caputo. *Cross Currents* 56, no. 4 (Winter 2007): 133–39.

———. *Cloud of the Impossible: Negative Theology and Planetary Entanglement*. New York: Columbia University Press, 2014.

———. *The Face of the Deep: A Theology of Becoming*. London: Routledge, 2003.

———. *From a Broken Web: Separation, Sexism, and Self*. Boston: Beacon, 1988.

Kessler, Michael, *Mystics: Presence and Aporia*. Chicago: University of Chicago Press, 2003.

Kojeve, Alexandre. *Introduction to the Reading of Hegel: Lectures on the Phenomenology of Spirit*. Ithaca, NY: Cornell University Press, 1980.

LaCapra, Dominick. "Trauma, Absence, Loss." *Critical Inquiry* 25, no. 4 (Summer 1999): 696–727.

Lahens, Yanick. "Exile: Between Writing and Place." *Callaloo* 15, no. 3 (Summer 1992): 735–46.

Latour, Bruno. "Whose Cosmos, Which Cosmopolitics: Comments on the Peace Terms of Ulrich Beck." *Common Knowledge* 10, no. 3 (2004): 450–62.

Lauer, Christopher. *The Suspension of Logic in Hegel and Schelling*. New York: Continuum, 2010.

Levinas, Emmanuel. *Totality and Infinity*. Dordrecht: Kluwer Academic Publishing, 1991.

Lindsay, James. "The Philosophy of Schelling." *Philosophical Review* 19, no. 3 (May 1910): 259–75.

Lloyd, Vincent. *Race and Political Theology*. Stanford, CA: Stanford University Press, 2012.

Magee, Glenn. *Hegel and the Hermetic Tradition*. Ithaca, NY: Cornell University Press, 2008.

Malabou, Catherine. *The Future of Hegel: Plasticity, Temporality, and Dialectic*. London: Routledge, 2004.

———. *The Heidegger Change: On the Fantastic in Philosophy*. Albany: SUNY Press, 2011.

Malabou, Catherine, and Judith Butler. "You Be My Body for Me: Body, Shape, and Plasticity in Hegel's Phenomenology of Spirit." In *A Companion to Hegel*, edited by Stephen Houlgate and Michael Baur, 611–40. Malden, MA: Blackwell, 2011.

Maldonado-Torres, Nelson. "On the Coloniality of Being: Contributions to the Development of a Concept." *Cultural Studies* 21, nos. 2–3 (2007): 240–70.

Marion, Jean-Luc. *Idol and Distance: Five Studies*. Translated by Thomas A. Carlson. New York: Fordham University Press, 2001.

May, Todd. "Badiou and Deleuze on the One and Many." In *Think Again: Alain Badiou and the Future of Philosophy*, edited by Peter Hallward, 67–76. London: Continuum, 2004.

McGrath, S. J. *The Dark Ground of Spirit: Schelling and the Unconsciousness*. New York: Routledge, 2002.

Meister Eckhart. *The Essential Sermons*. Translated by Edmund Colledge and Bernard McGinn. Mahwah, NJ: Paulist Press, 1981.

———. *Meister Eckhart: Teacher and Preacher*. Edited by Bernard McGinn. Mahwah, NJ: Paulist Press, 1986.

Mendieta, Eduardo. *Latin American Philosophy: Currents, Issues, Debates*. Bloomington: Indiana University Press, 2003.

Mignolo, Walter. *The Darker Side of Western Modernity: Global Futures, Decolonial Options*. Durham, NC: Duke University Press, 2011.

———. "Geopolitics of Knowledge and Colonial Difference." *South Atlantic Quarterly* 101, no 1 (Winter 2002): 57–96.

———. *Local Histories/Global Designs: Coloniality, Subalternity, and Border Thinking*. Durham, NC: Duke University Press, 2000.

———. "Philosophy and the Colonial Difference." In *Latin American Philosophy: Currents, Issues, Debates*, edited by Eduardo Mendieta, 80–87. Bloomington: Indiana University Press, 2003.

Miller, David. "Theopoiesis: A Perspective of the Work of Stanley Romaine Hopper." In *Why Persimmons and Other Poems*, edited by Stanley Romaine Hopper. Atlanta, GA: Scholars Press, 1987.

Mills, Jon. *The Unconscious Abyss: Hegel's Anticipation of Psychoanalysis*. Albany: SUNY Press, 2002.

Monahan, Michael. *The Creolizing Subject: Race, Reason, and the Politics of Purity.* New York: Fordham University Press, 2011.

Moraña, Mabel, Enrique Dussel, Mabel Moranifa, and Carlos Jauregui. "Colonialism and Its Replicants." In *Coloniality at Large: Latin America and the Postcolonial Debate*, edited by Mabel Moraña, Enrique Dussel, and Carlos Jauregui, 1–22. Durham, NC: Duke University Press, 2008.

Murdoch, H. Adlai. "(Re)Figuring Colonialism: Narratological and Ideological Resistance." *Callaloo* 15, no. 1 (1992): 2–11.

Nancy, Jean Luc. *Hegel: The Restlessness of the Negative.* Translated by Jason Smith and Steven Miller. Minneapolis: University of Minnesota Press, 2002.

Nietzsche, Friedrich. *Beyond Good and Evil: Prelude to a Philosophy of the Future.* Edited by Rolf Peter and Judith Norman Horstmann. Translated by Judith Norman. Cambridge: Cambridge University Press, 2002.

Norman, Judith, and Alistair Welchman. *The New Schelling.* London: Continuum, 2004.

Nussbaum, Martha. "Kant and Stoic Cosmopolitanism." *Journal of Political Philosophy* 5, no. 1 (1997): 1–25.

———. *Therapy of Desire: Theory and Practice in Hellenistic Ethics.* Princeton, NJ: Princeton University Press, 1996.

O'Meara, Dominic. "Scepticism and Ineffability in Plotinus." *Phronesis* 45, no. 3 (August 2000): 240–51.

O'Neill, John. *Hegel's Dialectic of Desire and Recognition: Texts and Commentary.* Albany: SUNY Press, 1995.

Pahl, Katrin. *Tropes of Transport: Hegel and Emotion.* Evanston, IL: Northwestern University Press, 2012.

———. "The Way of Despair." In *Hegel and the Infinite: Religion, Politics, and Dialectic*, edited by Slavoj Žižek, Clayton Crockett, and Creston Davis, 141–58. New York: Columbia University Press, 2011.

Panteleimon Manoussakis, John, ed. *After God: Richard Kearney and the Religious Turn in Continental Philosophy.* New York: Fordham University Press, 2006.

———. *God after Metaphysics: A Theological Aesthetics.* Bloomington: Indiana University Press, 2006.

Paslick, Robert. "From Nothingness to Nothingness: The Nature and Density of the Self in Boehme and Nishitani." *Eastern Buddhist* 30, no. 1 (1997): 13–31.

Pizarnik, Alejandra. *Diarios.* Buenos Aires: Lumen, 2003.

Plato. *The Parmenides of Plato.* Glasgow: James Maclehose and Sons, 1894.

———. *The Republic.* Edited by G. R. F. Ferrari. Translated by Tom Griffith. Cambridge: Cambridge University Press, 2000.

———. *Timaeus.* Translated by Donald J. Zeyl. Indianapolis: Hackett, 2000.

Plotinus. *Plotinus.* Translated by Stephen MacKenna and B. S. Page. The Greatest Books of the Western World 17. London: Encyclopedia Britannica, 1952.

Plotinus. *Plotinus: The Six Enneads.* Translated by Stephen MacKenna and B. S. Page. Blacksburg: Virginia Tech Press, 2001.

Pollock, Sheldon, Homi Bhabha, Carol Breckenridge, and Dipesh Chakrabarty. "Introduction: Cosmopolitanisms." *Public Culture* 12, no. 3 (Fall 2000): 577–89.

Popper, Karl. *The Open Society and Its Enemies*. Vol. 2. *Hegel, Marx, and the Aftermath*. Princeton, NJ: Princeton University Press, 1966.

Pseudo-Dionysius. *The Complete Works*. Translated by Colm Luibheid. New York: Paulist Press, 1987.

Quijano, Anibal. "Coloniality of Power, Eurocentrism, and Latin America." *Nepantla: Views from South* 1, no. 3 (2000): 550–51.

Radler, Charlotte. "Living from the Divine Ground: Meister Eckhart's Praxis of Detachment." *Spiritus* 6, no. 1 (Spring 2006): 25–47.

Radovic, Stanka. "The Birthplace of Relation in Edouard Glissant's *Poetique de la Relation*," *Callaloo* 30, no. 2 (Spring 2007): 475–81.

Rae, Patricia, ed. *Modernism and Mourning*. Cranbury: Associated University Press, 2007.

Ralkowski, Mark. *Heidegger's Platonism*. New York: Continuum, 2009.

Rosen, Stanley. *Plato's Republic: A Study*. New Haven, CT: Yale University Press, 2008.

Roth, Michael. *Knowing and History: Appropriation of Hegel in Twentieth Century France*. Ithaca, NY: Cornell University Press, 1988.

Sacks, Peter. *The English Elegy: Studies in the Genre from Spenser to Yeats*. Baltimore: John's Hopkins University Press, 1987.

Said, Edward. *Culture and Imperialism*. New York: Vintage, 1993.

Santos, Bonaventura de Sousa. "Beyond Abyssal Thinking: From Global Lines to Ecologies of Knowledge." *Review* 30, no. 1 (2007): 45–89.

Schelling, F. W. J. von. *The Ages of the World*. Translated by Jason Wirth. Albany: SUNY Press, 2000.

———. *Philosophical Investigations into the Essence of Human Freedom*. Translated by Jeff Love and Jonathan Schmidt. Albany: SUNY Press, 2006.

Schraffman, Ronnie. "Aime Cesaire: Poetry Is/and Knowledge." *Research in African Literatures* 41, no. 1 (Spring 2010): 109–20.

Schurmann, Reiner. *Wandering Joy: Meister Eckhart's Mystical Philosophy*. Great Barrington: Lindisfarne Books, 2001.

Sedley, David. "The Two Conceptions of Vacuum." *Phronesis* 27, no. 2 (1982): 175–93.

Sells, Michael. *Mystical Languages of Unsaying*. Chicago: University of Chicago Press, 2002.

Soelle, Dorothee. *The Silent Cry: Mysticism and Resistance*. Minneapolis: Fortress Press, 2001.

Solomon, Robert. *In the Spirit of Hegel*. Oxford: Oxford University Press, 1983.

Stang, Charles. "Being Neither Oneself nor Someone Else." In *Apophatic Bodies: Negative Theology, Incarnation, and Relationality*, edited by Chris Boesel and Catherine Keller, 59–77. New York: Fordham University Press, 2010.

Thomas, Bonnie. "Edouard Glissant and the Art of Memory." *Small Axe* 13, no 3 (November 2009): 25–36.

Trozzo, Eric. *Rupturing Eschatology: Divine Glory and the Silence of the Cross.* Minneapolis: Fortress Press, 2014.

Turner, Denys. *The Darkness of God: Negativity in Christian Mysticism.* Cambridge: Cambridge University Press, 1995.

Van der Kolk, Bessel, Alexander McFarlene, and Lars Weisaeth, eds. *Traumatic Stress: The Effects of Overwhelming Experience on Mind, Body, and Society.* New York: Guilford Press, 1996.

Villet, Charles. "Hegel and Fanon on the Question of Mutual Recognition: A Comparative Analysis." *Journal of Pan African Studies* 4, no. 7 (November 2011): 39–51.

Villiers Pistorius, Philippus. *Plotinus and Neoplatonism: An Introductory Study.* Cambridge: Bowes and Bowes, 1952.

Walcott, Derek. "The Antilles: Fragments of Epic Memory." (Nobel Prize Lecture, December 7, 1992). In *The Routledge Reader in Caribbean Literature,* edited by Alison Donnell and Sarah Lawson Welsh, 503–6. London: Routledge, 1996.

———. *The Poetry of Derek Walcott, 1948–2013.* New York: Farrar, Strauss and Giroux, 2014.

Westphal, Merold. *Transcendence and Self-Transcendence: On God and the Soul.* Bloomington: Indiana University Press, 2004.

Widder, Nathan. "The Rights of Simulacra: Deleuze and the Univocity of Being." *Continental Philosophy Review* 34 (2001): 437–53.

Wiesel, Elie. *Night.* Translated by Marion Wiesel. New York: Hill and Wang, 2006.

Wilder, Amos. *Theopoetic: Theology and the Religious Imagination.* Philadelphia: Fortress Press, 1976.

Wilder, Gary. "Race, Reason, Impasse: Césaire, Fanon, and the Legacy of Emancipation." *Radical History Review,* no. 90 (Fall 2004): 31–61.

Williams, Patrick, and Laura Chrisman, eds. *Colonial Discourse/Post-Colonial Theory: A Reader.* New York: Columbia University Press, 1994.

Williams, Robert. *Hegel's Ethics of Recognition.* Berkeley: University of California Press, 1997.

———. *Recognition: Fichte and Hegel on the Other.* Albany: SUNY Press, 1992.

Wuthnow, Julie. "Deleuze in the Postcolonial: On Nomads and Indigenous Politics." *Feminist Theory* 3, no. 2 (2002): 183–200.

Young, Robert C. *White Mythologies.* London: Routledge, 1990.

Žižek, Slavoj. *The Abyss of Freedom/Ages of the Word, F. W. J. von Schelling.* Ann Arbor: University of Michigan Press, 1997.

———. *The Fragile Absolute: Or Why Is the Christian Legacy Worth Fighting For.* London: Verso, 2000.

———. *Indivisible Remainder: On Schelling and Related Matters.* London: Verso, 1996.

————. *Less Than Nothing: Hegel and the Shadow of Dialectical Materialism*. London: Verso, 2012.

————. *The Parallax View*. Cambridge: MIT Press, 2009.

————. *The Sublime Object of Ideology*. London: Verso, 1989.

————. *Tarrying with the Negative: Kant, Hegel, and the Critique of Ideology*. Durham, NC: Duke University Press, 1993.

————. *The Ticklish Subject: The Absent Centre of Political Ontology*. London: Verso, 1999.

Žižek, Slavoj, Clayton Crockett, and Creston Davis, eds. *Hegel and the Infinite: Religion, Politics, and Dialectic*. New York: Columbia University Press, 2011.

Žižek, Slavoj, and John Milbank. *The Monstrosity of Christ: Paradox or Dialectic?* Edited by Creston Davis. Cambridge: MIT Press, 2009.

Index

Perspectives in Continental Philosophy
John D. Caputo, series editor

Karl Jaspers, *The Question of German Guilt*. Introduction by Joseph W. Koterski, S.J.

Jean-Luc Marion, *The Idol and Distance: Five Studies*. Translated with an introduction by Thomas A. Carlson.

Jeffrey Dudiak, *The Intrigue of Ethics: A Reading of the Idea of Discourse in the Thought of Emmanuel Levinas*.

Robyn Horner, *Rethinking God as Gift: Marion, Derrida, and the Limits of Phenomenology*.

Mark Dooley, *The Politics of Exodus: Søren Kierkegaard's Ethics of Responsibility*.

Merold Westphal, *Overcoming Onto-Theology: Toward a Postmodern Christian Faith*.

Edith Wyschogrod, Jean-Joseph Goux, and Eric Boynton, eds., *The Enigma of Gift and Sacrifice*.

Stanislas Breton, *The Word and the Cross*. Translated with an introduction by Jacquelyn Porter.

Jean-Luc Marion, *Prolegomena to Charity*. Translated by Stephen E. Lewis.

Peter H. Spader, *Scheler's Ethical Personalism: Its Logic, Development, and Promise*.

Jean-Louis Chrétien, *The Unforgettable and the Unhoped For*. Translated by Jeffrey Bloechl.

Don Cupitt, *Is Nothing Sacred? The Non-Realist Philosophy of Religion: Selected Essays*.

Jean-Luc Marion, *In Excess: Studies of Saturated Phenomena*. Translated by Robyn Horner and Vincent Berraud.

Phillip Goodchild, *Rethinking Philosophy of Religion: Approaches from Continental Philosophy*.

William J. Richardson, S.J., *Heidegger: Through Phenomenology to Thought*.

Jeffrey Andrew Barash, *Martin Heidegger and the Problem of Historical Meaning*.

Jean-Louis Chrétien, *Hand to Hand: Listening to the Work of Art*. Translated by Stephen E. Lewis.

Jean-Louis Chrétien, *The Call and the Response*. Translated with an introduction by Anne Davenport.

D. C. Schindler, *Han Urs von Balthasar and the Dramatic Structure of Truth: A Philosophical Investigation*.

Julian Wolfreys, ed., *Thinking Difference: Critics in Conversation*.

Allen Scult, *Being Jewish/Reading Heidegger: An Ontological Encounter*.

Richard Kearney, *Debates in Continental Philosophy: Conversations with Contemporary Thinkers*.

Jennifer Anna Gosetti-Ferencei, *Heidegger, Hölderlin, and the Subject of Poetic Language: Toward a New Poetics of Dasein*.

Jolita Pons, *Stealing a Gift: Kierkegaard's Pseudonyms and the Bible*.

Jean-Yves Lacoste, *Experience and the Absolute: Disputed Questions on the Humanity of Man*. Translated by Mark Raftery-Skehan.

Charles P. Bigger, *Between* Chora *and the Good: Metaphor's Metaphysical Neighborhood*.

Shannon Sullivan and Dennis J. Schmidt, eds., *Difficulties of Ethical Life.*

Catherine Malabou, *What Should We Do with Our Brain?* Translated by Sebastian Rand, Introduction by Marc Jeannerod.

Claude Romano, *Event and World.* Translated by Shane Mackinlay.

Vanessa Lemm, *Nietzsche's Animal Philosophy: Culture, Politics, and the Animality of the Human Being.*

B. Keith Putt, ed., *Gazing Through a Prism Darkly: Reflections on Merold Westphal's Hermeneutical Epistemology.*

Eric Boynton and Martin Kavka, eds., *Saintly Influence: Edith Wyschogrod and the Possibilities of Philosophy of Religion.*

Shane Mackinlay, *Interpreting Excess: Jean-Luc Marion, Saturated Phenomena, and Hermeneutics.*

Kevin Hart and Michael A. Signer, eds., *The Exorbitant: Emmanuel Levinas Between Jews and Christians.*

Bruce Ellis Benson and Norman Wirzba, eds., *Words of Life: New Theological Turns in French Phenomenology.*

William Robert, *Trials: Of Antigone and Jesus.*

Brian Treanor and Henry Isaac Venema, eds., *A Passion for the Possible: Thinking with Paul Ricoeur.*

Kas Saghafi, *Apparitions—Of Derrida's Other.*

Nick Mansfield, *The God Who Deconstructs Himself: Sovereignty and Subjectivity Between Freud, Bataille, and Derrida.*

Don Ihde, *Heidegger's Technologies: Postphenomenological Perspectives.*

Suzi Adams, *Castoriadis's Ontology: Being and Creation.*

Richard Kearney and Kascha Semonovitch, eds., *Phenomenologies of the Stranger: Between Hostility and Hospitality.*

Michael Naas, *Miracle and Machine: Jacques Derrida and the Two Sources of Religion, Science, and the Media.*

Alena Alexandrova, Ignaas Devisch, Laurens ten Kate, and Aukje van Rooden, *Re-treating Religion: Deconstructing Christianity with Jean-Luc Nancy.* Preamble by Jean-Luc Nancy.

Emmanuel Falque, *The Metamorphosis of Finitude: An Essay on Birth and Resurrection.* Translated by George Hughes.

Scott M. Campbell, *The Early Heidegger's Philosophy of Life: Facticity, Being, and Language.*

Françoise Dastur, *How Are We to Confront Death? An Introduction to Philosophy.* Translated by Robert Vallier. Foreword by David Farrell Krell.

Christina M. Gschwandtner, *Postmodern Apologetics? Arguments for God in Contemporary Philosophy.*

Ben Morgan, *On Becoming God: Late Medieval Mysticism and the Modern Western Self.*

Neal DeRoo, *Futurity in Phenomenology: Promise and Method in Husserl, Levinas, and Derrida.*